THE FARMER FROM MERNA

A BIOGRAPHY OF GEORGE J. MECHERLE

AND A HISTORY OF THE STATE

FARM INSURANCE COMPANIES

OF BLOOMINGTON, ILLINOIS

THE FARMER
FROM MERNA

BY KARL SCHRIFTGIESSER

RANDOM HOUSE · NEW YORK

CONTENTS

FOREWORD

This book, which is both a biography of the late George Jacob Mecherle and a history of the State Farm Insurance Companies of Bloomington, Illinois, which he founded, was undertaken at the request of the State Farm Mutual Automobile Insurance Company. It is, therefore, an authorized biography and history. I should like to point out to the general reader, however, that in the preparation of this typically Midwestern story and in its writing I have been given the fullest latitude and utmost freedom in the choice of material and the use to which I have put it. The executives of the company opened its files to me and let me examine them without direction. This freedom from censorship on their part has been an enjoyable experience. I hope the result may be considered a slight contribution to the history of the Middle West.

I would like to thank personally scores of persons who have in one way or another helped me with this book, but that would be impossible. Some have helped me without knowing it; others have dug willingly into their files and memories for material which they have freely given.

I would be ungracious if I did not mention some who have been most helpful. Most of all I would like to thank Mr. Thomas C. Morrill, vice president and former Deputy Superintendent of Insurance of the state of New York, and a deep student of what Mr. Erwin A. Meyers (who knows how grateful I am for his assistance) has called the esoterics of insurance. Without Mr. Morrill's guidance through the fine type I would have been lost.

Others who have gone out of their way to aid me are Mrs. Sylvia Caldwell Mecherle, the late Ramond Perry Mecherle, and G. Ermond Mecherle. Mrs. Mary Dearth, George Mecherle's secretary, was especially helpful. Others whom I would like to thank are the Messrs. Rust, senior and junior, Tompkins, Fuller, Campbell, Parsons and Coleman, among the company's higher echelon; the late William R. Gould, whose accurate memory went far back; H. E. Curry; J. K. McLean; the late Charles E. Wonderlin; William Lausterer, who knew Merna, Illinois, for more than eighty years; Miss Pauline Schmidt, Mrs. Wilma Dooley and the entire secretarial staff of the twelfth floor of the State Farm Building; the staff of the Withers Memorial Public Library of Bloomington; and the McLean County Historical Society. The Messrs. Walter Dornaus and Harold Hayslip gave much valued personal assistance. And a private word of thanks to Louis Ruppell and Miss Diana Hirsh.

THE FARMER FROM MERNA

1

ACROSS THE PRAIRIE

In the decade between 1850 and 1860 two and one-half million immigrants arrived in the United States. Of this vast horde, which streamed from the famines and political upheavals of Europe, 951,667 were Germans. The majority of this latter group were able-bodied, clear-minded men and women in the prime of life. Crowded in the cramped quarters of sailing vessels and often without any means of support except their willing hands, they came to America for a variety of reasons. In those turbulent years which followed the abortive revolution of 1848 and preceded the rise of Bismarck to power, some of them sought that ephemeral something which—since the early days of the nineteenth century when opposition to monarchy and rule by the few had stirred the intellectuals and fired lesser men to revolt—had been known as Liberty. At the same time others were impelled to uproot themselves for more selfish reasons, among which hunger or the threat of hunger played an important part, while still others were lured from relative security by dreams of easy wealth. But still others came because they were swept away by the excitement of the times, with no overwhelming intellectual, political, or economical reason clearly determined in their own minds. They just came, carried by the tide, hopeful for something they could not put into words, seeking some justification of their existence which could not be found in the cramped streets of their German cities or on the pinched acres of their German farms.

Among these 951,667 German immigrants in their Old World costumes and with no words but their native dialects on their tongues were two young brothers and their younger sister, strong, rosy-cheeked products of the rolling and rustic countryside of the province of Württemberg. The oldest of this little group was Johann Christian Thomas Mögerle, who had just passed his twenty-second birthday on the 15th of January, 1852, the year of their departure. His brother, Johann Christian Friedrich Mögerle, was one year and two months his junior. Their sister Rosine, or Rosa as she was known, was a little more than nineteen years old at the time.

The passage of time has obliterated all details of the life of the Mögerle family up to the time the three youngsters undertook their journey to America in the spring of 1852. Only the bare records of their birth remain in the church archives at Untermasholderbach. Family legend, however, helps round out the picture. The Mögerle family had been farmers in the province of Württemberg for generations. Johann George, the father of this little group (there were two other brothers and two other sisters in the family) had been born in the tiny village of Untermasholderbach in 1800. His wife, who had been Maria Margaretha Denger, was, presumably, also a native of this region. They were farmers who apparently did not find life too grim in the fertile province (which, incidentally, is just about one-eighth the size of the state of Illinois). What their political beliefs were we do not know. They must have been anti-monarchists, however, and touched with the belief in Liberty as it swept down from the north. Both Christian and Friedrich, as the boys were known, had passed their twenty-first birthdays without having been called for military duty. It was primarily to escape the army that the two boys set out on their journey. That they had the full approval of the family, which must have sat for many nights in worried council in the farm kitchen, is indicated by the fact that Father Mögerle gave them, in addition to their passage money, about the equivalent of one hundred dollars, and that sister Rosine left for the New World with them.

At least they were free people seeking even greater freedom, possibly hopeful of becoming a part of one of the New Germanys that so many immigrants of this decade expected to establish in Wisconsin, Missouri, and Minnesota. They did not leave with a price on their heads, as Carl Schurz did a year later. The iniquities of contract labor, through which evil system thousands of poor Europeans were later to be brought across the ocean for exploitation, had not yet become widespread. But even so their way was not to be easy. In 1852 the path of the immigrant was rough, but by that year it already led in several well-trodden directions. Already a steady stream of Germans was flowing toward Wisconsin. Others had settled in southern Ohio, in the region of St. Louis in Missouri, and in Chicago and elsewhere in the comparative emptiness of Illinois. There was already a German newspaper in Alton, Illinois. There were increasing numbers of Germans, who had entered through Southern ports, starting colonies in Texas and Louisiana. But most, like the Mögerles—who somewhere along the line changed their name to Mecherle, which from the first has been pronounced ma-HURL—entered through the great port of New York with no definite further destination in mind, except to move inland, by immigrant train or otherwise, to some place where, for some reason, they believed golden opportunity lay in wait.

In 1852 there was no single landing-place for the immigrants. Castle Garden was not set aside for this purpose until four years later, after a series of investigations by press and Congress had shocked a nation into action. At the time the Mecherles clambered ashore—on June 17— all immigrants, with or without funds or friends, were at the mercy of a clamorous tribe of runners, ticket-agents, and boarding-house sharps whose frauds and outrages plundered the immigrants of money and property, deluded them with false offers of employment, and often sent them into the western wilderness stripped of all their goods, penniless and starving, to make out as best they could.

Chris and Fred Mecherle, being farmers, had no intention of remaining in New York. Their star lay westward. There is no record of their stay in the great city or of how they got to Ohio, where their American trail begins. Rosine, their sister, left an even fainter trace of herself in the brutal New World for which she had had no preparation in the valley quietude of Untermasholderbach. Her brothers trustingly registered her with a German "employment agency" and went their way. But that was the time when New York was filled with Germans preying upon the Germans, as unscrupulous Irish were preying upon the Irish, and greedy

English were preying upon the English, in the hard, unregulated, un-scrupulous port of New York. Whatever her fate, they never knew. She dropped from sight. They did not hear from her again.*

Of the brothers' early days in America no documentary evidence now exists. Neither Chris nor Fred had much more than a rudimentary common school education and, although they could read and write, they were not by nature given to retrospection. They kept no diary or notes of their adventures. If they wrote back to Württemberg their letters have long since disintegrated. They were to spend the next six years in the wilderness, leaving few markers behind on the long trail which finally brought them to McLean County, Illinois. Most of the time they worked as farm hands, never staying long in any one place. Where they farmed in Ohio is not known. Some time during these first American years they became fishermen on Kelleys Island, which stands windswept in Lake Erie some ten miles north of Sandusky, Ohio. They stayed there for a year.

Those were restless days in the Republic and soon the Mecherle broth-ers, then as later inseparable partners in everything they did, moved on-ward together. At first they probably trekked toward the south, wander-ing as itinerant farm hands through Kentucky, Tennessee, Mississippi. They were strong young men, willing and able to do the hard work re-quired of them as they tramped the countryside. But in spite of their restlessness they were always searching for a place to settle down. Some-where along the way they acquired a pair of horses, and it was on horse-back that they passed through many of the seventeen states† which, so the family legend says, they traversed during the five years between their landing in New York and their arrival in Bloomington, Illinois.

They were enamored of the new country, but their thoroughgoing German nature made them choosy. In those days there was plenty of country to choose from. They wanted only the best. As they wandered they acquired much knowledge. They learned to speak English, but what was even more important they learned that all the soil of this

* The records at Untermasholderbach record the death of a Rosine Mögerle in 1839. Her name is given as Rosine Elisabeth Barbara Marie and her birth date is given as February 12, 1833. Another sister, Marie Rosine Barbara Elisabeth, was born in 1839. Her death is not recorded. If she were the sister who accompanied the brothers she would have been less than thirteen years old at the time they came to America, her birth date being given as July 16, 1839. Unfortunately the late George Mecherle was unable to clear this matter up on his visit to the family town in the summer of 1949.
† Some had not become states at that time.

new country was not alike. Like many another pioneer crossing the prairies with a dream of homestead they carried with them a spade. Whenever they came to a likely place they would dig down through the topsoil, filtering the good earth through their hands, studying it with the inherent wisdom of men born to grow crops. They would assess the growth of the trees and the plants nourished by this soil and with their farmers' minds figure out the future potentialities of the region. But for some reason no place held them—not even the rich soil of Kansas, over which they must also have passed.

Perhaps it was because, in their wanderings, they never acquired enough cash money with which to buy a farm. What they did acquire was a deep love for the flat, windswept prairie of Illinois, which had attracted so many of their fellow Germans who were already wrestling with the black, rich soil. No one knows from which direction they came, whether up from St. Louis or down from the north, nor how they traveled. But one day in 1857 they stood together on the board sidewalk in front of the cupola-topped old brick Court House in Bloomington, Illinois. Lean, muscled, big-handed, and as inseparable as ever, they were two likely workers for any farmer who might pass by looking for someone to help drain his share of the prairie that stretched in undulating waves in every direction.

During the five years the Mecherle brothers had wandered and worked their way across the vast uncultivated territory of what was then western America, great history was in the making. Of much of it, the strange doings of an unfamiliar democracy, the brothers—strangers in a strange land—were probably happily unaware. But all of it was to affect their lives and fortunes, although they were never to be personal participants in any of these terrifying events, no matter how close geographically or economically they came to them. They were growers of corn and feeders of cattle, simple, stolid men who were content to go about their backbreaking chores in summer heat or wintry blasts and let others who had the talent for such things do the talking and moving of destiny.

These five years were years of national upheaval, of industrial expansion, of agricultural advance. Two years before their arrival President Millard Fillmore had signed the Compromise acts of 1850, thus apparently setting at rest the great agitation over slavery which had threatened to divide the Union. Five months after they had landed in New York, Franklin Pierce of New Hampshire had become President. If the Mecherles gave the matter any thought they, too, like the ma-

jority of German immigrants, aligned themselves at least in sympathy
with his political party, the Democratic. But two men from Illinois, the
state toward which destiny was drawing the brothers, were to change all
this and set the pattern out of which was to be shaped the new Republican Party, to whose principles they and their sons and grandsons were
to adhere unwaveringly in the years to come.

One of these men was Stephen A. Douglas, senior Senator from the
Prairie State, the swaggering "Little Giant" whose speculations in Chicago real estate and western lands sharpened his vision of an inland
United States served by a transcontinental railway passing over the central route. Out of this mercenary vision came the Nebraska Bill, out of
which, in turn, came the Kansas-Nebraska Act which repealed the
Missouri Compromise and, in the words of Senator Sumner, put "freedom and slavery face to face, and bids them grapple." To the German
immigrants the issue was obvious. They broke away from the Democratic Party by thousands in protest, making it clear, as Allan Nevins
has put it, that "they meant to settle the West thickly themselves and
did not want Negroes there—much less slaves."

How much of this concerned the Mecherle brothers, we do not know.
But they cannot have helped being influenced by it in some measure,
for the new German-Americans were among the most vocal supporters
of the new party and of Abraham Lincoln, its standard-bearer, after both
emerged from the political and economic struggle that was then taking
place. And Bloomington, no longer a sleepy village nestling in its grove
of trees in the midst of the prairie, was in the very heart of this battle of
words that was to lead to Civil War and Union. The very air that swept
over it was charged with its electricity. Its streets were crowded with men
whose lives and fortunes, great or small, depended upon which way the
prairie wind, stirred as it was by the western voices of Abraham Lincoln
and Stephen Douglas, should blow. It was whistling in every direction,
working itself up to a prairie tornado, when the brothers Mecherle stood
in front of the courthouse up whose steps both Lincoln and Douglas
had trudged so many times.

They probably were far more interested in where their next meal was
coming from than they were in the political issues agitating the lawyers
and politicians, merchants and farmers who jostled them in the hum-
ming square. For Bloomington, set as it was almost halfway in a straight
line between Chicago and St. Louis, was a bustling and busy town in
the decade before the Civil War. Two husky men of twenty-six and

twenty-seven, toughened and matured by their years of wandering, need have had little to worry them. Bloomington, although far from being a "boom" town, was then both prosperous and expanding. The past decade had seen its population increase from 1,000 to 6,000, and the same period had seen hundreds of settlers moving out on the open prairie, where dangerous Indians no longer lurked. A vast change was indeed taking place on this prairie. Four years before one could stand on a hill near Peoria and look over the undulating plain in any direction and see neither house nor tree as far as the eye could reach. Now, the scattered smoke from farmhouse chimneys, especially to the east and south, blurred the unbroken sky, and the smoke of the wood-burning engines of the new railroad traced the pattern of its right of way through the changing land.

The reason for all of it was this new road. In 1850 Douglas and his allies in and out of Congress had pushed through a measure which made huge tracts of public land available to the states of Illinois, Mississippi and Alabama for transfer to railroad corporations. As a result of this act, managed so adroitly by Douglas* and backed by a powerful lobby of Eastern financiers, the Illinois Central Railway was generously bestowed with some 2,595,000 acres of rich, virgin soil along its right of way. Thus endowed, promoter Robert Rantoul of Massachusetts found ready money on Boston's State Street and New York's Wall Street, and soon 10,000 laborers, mostly newcomers from Ireland, were hammering the track tight to the prairie from Chicago to Cairo. Within three years trains were running from LaSalle to Springfield, with Bloomington as the main intermediary shop. Late that same year, 1853, the Chicago & Alton began setting down its line, with Bloomington as the headquarters for the contractors. Four years later it was to establish its main shops in Bloomington, giving employment to nearly 200 men.

Another reason for the settling of the open prairie was the passage by Congress in 1850 of the Swampland Act, which gave to the state of Illinois thousands of acres of land generally considered unfit for development. Two years later the Illinois legislature granted 28,793 of these soggy acres to McLean County. These were to be reclaimed by the building of dams and by a proper system of drainage, but no effective methods for doing this to any great extent were then available. Later, how-

---

* He cleverly disarmed Southern opposition by linking the interests of the Mobile & Ohio Railroad project with his own. See *Ordeal of the Union*, by Allan Nevins, p. 201, and notes.

ever, the lands were sold off to individual settlers, the county getting $127,716 for them. Of this amount some $70,000 was spent to establish Normal University in North Bloomington and the rest was split up among the townships for the use of their schools. Not only did this activity spell prosperity for the village of Bloomington, the seat of McLean County, but it opened up for development some of the most fertile territory in the United States. The future looked bright indeed. New streets were laid out north and south of Courthouse Square; homes were built; stores were established in new buildings; and Bloomington became the center of what was soon to be a flourishing agricultural region served by two railroads. Before all this, land had been available almost for the asking, but the isolation of the uncultivated area made the asking precarious. Even from the hungry railroads the price of the land was now within the reach of homesteaders willing to take it and turn it through the sweat of their toil into profit.

Among those who, within the last few years, had been attracted by the cheap, rich land were a number of German immigrant families. One of them, that of Gottlieb Arnold, had come to McLean County from the Mecherles' native province of Württemberg, but Gottlieb was then working rented land and had no means of giving his fellow landsmen the opportunity they were looking for. There was Frank Kraft, who had arrived in the United States a year before from Baden; he was working by the month, saving his money toward the purchase of his first eighty acres, on which he already had his eye in Towanda. He, too, was to labor five years before he could start in farming for himself. Perhaps the Mecherle brothers sought out Gottlieb, or Kraft, or even George Schlosser, another German who was working as a hired man in Towanda, and talked matters over with them, learning from their years of experience on the prairie that, no matter where they went, they would find no better place than right there for settling down. But there was another newcomer to the region who was to end their indecision for them once and for all time.

Among those who had found this area worthy of their talents and brawn was a devout, church-building Quaker named John R. Benjamin. He was six years older than Chris Mecherle and had come to the prairie with his wife Sarah from the East in 1855. Now he was rearing his family on his homestead on undrained land some ten miles over the quagmire road east of Bloomington, in what is now Dawson Township but was then called Padua. Although he was to bring up several strong sons—his oldest boy, Timothy, was then just eight years old—and they were to till this rich soil with satisfaction, he was looking for hired help the day the Mecherle brothers stood outside the Court House. From whatever direction they had come, and by whatever means, whether by horseback or on the new railroad, they had passed through miles and miles of flat country which their experienced farmers' eyes must have told them was as good as any they had yet seen. They had made up their minds that McLean County was where they wanted to stay. When the stout, round-faced, bearded Benjamin, his coarse trousers tucked in his high boots and his fur cap perched on the back of his head, walked up to them and offered them work on his farm east of Bloomington they knew that they had at last reached the end of the trail.

Chris and Fred Mecherle chose an ideal place at an ideal time to become American farmers. Not only was McLean County geographically the largest subdivision of the state of Illinois, but it was one of the highest, being in some places more than 900 feet above sea level. The Mackinaw River, then as now, drained the northern section, except in the northeast corner where the branches of the Vermilion cut through the prairie. Flowing to the east was the historic Sangamon, and flowing southward was a branch of Salt Creek. South of the ridge that cuts through the Bloomington moraine were other streams that partly drained the rich land into Sugar Creek, the Kickapoo, and Salt Creek again. Once, not many years before, the Illinois-Wabash Indian trail snaked through this region; and even in the years since the arrival in America of the two brothers, the crowded emigrant wagon-trains rumbled over this quagmiry route on the way to the west.

The little Quaker community of Benjaminville stood in the flat country, surrounded by the low hills of Danvers, Downs and Saybrook. It was soggy land, the water oozing out of the coal-black soil that was later to make McLean one of the richest farming counties in all the United States. But the vision of American inventors was already making the conquest of the prairie by the successors of the scarred frontiersmen a comparatively easy battle. The McCormick reaper was just ten years old. Marsh's harvester and Appleby's self-knotting binder were on the market, and the steel-toothed cultivator was available.

But most important of all to farmers like Quaker Benjamin and farm hands like the Mecherle brothers was the development of the improved large plow. This huge affair was designed to cut through the prairie sod in great swaths. Sixteen to thirty oxen were needed to pull it through the ground along the natural waterways, sometimes traversing the whole length or width of several farms. Thus great open ditches were cut through the swamps and the water drained off into the streams and river branches. But even this plow was not enough to drain the swamplands adequately, and so Yankee ingenuity invented the mole ditcher. In the late 1860's and early 1870's this was in wide usage as the farmers struggled to eliminate the buffalo wallows and frog-filled ponds still left in the lower bottoms even after the wide ditches had been cut through.

Compared to modern tractor-driven farm machinery these ditchers were cumbersome and unwieldy devices, but they helped wrest the prairie into usefulness for mankind. Again great teams of oxen were used to drag the heavy wooden beam, to which was firmly bolted a five-foot steel bar, seven inches wide with an edge like a sharp knife. At the lower end of this heavy knife rivets secured two bars of heavy steel. This was the mole, or shoe, which gave the contrivance its name. The farmers could sink this to the required depth in the ground, and then the oxen, attached by chain or cable to the oaken beam, would strain and haul it through the sod, leaving behind them a ditch six inches wide through which the water was supposed to flow away. Sometimes even thirty oxen could not directly move the ditcher, or the heavy plow, and then capstans were called into play. Not every farmer owned his own ditcher. The cost for hiring this necessary work done was twenty-five cents a rod.

But even this refinement did not leave the prairie as dry and tillable as it ought to have been for raising the best crops. Something else was needed when the blind ditches began to fill up as the crawfishes caused the soil to crumble and cave in. In 1879 Edgar M. Heafer began making drain tile in Bloomington and the next decade and a half saw the reclamation of the wastelands move at rapid pace even though, at first, the tiles were too small. Before the turn of the century most farms in McLean County were well drained.

There had been white settlers in McLean County since 1822—two years after Illinois became a state—but most of them had huddled along the streams, where the trees grew and where they could find protection from the Indians who then still roamed the territory, marauding and massacring even as they had done when LaSalle first sank his legs into the Illinois bogs. Now there were close to 28,000 persons living in the county, many of them on farms far from the sporadic groves so eagerly sought by the first comers. Like these others, Benjamin and his family had "dared to brave public opinion and the prairie wolves" out on the open land. It was still a wet, rough country, however, with thousands upon thousands of acres yet to be made tillable, when Chris and Fred sat down to their first supper in the Benjamin kitchen.

For the next six years the brothers lived in John Benjamin's tenant house and little that was eventful took place in their lives. Abraham Lincoln, whose lanky figure was a familiar one to the men and women of Bloomington, where he had practiced law, became President. The Civil War split the nation, and drew hundreds of young men from the farms of Illinois into the uniform of the North. But these grim happenings seemed to have passed over the brothers without touching them. Chris was already thirty years old when Lincoln was elected, and the fact that he was under the influence of a Quaker undoubtedly added to his own peaceful and unmilitary inclinations. And so the brothers Mecherle worked, winter and spring, summer and autumn, on the Benjamin farm, seldom straying farther away from its acres than nearby Bloomington, which was metropolis enough for their simple wants.

In those first years on the farm, ushered in as they were by the Panic of 1857, and followed by its aftermath and the outbreak of civil strife, cash money was scarce indeed. Gold almost went out of circulation in 1862 and the gold value of greenbacks dipped down to thirty-five cents on the dollar. Nearby Bloomington—where the panic of 1857 had been keenly felt and many fortunes, built up since the coming of the railroads, had been wiped out—felt the pinch of depression almost as badly as did larger communities. When corn dropped to ten cents a bushel the newly settled farmers suffered. It was not really until about 1873, more than a decade after Abraham Lincoln's first call for volunteers, that prosperity returned to the prairie, which by then was so well settled that the hungry and adventurous were already streaming into the lands of the Far West.

Such money as the striving Benjamin accumulated went into the purchase of land. His honesty was a byword in the region and the Mecherle brothers were content to let their wages stay marked down in his ledger. They did not, then, need money. They were biding their time and they knew that when the day of reckoning arrived they would receive their just settlement of the lengthening account.

This day was hastened by the appearance in their lives of a young lady schoolteacher who charmed them both but who had eyes only for Chris.

Susanna Johnson Hull, just turned twenty when Chris first met her, was a typical child of the Middle West. In the American manner her blood was a mixture of solid Yankee, stolid Dutch, and sound Scot. She had been born on a farm in Butler County, Ohio, north of Cincinnati and near the Indiana line. When she was seventeen years old her Quaker parents moved westward to settle on a new farm in Blue Mound, a treeless rise in the plain twelve miles or so east of Bloomington. In her little Quaker bonnet she made a pretty picture when Chris met her while she was teaching school in adjoining DeWitt County. The fact that he was a Lutheran made no difference, but the fact that he was just a "hired hand" did. The brothers decided that they would settle accounts with John Benjamin and strike out on their own.

The settlement was made in December, 1862, when John Benjamin deeded one hundred acres to the two brothers. The recorded cost to them was $1,800, which they may have paid in cash. The family legend, however, is that Chris and Fred had foregone most of their wages during the past five years, probably taking in cash only what they needed for clothes and staples, and then had settled with Benjamin for 160 acres of land. Like so many legends this is not quite accurate. The first acquisition of land was one hundred acres. Six years later they bought from Benjamin another sixty-acre tract adjoining their original purchase, and so it was not until eleven years after their arrival in McLean County that they owned, in their own right, a quarter section.*

It was a good farm to which they moved in the spring of 1863, but by no means the best at that time in the vicinity of the tiny village of Merna in Towanda township, which clustered two miles north of the farm's furthermost fence. Much of it was rich slough land that would be of little value until it was drained. On a slight rise near the rutted trail or road which ran past the acreage the brothers built a shack (later they were to build their own house, which still stands) and there, for two more years, they existed as bachelors until the farm was ready for use.

Chris and Susanna were married in the Quaker church in Benjaminville on December 6, 1864, and went at once to live on the new farm. Brother Fred soon joined them. The close partnership of the brothers was not disturbed by Chris's marriage, then or ever. Fred never married, nor did he ever leave the home which he and his brother built, being happy to stay there, working his acres and tending his stock, until his death fifty-one years later in January, 1916. It was a happy home, a tight

* This quarter section still belongs to the Mecherle estate.

little place where there was no one to bother them, no one to criticize them, and where, over the years, they could cling to such Old World customs as were not rubbed off by the roughness of their isolated prairie life.

Although Bloomington, the county seat, site of the Alton railroad shops, and gathering-place of all the farmers of the region, was only nine miles away, the Mecherles ignored it. The farm was the center of their lives, and Merna, a crossroads handful of houses, a store, and a school, gave them such community life as they needed. Not that they were antisocial. Far from it. They knew all their neighbors, the Germans and the Irish who mostly made up the settlement. As the years passed they became the most respected citizens, in more ways than one. They added to their acreage until they became among the largest landholders in the region. They prospered. Thrifty but not mean, conservative but not reactionary, they saved their money, nurtured their soil, fed their cattle, and grew relatively rich. The neighbors came to depend upon them not only for advice but for material aid. They acted as the local bankers. Any good farmer, needing cash, could come to them and from their store, always kept in a box and never in a Bloomington bank, they would supply the needed cash. They boasted that they were never robbed and never cheated, that all the debts owed to them were paid. Their fame never extended far beyond Merna, but there they were men of good will.

In another way good fortune came to them. To Chris and Susanna were born seven children.* To them Chris was a stern but kindly father, who expected them to do their duty and their chores, who brooked no nonsense but who also understood their problems in his silent way. Uncle Fred adored them. But it was their mother, Susanna the Quaker, who shaped their way of life. The rule of her household was integrity. The joint Christianity of John Fox and Martin Luther pervaded the lives of them all. Chris, a slim man with a neat beard that was growing white with the passing years, dominated. But Uncle Fred, with his tales of the old country and wanderings in the new, acted as leavening during the long winter evenings, while Mother Mecherle, with her brown hair neatly parted in the middle, benignly influenced them all, making them mind their manners and their morals.

---

* Frederick C., b. 1866, d. 1923; Willis F., b. 1867, d. 1944; Lucy Belle, b. 1870, d. 1920; Laura, b. 1872, d. 1942; George Jacob, b. 1877, d. 1951; Walter R., b. 1880, d. 1943; and Lilly, b. 1884, died at birth.

In most respects the Mecherle farm was little different from hundreds of others drained and planted by the Forty Eighters. It was as American as the corn that all but hid it in the August sun, but it still had its ties with the Germany the brothers had deserted so many years before. Gradually Chris and Fred lost almost all trace of their German accent. English was spoken by the family, although the brothers sometimes lapsed into their native tongue. But every Easter Eve—as long as he lived—Chris would place an apple beside the bed of every member of the family, and near the barn he would set out a bushel of oats and corn so that no beast would go hungry on Easter day. Father Mögerle had done so at Untermasholderbach, and he would do so in Merna, Illinois.

George Jacob Mecherle, who was named for both his German grandfather and his mother's brother, Jacob Hull, was the next to the youngest of this brood. When he was born on June 7, 1877, twenty years after his father and uncle had first arrived in Bloomington, his brother Fred was eleven years old and his brother Willis was going on ten. Sister Lucy Belle, who had an unfortunate affliction in that one of her arms was slightly withered, was seven, and sister Laura was a determined moppet of five. At least until his brother Walter came along three years later, George was the pet of them all and from the first showed signs of being the brightest. He was the favorite of his Uncle Fred, who early spotted in him evidences of vast curiosity about everything that went on around him, in the house, the barns, and the fields, and a natural inclination toward leadership. He also was, in his way, a student, with a quick and absorbing mind, who devoured all the meager reading matter which found its way to the crowded household. He was a stout lad, with a good appetite both for the abundant food on the table and the hard work that was the lot of himself and his brothers from the time they were old enough to drive in the cows or follow the hay wagon to the barn.

Schooling was scanty for farm children in the Middle West in the 1880's. Classes did not begin until the corn was shucked and in the cribs or hauled to the siding at the station on the branch of the Illinois Central. They ceased with the advent of spring ploughing. School was a one-room affair. It was a rough place. The boys, farm-grown and hardened, were almost always big for their age and restless with their confinement. But they were held to a rigid, old-fashioned routine. Outside the classroom there were hunting, fishing and baseball.

It was a good time to be growing up in the Middle West—the last decades of the nineteenth century. They were years mostly of peace, prosperity, and confidence. George Jacob Mecherle was a true child of his time.

2

THE MERNA FARM

The Mecherle farm on the Empire road in Merna, now doubled in size from its original 160 acres, was a comfortable if crowded home. The ugly white house, the rutted barnyard, the barns, the cattle pens, the dug well, hardly differed from those on scores of other farms scattered over what was no longer the prairie. In the summer for miles around the pale yellow corn rose high in the heat; and in winter snow covered the limitless acres. Sun, wind and rain had weathered the buildings and an air of permanency had settled on them, far different from the unkempt look Chris and Fred and old John Benjamin had known a scant score of years ago when the prairie grass still grew, tall and tough.

The devout Susanna, in her long brown skirt and with her Quaker bonnet perched on her brown hair, ran the house with a benevolent hand, determined that her children should all have the learning that she, who had been a schoolteacher, and the crowded one-room school at the Merna crossroads together could give them. What her secret horizons were none knew, but her brother was a successful doctor in Chicago, and another brother had gone all the way from the prairie to Fresno, California. Perhaps she dreamed that her boys, too, would leave this flat country to climb distant peaks. But, of course, it is also possible that she, who had known this land from her girlhood, loved it so deeply that she hoped they would stay to tend it, like their father and uncle, with steady hands. Whatever her dream, Susanna had little time from the busy daily round of the farm wife to indulge in it too often.

But there was time enough to see that her children should have all the advantages the community offered, all the health and happiness her own cheerful nature could impart. She taught them to read and write at an early age, and to do simple sums, so that when it was time for them to go to school they had as good a start as anyone. She was particularly attentive to her second youngest, George, who early showed an aptitude toward learning. Perhaps, she felt, he might someday become a teacher, even a college professor. To this stimulus he responded. He loved to read and, had he had a more cultured guidance and better opportunity, he might well have turned his path in this direction. But, as he later confessed to an old schoolmate, "there were too many things to do to spend my time in school, at least that was the way I looked at it at that time."

The Mecherle farm was not one of those grim, man-killing, dream-shattering, unlovely, sour warrens that Hamlin Garland and other writers of this period were to find in such sad plenitude up and down the Middle Border. Its fertility responded to the sure hands of Chris and Fred, whose draft horses were the envy of their neighbors, whose cattle were sleek, whose hogs were fat, and whose profits were steady. By neighborhood standards they were even rich. No threat of poverty or insecurity ever threatened them. The banks owned no part of their land. They were shrewd brother-partners, frugal in many ways, but never mean. They had an abiding love for their land and no fear of the hard work that its care required. To the son and nephew George they imparted this love and this lack of fear. Whatever *his* secret horizons, they cannot have extended far beyond the rim of the undulating prairie. He was marked for a farmer and he knew it, or so he thought in those days on the Merna farm.

Merna, then as now, was a tiny community. When the prairie had been opened for settlement much of the land in this vicinity had been taken up by sturdy Irish immigrants, most of whom had come to Mc-Lean County with the gangs whose brawn had laid the iron track of the railroads through the wilderness. Having saved their money and sent to the Old Country for their girls or wives, they had made this, as some of them put it, a little bit of the old sod. Like their solid German or silent Yankee neighbors they had ditched and drained and now they were raising their families on their farms, sending them to the public school at Merna,* and teaching them their ancestral faith in the Roman Catholic Church they had erected in 1870. Thus George and his brothers and sisters, children of a German Lutheran immigrant and a devout Quaker mother, grew up with children of Irish immigrants as playmates through most of their formative years. If nothing else, it taught George that tolerance toward all races and creeds which he was so often to express and exemplify in his later years.

George was a strapping lad, tall, big-framed, with thoughtful hazel eyes. In the crowded school—the one-room Merna school had one of the largest enrollments in the township of Towanda—he was one of the best scholars: a clear penman, an able arithmetician, a fair grammarian, and a more than "passing" student of "modern geography" and United States history, which were the subjects taught in those days. Dominating the studies, in spirit at least, were the McGuffey Readers, then the mainstay of education throughout all the Middle West. All the glory of the most acceptable English poets, the homilies of temperance, the virtuous propaganda in behalf of honesty and patriotism, of which these Readers were compounded, he absorbed with pleasure. It was not just nostalgia that caused him, in later years, to reread them with profit and speak of them with reverence. In the late 1880's in the Merna school they had been for him an intellectual experience never to be repeated. He kept his own well-thumbed copy of the Fifth McGuffey Reader among his treasured possessions all his life. His later eloquence and even the phraseology of his speech came in great measure from these eclectic books that had so much to do, sixty and seventy years ago, with forming the middle-class Midwestern mind. Their virtues were his virtues and their limitations his limitations, the hard core of the place and the period that was McLean County when he was a growing boy.

Education, in those days, was simple, uncomplicated, without teach-

---

* A Roman Catholic parochial school had been established in Bloomington in 1863, but in those days of bad roads few if any Catholics living on the outlying farms were able to attend. The German Lutherans had built their first parochial school in Bloomington in 1858. See *McLean County and Its Schools*, by William B. Brigham (Bloomington, McLean County Historical Society, 1951), pp. 48-9.

ing aids or standard textbooks beyond the McGuffey Readers. Almost
any bright youngster could become a teacher in those days when the
sheepskin eraser and the hickory stick were uniform equipment in every
free school. In 1840 Abraham Lincoln had asked the state legislature to
pass a law "for the examination as to their qualifications of persons offering themselves as school teachers," and a few years later the state pro-
claimed that teaching certificates should be granted to "persons of good
moral character" who could "properly teach" the simple subjects in the
free schools. That these requirements were not severe, and that George
Mecherle was a bright student by the standards of the time, is proved
by the fact that at the age of thirteen he was able to pass the tests and
receive a teacher's certificate. This accomplishment, however, was merely
a gesture, undoubtedly performed at the instigation of his mother. He
never made use of the piece of paper from the Superintendent of Towanda Schools. Nevertheless, as we shall see, teaching school was then
his major, if subconscious, aim in life.

There were, as he said, so many other things to do. Among the other
things was the chastening of Frank Gahagen. In his history of McLean
County schools Dr. Brigham recalls that at the Merna School "fighting
and promoting fights was the order of the day." One year, after the
corn-shucking season had ended and the big boys tromped off to school,
young Frank, who was one of the bigger boys and a nearby neighbor of
George, challenged him to a fight. There was no animosity behind the
challenge. It was merely a part of the order of the day, for George was
as big as Frank, who claimed the championship of the school. The fact
that George was a Quaker (or at least an attendant at the Friends'
church at Benjaminville) may have had something to do with it. It did
not, however, keep George from accepting the challenge. The boys
started fighting in December. They kept it up each day at the noon re-
cess. Neither gave, and neither triumphed, and it went on until spring.
At last Frank admitted that he had met one boy he could *not* lick. Thus
the ultimate victory was George's and it marked him as the new cham-
pion of the school.

Then there was hunting and fishing. George was adept at both but
he was especially good at hunting. Once he and a crowd of boys, including his older brothers Fred and Will, went after rabbits when the temperature was ten degrees below zero. His younger brother Walter tagged
along. George bagged eight rabbits that frosty day. On the way home

he spotted another rabbit in the brush. Giving Walter a gun, he told him to sneak up on it and shoot. Walter did, and then went up to pick up the rabbit only to find it frozen stiff, having been dead a long time as George had known it was all the time. This penchant for the practical joke, which never had a very nasty sting in it, lasted all his life.

But the greatest delight of his boyhood days was baseball. Spring or autumn there was always a game of baseball going on in some back pasture or empty field. His powerful shoulders made him a great hitter, in his class, and he was quick and adept at every position. His contemporaries thought he had big league "stuff." At least, he was the best ball player in Merna and good enough to be recognized as a potent rival by other teams in the township when they met on a summer Sunday afternoon in the field near the depot on the Kankakee branch.

When George was seventeen years old the family decided that he should continue his education. In the autumn of 1894, having finished all the schooling that Merna afforded, he enrolled in the high school at the State Normal University. His ostensible purpose was to become a teacher, although many young people went there without any serious intention of following this underpaid profession. Because of the uncertainty of the roads it was out of the question for him to travel back and forth the nine miles between the farm and the school. With another boy named Charles Andrew he took a room in a boarding house conducted by two old maids in the town of Normal within quick walking distance of the classrooms. This was the first time he had ever been away from the Merna farm.

On September 11, 1894, very soon after the school opened, he addressed the following letter to his sister Lucy:

Dear Folks:
I am here, by here I mean in the northeastern part of Normal, and I am about as tough feeling mortal as you ever seen, I feel as if there were a thousand of Bricks resting on my head, but it is some better now. I didn't eat any dinner today. Now I dont want you to get scared, as I didn't feel hungry and I thought Pa would be in town today and I walked up to Bloomington, because the street cars weren't running, and got back just in time for my Grammar class. I wanted to see Pa awful bad because I haven't got any more money than I can spare. After this letter is mailed I will just have four cents. I want about twenty dollars as my tuition will cost me fifteen dollars for this term. I want this money right away either send or bring it as quick as possible for I am in a desperate state of affairs, without hardly a cent.

The reason I am so nearly strapped is because I had to get every one new books and they cost me over four dollars.

Hoping you will send immediately I remain

George J. Mecherle.

"Pa" must have come to town with the money, for George stayed at Normal for the rest of the semester. Fifty-six years later George Mecherle recalled his days at Normal in a letter to John Page, who had been in his class.

> . . . I never was in Normal over the week end. I always went home; my family lived just nine miles from Bloomington and that is the reason I failed to be in Normal the night they hung Altgeld in effigy, which caused such furor and compelled Mr. Cook to expel so many of the boys who had been engaged in that escapade. Some of my boy friends were expelled and had to go elsewhere for their further education. That was largely the reason why I discontinued my schooling in Normal after the first semester. In fact I never did go to school elsewhere. . . . I went back to the farm and continued as a farmer until I was 40 years of age. . . .

The hanging of Altgeld in effigy was not in protest over his pardoning of the two Chicago "anarchists," for that happened in 1893, nor was it because the High School students disapproved of his opposition to the use of the U.S. Army to put down the Pullman strike in the summer of 1894. It was a much more personal and local matter. For some time President John Williston Cook had been trying to abolish the High School. Most of the instruction there was given by the regular Normal teachers, with the results that already overcrowded classes were disrupted by the presence of the secondary students. Three years previously President Cook had got the tuition raised to thirty-six dollars a year and the attendance limited to 160 students. Now the matter was called to the attention of Governor Altgeld, who advised the abolition of the school. The youngsters signified their disapproval in their week-end flare up with the consequences remembered by George Mecherle. He could not have gone through the entire four-year course if he had wanted to. The Governor's recommendation was followed and the High School was permanently closed in June, 1895.

Having thus made his final decision, having thus determined the course of his life, he settled down to the hard work of helping to operate the Mecherle acres. His father was now sixty-four years old and Uncle Fred was sixty-three, and both were ready to ease off. There were, of course, the other brothers to help out. The menfolk were glad to have George back, even if Mother Mecherle must have felt a twinge of sadness at his forsaking his books. For one thing, young as he was, they respected his judgment. A few years earlier the brothers had raised a bumper corn crop, but when it was ready to market the prices were lower than they thought they ought to get. Pa and Uncle Fred were discussing what to do when the latter turned to George and said, "Well, George, what would you do if it were your corn?" His reply was typical: "If it were my corn and I had your money, I'd spend some for lumber, build me some corn cribs, and hold it until the price went up." They did.

In those days George was known as "quite a talker," and one who was apt to be persuasive in his arguments. He was a familiar figure at Gould's store, down by the Merna depot and corn crib, where he used to walk across the fields for the mail each day. He had then an absorbing interest in politics, and it was his great pleasure to sit in the store and discuss the affairs of the day with the gathered farmers. His favorite antagonist was J. A. McAvoy, a retired schoolteacher, and the pair would go at it hot and heavy. McAvoy was a Democrat and George was a Republican, who read, revered, and relished his *Chicago Tribune* every day.* He read a great deal then, as he did later, but in his choice of material he was a seeker of information rather than a romanticist or escapist. He liked best to read the progressive farm journals—the *Prairie Farmer* was his favorite and he remained a faithful reader all his life— and to study up on new ways of raising corn or cross-breeding hogs or cattle. He wanted very much to have his own farm where he could carry out some of the experiments he was reading about.

His was, then, a happy, if busy, youth. The Mecherle farm more nearly resembled the Middle West of James Whitcomb Riley, with its "genial atmosphere of the horse and buggy age, warm, kindly, tranquil, neighborly, unhurried," as Van Wyck Brooks has described it, in *The Confident Years*, than the Sangamon country which Edgar Lee Masters was, in the *Spoon River Anthology*, to describe as "a festering sore." There was no hint there of the wretchedness of Theodore Dreiser's teutonic upbringing on the banks of the Wabash. It was an age when wealth was still modest both in villages like Merna or in bigger towns like Bloomington, where men still sat on fence rails, whittling, in alpaca

* This was a lifelong habit.

coats, and there were always loungers in tilted chairs in front of the Illinois House. On Saturday farmers, like the Mecherles or the Gahagans, the Benjamins or the Carmodys, drove to town and hitched their teams in Courthouse Square.

Most of the intellectual excitement of the era seems to have passed lightly over the Merna farm. The religious apostasies of Robert Ingersoll, the political heresies of William Jennings Bryan, the urban cynicisms of Mr. Dooley, were undoubtedly discussed at Mr. Gould's store, but George Mecherle was not charged with any of the intellectual restlessness of the times. The Populism of the 1880's did not ruffle a tassel of Mecherle corn. The Mecherles were independents, but they had been schooled from their earliest Illinois days in the traditions of Republicanism, and were staunch believers now in McKinley's stability, almost completely unaware of riotous Chicago to the north, except as a place where the price of corn and hogs was dictated by the immutable laws of supply and demand. These traits and these beliefs they passed on to their children, who saw peace and prosperity in the good, black McLean County soil—if they were willing to work for it.

And so, in work and play, the prairie seasons passed. And then George fell in love.

Mae Edith Perry lived on a farm about a mile and a quarter from the old Mecherle place. Mae was a pretty girl and very popular among the Merna and Benjaminville swains. Her father, John Perry, was a successful farmer and cattle breeder, and an old-timer in the neighborhood. Mother Perry, who had an especial fondness for George, was an Orendorff, which meant that her roots went deeper into the Illinois soil than those of most of the families settled in the Bloomington area. She was proud of her family which, by Midwestern standards, was an old one.

Christopher Orendorff, son of a German Army officer, had come to this country about the time of the Revolution, and in 1791 had settled in Hagerstown, Maryland. There he married Elizabeth Phillips. He moved with her first to Georgia. Then he went on to South Carolina and farmed near Spartanburg for seven years. In 1807 he struck out with Elizabeth and their four sons and daughter for Tennessee. A little while later he pushed on to Kentucky. Still dissatisfied, he moved on again, and eventually arrived in St. Clair County, Illinois. But he still had not found a settlement to his liking. For a time he lived in Sangamon County. Then he moved on once more, for the final time at last, until he found a farm a few miles north of where the town of Lincoln now stands in Logan County. In spite of all this restless wandering he raised to maturity a family of twelve children.

Thomas, the fifth of the brood, was born at Spartanburg, South Carolina, in 1800. He and his brother William, during the family's stay in Sangamon County, did not find the countryside to their liking. One day they saddled their horses and set off to find themselves some better land. They came at last to a place called Keg Grove. Not knowing the grove had a name, they sat down to write a letter back home.

"How will we start our letter?" William asked his brother. "We have no name for this place."

Thomas cast his eyes over the trees, whose brilliant spring blooms were a riot of color in the midst of the prairie, and said, "Let's call it Blooming Grove."

The spot still bears this name, and Bloomington—which was first called Bloomingtown—probably took its title from the brothers' inspiration. Two settlers had preceded the Orendorff brothers and had built their cabins near the spot where the brothers halted their trek on horseback. After talking with these men, who said the place was a paradise, Thomas staked a claim south of what is now Bloomington and lived there for many years until he bought a farm east of Blooming Grove. There he lived until his death in 1891. This spare and rugged old man, who stood six feet four inches high, and his wife, who had been Mary Malinda Walker, the daughter of William Walker, one of the earliest settlers in Blooming Grove, raised a family of thirteen children. He was the grandfather of Mae Edith, whose mother, Clarabelle Orendorff, had married John Perry.*

* At a reunion of the Orendorff family a few years ago, G. J. Mecherle gave the following interesting and intimate description of Thomas Orendorff: "Thomas Orendorff was a man 6 feet 4½ inches tall, athletic, faithful in all relations of life. He was very apt in mathematics and never required paper and pencil to figure any transaction. He was religiously inclined, being a Methodist. I never saw him angry or heard him use a profane word. He was honest, kind, and considerate and loved his home and family and theirs was a very happy home, one I dearly loved to be in. He was very regular in his habits always retiring at eight and arising at four. The children could remain up later but had to be very quiet. He would arise of a morning, kindle the fires, light his cob pipe, and smoke and read until the rest of the family was ready to get up. He raised his own tobacco, cut and cured it and made it into twists. He never aspired to great riches but always had an abundance for those times and was ever ready to help with anything toward the betterment of the locality. He gave land for school and church purposes, where the Walker schoolhouse now stands, which was named for his wife's father, William Walker. The

Mae Perry had been George's "girl" for some time, but he began to take her seriously about the time he left Normal. He was always cutting across fields to visit at her home, and pretty soon what had been a boy-and-girl affair became the most widely talked-about romance of the neighborhood. As soon as work and supper were done George would be over at her house, and it was not long before she was making candy for him. Mae had the reputation of baking the best cream puffs of any-one for miles around, and when she began making them for George, who adored them, people knew that the romance was getting ahead in proper order.

But, like his father before him, George had to establish himself before he could ask Mae to marry him. Having made up his mind to be a farmer, all he now had to do was to acquire a farm. He had been able to save a little money, but not enough with which to strike out for him-self. Uncle Fred, the old bachelor, came to his rescue. Over the years Fred had acquired a considerable amount of property, and among his holdings was a farm, with buildings, which was just the place for a young couple to have when starting out life together. It was located four and a half miles from Bloomington, and was in good condition, but not so good but that a husky lad like George could greatly improve it.

Uncle Fred turned this farm over to George on a business basis. He was to pay rent at first, but there was an option to buy. Everyone in the family knew that George would soon own it outright. It was in 1899 that he took over the farm. Uncle Fred presented him with a fine pair of draft horses and, even as Father Mögerle had done when he and Chris set out for America, made him a present of some cash. It was a good start, but George was an independent sort of lad who had no in-tentions of long remaining under obligation, even to his own family. That summer he worked as separator man with Harrison Lott's threshing crew, which went about the county threshing wheat and oats. Lott's was one of the biggest outfits anywhere around. It took ten men to operate the big steam engine and the thresher that was attached to it by a 150-foot belt. Six other men sweated to pick up the stacked grain and feed it to the great, clanking, snorting machine. It was hard work, but George was a big fellow, with powerful shoulders and untiring energy, and that

Orendorff family were close friends of Abraham Lincoln, who did much of his rail splitting for Joseph, a brother of Thomas; and a sister, Polly Cameron, financed Lincoln in his first office, that of Justice of the Peace, when he was a member of the Cameron family and a young law student at Springfield."

summer, out on John Perry's farm, in three runs they threshed 75,000 bushels of oats.

In June, 1900, Chris—he was now just seventy years old—"took sick." The years of toil were demanding their pay at long last. Throughout the summer he lay in his bed on the "old place," as the first Mecherle farm was affectionately known by the family and neighbors alike. Late in September he died. He was, as the *Daily Pantagraph* said, "a man who had acquired a considerable fortune and whose business dealings had been known for their integrity and straightforwardness." They buried him in the old churchyard of the Friends Meetinghouse in Benjaminville, which his first friend in McLean County, John Benjamin, had established nearly half a century before. His brother Fred, who had always been his partner and who was to continue to operate the farm, was to survive him by sixteen years. The gentle Susanna was to wait fifteen years until she joined him there.

The next year, his present security assured and his future seemingly bright, George and Mae were married.*

For the first eighteen years of the twentieth century George Mecherle

* When George and Mae were married, George's brothers Willis and Walter stayed on at the "old place" to help Uncle Fred. Lucy, who never married because of her infirmity, also remained, and for years after Mother Mecherle's death was Walter's companion and housekeeper. Walter also never married. After his mother's death he continued to farm the "old place," and for several years specialized in raising shorthorn cattle and purebred hogs. A contented bachelor, he stayed there even after Lucy's death, at the age of fifty, in 1920. She was buried with her parents in the Friends cemetery at Benjaminville. In 1932, when he felt he could no longer farm the "old place," Walter (who had inherited it at the death of Fred Mecherle, his uncle) deeded it to George who, in return, set up a trust fund for Walter on which the latter lived comfortably in Bloomington for several years. He died at his brother George's home at the age of sixty-three in 1942. Walter never associated himself with George in any of the latter's business activities, but they were always close to each other. Willis, on the other hand, was to become closely associated with his younger brother George. He married five years after George did, his wife being the former Erma Tompkins. They lived for several years on a farm at Randolph, six miles south of Bloomington on the Decatur road. In 1922 he became his brother's associate in the insurance business. His children were: Elizabeth Lillian, 1905; Willis Harold, 1907; Alwillah Irene, 1908.

George Mecherle had strong family attachments. For many years he watched over the fortunes of most of the members of his family, except those of Willis, who was a shrewd and competent business man in his own right. He cared for the varied farming and business interests and investments of his sister Laura for many years. Laura, born in 1872 and thus five years George's senior, married William F. Young, whom she survived by several years. They had two children, William Young, who lived in Canandaigua, N. Y., and Irma (Mrs. Cordes) who died several years before her mother's death in 1942.

worked, improved, and enlarged his farm, raised a family, and tended to the duties of a conscientious citizen. His first child, Ramond, was born in 1904, and the next year his second son, George Ermond, came along. Four years later a sister, Mildred, was added to the family, and two years after that twin sons, Hubert and Herbert, completed the second generation of American-born Mecherles.*

One day in the winter of 1915 Susanna invited all her children to the "old place" for dinner. She was then in her seventy-fourth year—a quaint old lady now, who still wore the plain brown clothes, the little bonnet and the full-gathered skirt with the large pocket where, as youngsters, George and his brothers and sisters had often found sweets or pennies waiting their grubby hands. Her eyes that had looked across the prairie so many years were filled with love for those gathered around her. They talked of the old days, laughing and joking, teasing each other as they had done when they were children. But they knew something was in her mind.

After dinner Susanna drew twenty-dollar gold pieces from her pocket, one for each child. No one said anything as she passed them around. At last George found words.

"Ma," he said, "we'll never need anything like that to remember you by."

Susanna looked at him, smiling, and said, "I want you to have it. Remember, if you keep this you'll never be 'broke.'"

George, at least, was never broke. He carried his with him the rest of his life, until the gold had worn thin.

A few weeks later Susanna passed away. Uncle Fred, now retired from active farming, was the last of the little triumvirate of pioneers whose lives had stretched over so many exciting years of history, who had seen the prairie change from wilderness to unbroken miles of fertile growth. He was almost eighty-five years old, when, after a long illness, he died

---

* Ramond Perry Mecherle: born, February 19, 1904; married, Mildred Murray; children—Ramond Perry and (Mrs.) Georgia Lou (Garland); died, May 15, 1954.

George Ermond Mecherle: born, August 20, 1905; married, first, Marguerite Henderson; children—George Robert and Douglas Ermond; married, second, Marcella Noonan.

Mildred Mecherle: born, February 18, 1909; married, Kenneth Noll; child—Kenneth.

Hubert C. Mecherle: born, May 27, 1911; married, Ruth Colville; died, January 5, 1943.

Herbert L. Mecherle: born, May 27, 1911; married, Pearl Buttorf; children—Victoria Ann and Julie Lynn.

on January 13, 1915. Like his brother and the gentle Susanna, he was buried in the Friends' burial ground at Benjaminville, not far from the site where he and Chris first put their shoulders to John Benjamin's plow in 1857.

From the beginning of his own farming career George was known as a "doer," and as a man who not only wanted the best equipment but who would take care of it after he got it. His farming methods were the best. He was a careful worker who believed that efficiency counted. His neighboring farmers knew him as a man who never allowed the harnesses of his magnificent draft horses to get out of kilter. Later, when he added gasoline-powered machinery, he saw to it that it was kept in first-rate repair. Most good farmers, of course, work this way; but George Mecherle was more meticulous than most, as his neighbors never tired of pointing out.

He was not content to do things one way just because that was the way his father had done them. He was always studying and reading about what the other fellow had done. His desk was littered with Department of Agriculture brochures, columns of advice torn from the *Prairie Farmer* or from the farm page of A. J. Bill in the *Daily Pantagraph*. He was interested in the work of the McLean County Better Farming Association from its inception in 1914, and made good use of the technical advice offered by it and by its successor, the McLean County Farm Bureau. He understood how to restore tired and worn-out soil, through the use of phosphates and limestone, and he was an early believer in the principle of crop rotation. Many years later he was to lend his wholehearted support to the development of hybrid corn.

Once, long after he had given up active farming, he went out to the "old place," then under the competent hands of his tenant farmer—one of the most profitable farms in the United States. It had, of course, cost him thousands of dollars to bring it to the point of perfection. He stooped down and scooped up a handful of the rich, tar-black soil, and let it run through his fingers. He looked across hundreds of acres where the soil was all as rich as that which he was admiring.

"By golly," he said, a little wistfully, "if I'd had a farm like this there would never have been a State Farm Insurance Company!"

The truth is, he did have one of the best farms in the county, for he was, as an old neighbor once said, "a scientific farmer without a scientific education."

Not only was he a good farmer, but he was a good businessman. He always felt that agriculture, big or little, was a part of big business, perhaps the biggest and, in his mind, surely the most important business of mankind. He made money by the application of the same rules that had led him to persuade his father to spend money for lumber to crib his corn rather than let it go at a low price.

This child of the Middle West learned farming and, what is perhaps even more important, he learned about farmers. A gregarious, extroverted, volatile man, he looked, walked, talked and acted like the farmer he was, and he was never happier than when discussing farming problems—crop prices or the new science of soil management—with his fellow farmers. He was a familiar figure, even then, on the streets of Bloomington, where all his friends knew him as George. He made friends wherever he went, which in those days was seldom far from the Bloomington-Merna area, and hardly ever beyond the narrow limits of McLean County.

Like Chris Mecherle before him he had a reputation for integrity in his business deals, whether for himself or for Old Town Township, where his farm was located, south of the "old place," which was now being farmed by his brother Walter. He always had time to interest himself in township affairs. For several years he was the road commissioner, a post of exceeding importance in a farming community, and especially at this time, when the automobile was changing the economy and the face of the nation. George Mecherle had started farming for himself about the time the commercial production of automobiles had started. His career as an independent farmer (1900-18) covered the years which saw the automobile completely revolutionize the American way of life. In his book, *An American Story*, Albert Williamson tells the following story that epitomizes his way of doing business:

> One day a tractor salesman drove up to the Mecherle farm and found the road commissioner busy plowing a field. He went across the field and approached Mecherle as he came to the end of a furrow. Those who witnessed the event couldn't hear the conversation, but suddenly they saw Mecherle wrap the lines around the plow handle and start towards the salesman, who cleared the fence at a jump, got into his rig and hurried down the road.
>
> A few days later another stranger drove up to the Mecherle farm as the family was finishing dinner. He and the road commissioner went out on the porch. After they had lighted up cigars, the stranger began.
>
> "Mr. Mecherle, I'm sorry about what happened the other day. That fellow who approached you about buying a tractor works for me—I'm the

sales manager—and he was never authorized to offer you a split on the commission if you would buy a tractor for the township."

Mecherle snorted and bit into his cigar.

"You see," the salesman went on, "if you would buy a tractor for use here in Old Town Township and it worked well, it would be a fine recommendation for my company. Now, what we had in mind was, that if you could see your way clear to do that, it would be worth something to us to have your recommendation to show other townships."

About that time the chair in which Mecherle was lounging tipped back against the house, hit the floor with a bang.

"Bah!" he spat, "You know darned well you sent that fellow out here the other day and he was authorized by you to offer me a split on the commission. Now you're just trying to smooth it over and bribe me in a little different way. The only thing you've done is made it impossible for the township to buy a tractor from anyone as long as I'm road commissioner. Now, get out of here quick, before I really lose my temper!"

He carried this innate honesty into his other interests. For many years he was a member of the Old Town Farm Mutual Fire Insurance Company. He was never an officer or director of the company, but he had all his farm buildings insured with it and was generally consulted by the directors on matters of policy. It was with this group of neighbors banded together for their own protection against the ravages of fire, which then, as now, was one of the greatest menaces the farmer faced, that he had his first experience—if it could be called that—with the business to which he was to devote the later years of his life. And, for a number of years, while his children were attending the country school a mile or so down the road from the house, he was school commissioner. All these extra-curricular activities brought him in contact with people, spreading his reputation as a community leader and as a leading farmer in a little circle that grew ever wider as the years passed. But still his sphere was limited. Up to the age of forty he was just another McLean County farmer, prosperous, progressive, and seemingly with no ambition to move far from his home, his family, or his close associates, or even to change his rustic way of life.

3

THE SEED IS SOWED

The winter of 1917-18 was one of the bitterest to sweep across the prairie in many years. The twinges of pain which had been bothering Mae Mecherle with increasing regularity began to demand greater attention from the doctor. But medical science had not then any cure for, or even relief from, arthritis to offer her; except to suggest that a change of climate might be beneficial. Always deeply devoted to Mae since their marriage seventeen years before, George was ready to try anything that was in his power if it would alleviate her suffering.

The decision that was reached after many family conferences was, in its way, a drastic one. They would give up farming and go to Florida. That was a few years before the Florida "boom" of the 1920's and before the beaches and resorts of that semitropical state had become the winter sanatorium for thousands of persons from Maine to Minnesota to whom the chills of northern winters held no allure. There, it was hoped, the warm sun would do what medicos and medication had failed to accomplish at home.

George Mecherle did not think, at this time, that he was giving up farming forever. But he was prepared to stay away from the farm as long as necessary. He felt that he could afford to do whatever Mae's precarious health required. He owned 480 acres of fine, well-tilled, productive land; his home farm was well equipped with the best of machinery; and it was stocked with good shorthorn cattle and Poland China hogs, most of them of his own breeding. If he should liquidate his holdings, he figured, he would be worth—provided he got the best prices—about a quarter of a million dollars.

Sometime that winter he sold off his equipment and his stock. He did not sell the land, however, but rented his farmlands, thus assuring himself an income of sorts. Like most farmers George was an ingenious fellow, handy with tools and possessed of an inventive imagination. Since touring cars were not then equipped with sufficient storage space, he built a box of light but strong wood which he bolted to the side of the Willys-Knight. Then he loaded Mother and the children, Ray, aged fourteen, Ermond, Mildred and the twins, and headed toward the south. It was a gay group, carefree and hopeful of the future, that trekked down the southbound and mostly unimproved highways. As they passed through Macon, Georgia, the ringing of bells and whistles and the shooting of guns announced the Armistice of 1918. On the eve of peace they reached Del Ray Beach in Florida, the land of sunshine and, they hoped, of health.

None of the family had ever seen the sea before. None had ever been many miles from Bloomington in any direction. Chicago and St. Louis had, up until now, been the extent of George Mecherle's travels, and his visits to these metropolises had been few and far between. But he quickly adjusted himself to the carefree life. He bought a small boat and spent hours fishing. The children were happy and, for a time, Mae seemed to improve. But not for long. Hers, as it later turned out, was a progressive rheumatism which no change of climate could arrest. And she was homesick for the countryside where she had always lived. Besides, the children would have better schooling if they returned. Reluctantly George, who now had visions of becoming a Florida real-estate tycoon, and who actually contemplated selling his Illinois land and investing in Florida real estate, and who might have done so if it had not been for Mae's stubborn animosity toward the proposal, turned again northward with his family.

Instead of going back to the farm he took a house now known as "Victory Hall" on Hovey Avenue, just over the line from Bloomington in the college town of Normal. He was resigned, at the age of forty-two, to joining the growing number of retired farmers who even then made up so large a part of the population of the two communities. But he was too vigorous, too gregarious, too volatile to be happy in this role. Keeping his farm accounts, visiting his tenant farmer, and passing the long afternoons over the card tables of the Bloomington Club with his cronies was an empty sort of existence which had no appeal for him. He had worked all his life, he was still a young man, but here he was, desperately at loose ends.

But what could a man with his background, with no training except as a farmer, do? Well, he had always liked people, he was a "great talker" now, even as he had been back in Gould's store in Merna, and he had discovered he had a knack of persuasion that should stand him in good stead in some kind of business. He let it be known that he was, as it were, available. And soon he was offered a job selling insurance policies for the Union Automobile Indemnity Association of Bloomington.

The Union Indemnity was a small reciprocal insurance exchange that had been doing business in Illinois, Indiana, Iowa, and Missouri for about three years when George Mecherle became one of its agents. It wrote liability, property damage, fire, theft, and collision insurance on automobiles. Like most of the small insurance exchanges of the period it was managed by an attorney-in-fact; its plan of operation at that time called for a six months' premium to be paid in advance, with a guarantee to the insured that his net charge would not exceed 50% of the premium paid. Its assets were then limited mostly to cash in the bank and in the office and its annual business barely exceeded a quarter of a million dollars.*

George Mecherle experienced no difficulty in selling automobile insurance policies for this struggling young company. Inexperienced in salesmanship though he was, he is said to have made "as much as $1,500 a week." Although this undoubtedly was an exaggeration, there is no question that he showed unusual aptitude for the business. It is probable that most of his sales were made among his farmer acquaintances, but he was rapidly becoming well known in the city of Bloomington,

---

* In 1954, the company, still doing business from its main office in Bloomington, reported assets of $4,385,000, and was accorded an "excellent" policyholders' rating and financial rating by *Best's Insurance Reports*. L. F. Shepard, who was George Mecherle's first boss in the insurance business, was still attorney-in-fact. He and George Mecherle were good friends and neighbors until the latter's death.

where his daily appearance in the card room of the Bloomington Club was by now a fixture. There he mingled with the merchants, storekeepers, bankers, and professional men of the community, as well as with "retired farmers" like himself.

One thing about his new field of endeavor bothered him. Inexperienced as he was in insurance technicalities, he could not see eye to eye with his employers on details of their operations. Always outspoken, George Mecherle one afternoon expatiated on how *he* thought things should be done. Mr. Shepard laughed at him and said, "Well, George, if you don't like the way we run things, go start your own company. You'll find your ideas aren't practical."

Soon thereafter he quit Union as a salesman. It was a friendly parting. He did not start his own company then, nor was he to do so for several years. But the seed had been well planted.

Because he was once more at loose ends, because most of his wealth was tied up in land, rather than in readily available cash in the bank, and because he had a large and lively family to feed, he looked about for another position that he felt would suit his newly found talents as a salesman. His first taste of life as a businessman had been to his liking and, although he still looked like a farmer with his large frame straining at his business suit and with his necktie more often awry than not, he felt that delayed destiny beckoned him further in this direction.

George Mecherle found his next chance with the Illinois Tractor Company as a "bird dog" for one of that firm's regular salesmen, turning up likely customers among his farmer friends for the gasoline contrivances that were beginning to become standard equipment on many farms where horses and oxen or cumbersome steam engines had up to now done all the heavy work. At this time Henry Ford, who then marketed three-fourths of all the tractors sold in the United States, was engaged in bitter rivalry with International Harvester and General Motors for control of the trade. With the uprearing "Fordson" and the more costly "Sampson" in the market against the provedly better-built Harvester,* competition was keen and selling was a rough-and-ready business for which George Mecherle, with the soil of Old Town Township still clinging to his boots, was aptly equipped.

---

* The General Motors "Sampson" was withdrawn from the market in 1922, the company writing off its losses at $33,000,000; the "Fordson" was kept in the market, much to the consternation of Ford dealers who suffered heavy losses, until 1928. See Keith Sward, *The Legend of Henry Ford* (New York, 1948), pp. 211-12.

George Mecherle soon became a salesman in his own right and began invading territories where he was completely unacquainted with the local farmers. But he talked to them in their own language, and it was not long before he was the top salesman of the concern. He had to be a good salesman, for he was selling a tractor made by the Illinois Tractor Company in competition with the better-known makes of Ford, General Motors and International. In his Model T Ford he covered a great deal of ground, making friends, as always, wherever he went. In the long run this was more important than the commissions he earned. He got to know a lot of people far from home, in Illinois, in Indiana, and in Missouri. Unfortunately for his peace of mind, he found himself selling tractors faster than the company could deliver them and this did not set well with his rigid conscience. Once again he found himself throwing up his job because he was dissatisfied with the way his bosses ran their business.

All this time his subconscious mind had been dwelling upon a return to the insurance business. Wherever he went, he found the farmer complaining about the difficulties he encountered in acquiring adequate automobile insurance at a rate he could afford. But he realized he knew nothing about the insurance business. His experience in that line had not allowed him even to scratch the surface of the complex technicalities involved, and certainly his association with the Old Town Farm Mutual had taught him next to nothing. But still the theme, vague as it was, kept running through his mind. Without his really knowing what to do about it, the idea of an insurance business—a business that would draw upon his Midwestern background, his years as a farmer, his understanding of the farmer's mind and his needs—kept nagging him.

Historically he could have selected no better time than the year 1921 to embark upon an adventure such as he was about to undertake. And this was in spite of the fact that the country was undergoing the worst economic depression it had encountered since the 1890's, with thousands of bankruptcies taking place and nearly half a million American farmers losing their farms. Corn, which had sold on the farm at $1.88 in August, 1919, was down to 42¢ by the end of 1921, and wheat had fallen from $2.50 a bushel to $1 or even less. Nearly 5,000,000 persons became unemployed on this eve of the Age of Normalcy, as industrial production reached a point lower than it had been since 1914. But at the same time Henry Ford, who in February, 1920, had realized his life's desire of producing cars at the rate of one a minute, was cleaning house, inaugurating the "speed-up," and so pushing production that by the end of 1922 his balance sheet was to show $150,000,000 in cash in the bank and profits of close to $200,000,000 a year. In other words, the automobile industry was coming into its own.

There were, at the time he quit his job, hundreds of different automobile insurance companies, reciprocals, mutuals, and so-called Lloyds scattered throughout the country. In Illinois alone there were 290 stock and mutual fire and casualty companies and inter-insurance exchanges doing business, of which fifty-four were Illinois companies. Typical of these were two with which George Mecherle became acquainted as the idea of forming an insurance company for the protection of the farmers of Illinois—for his conception from the start was of a statewide farmers' organization—began to occupy his thoughts and stir his imagination sometime in 1921.

With neither of these companies did he have any direct association or even indirect connection, but inasmuch as both of them came under his scrutiny, one to serve as a warning and the other to provide him with inspiration, they are worth passing attention. From the ranks of one of them, also, he was to recruit his first partner in the insurance business, who was to serve him well, if briefly, in the formative stages of the State Farm Mutual Automobile Insurance Company.

Of these two companies the larger was the Illinois Automobile Insurance Exchange, which had come to Bloomington in 1917 with F. S. Larison, a friend of George Mecherle, as attorney-in-fact, or manager. Under that title it was the result of a merger of the Illinois Automobile Fire Insurance Exchange, which had started business in Dixon, Illinois, three years previously, and the Illinois Motor Vehicle Liability Exchange. At the beginning it had operated on the assessment plan, collecting from its subscribers at the end of each six-month period those funds needed to pay its expenses and losses. But in 1920 it switched over to the advance-premium plan of payment. In 1921 rumors began to spread throughout insurance circles that it was in difficulties, and in June of that year, after an examination, the Virginia State Insurance Department refused to renew its license on the grounds that it lacked the $200,000 surplus required by the laws of Virginia. As a result of this action a so-called convention examination was made by examiners from the insurance departments of Missouri, Illinois, Kentucky, Minnesota, Oklahoma, Oregon, Virginia, Wisconsin and North Carolina. They did not find things to their liking.* Their report was given wide publicity and in the following year the Illinois Department of Trade and Commerce, which had charge of all insurance affairs in the state, was forced to step into the picture. Eventually the Exchange was reinsured into the Continental Auto Exchange of Springfield, Illinois, which itself was to disappear in the depression of 1929.

Mr. Larison, struggling to forfend the debacle that faced his company, tried to persuade George Mecherle, whose growing interest in insurance was by now hardly a secret among his friends in Bloomington, to invest some money in the Exchange and to share in its management. George Mecherle showed equally good judgment by refusing. It was probably during these talks with Mr. Larison that he met Miss Minnie A. Jones. A spinster then approaching middle age, Miss Jones had been connected with the Exchange from the beginning. She was a shrewd, competent, even an expert technician, who knew the ins and outs of insurance-office management, although she probably could not have sold a policy if she had tried. The technical jargon of the trade did not faze her and, blessed as she was with a mathematical sense, she could scan a page of statistics with understanding and relish. For George Mecherle, who then knew little if anything about this aspect of insurance beyond what he had picked up in books borrowed from the Bloomington public library, Minnie Jones was, for a brief period, to be a godsend.

The other insurance company which had a definite influence upon George Mecherle's career was in direct contrast with the Illinois Exchange. It was organized in nearby Pekin, Illinois, under the insurance laws of Illinois on April 1, 1921, about the time that Mr. Mecherle was beginning to devote all of his attention to the insurance business, by a small group of farmers who were members of the Tazewell County Farm Bureau. Its avowed purpose was to "render a cost service to members of the Farm Bureau," which was very nearly the ideal toward which George

---

* The examiners found admitted assets of $356,265 and a net surplus of $21,363; they found that the Advisory Board took no part in management; that there were 1,316 unpaid claims pending; that "in some cases" there was a disposition to scale down, compromise, or deny liability and to contest claims, even in cases where, in the opinion of the examiners, the liability and extent of damage was determined beyond reasonable doubt; and that, in 1921, the amount of losses and claims were high and that disbursements exceeded the income. *Best's Insurance Reports: Casualty and Miscellaneous*, 10th Edition (New York, Alfred M. Best Company, Inc., 1923), p. 464; *Best's Special Bulletin Service* (Alfred M. Best Company, Inc., June 7, 1923.)

Mecherle aspired. It operated on a simple basis, one almost as simple as that of the farm mutuals like Mr. Mecherle's own Old Town organization, except that it was managed by an attorney-in-fact.* He, however, was responsible to a board of nine directors, all of whom were members of the Tazewell County Farm Bureau. Each member of the Association was assessed, at the end of each six months, his *pro rata* share of losses and expense. A simple operation which, as he discovered, was easily managed by one man and a girl employee of the Farm Bureau, the Tazewell setup greatly appealed to Mr. Mecherle. At that time he had no visions of founding a vast network. He did, though, visualize the extension of the Tazewell idea to the farmers of the entire state.

Like most farmers George Mecherle had grown up in an environment in which the "farmers' mutuals," perhaps the most democratic form of insurance ever invented, had a strong influence. Their history went back to the second decade of the nineteenth century when the first such organizations came into being in the New England and Middle Atlantic states. They spread throughout the rural areas of the East, sometimes successfully and sometimes disastrously. In 1857 New York State took them under its official wing when the legislature passed an act which allowed twenty-five or more persons, living in a given township and owning a total of $50,000 worth of property, to form a mutual insurance company. They were allowed to pay losses on buildings or goods contained therein, only when loss or damage was occasioned by fire. In the next sixty years the idea spread westward and Wisconsin, Illinois, Michigan, Iowa, Minnesota, Ohio and Indiana, in that order, enacted farmers' mutual fire insurance laws, generally with more liberal and practical provisions than the original New York law. Lightning hazard, as well as fire, was assumed in many states, although not in Illinois, and territories were not as limited. In Illinois farmers' mutuals were organized in three classes —township, county and district—all under the supervision of the Director of Trade and Commerce. By 1890 practically every state in the Middle West had its full share of farmers' mutuals. There were 216 such organizations in Illinois in 1921, and it was estimated that, of the $1,589,-000,000 worth of insurable farm property in the state, $559,000,000, or 35.2%, was carried by these small, local institutions.†

* The farm mutuals seldom employed anyone. They did pay a "surveyor" and sometimes a secretary, but these fees often were as low as twenty-five dollars a year.
† See *Farmers' Mutual Fire Insurance in the United States* (Victor N. Valgren, Chicago, University of Chicago Press, 1924), *passim,* and table, p. 24. As of 1921 Illinois

The Tazewell company was not, strictly speaking, a farmers' mutual, but it operated on the same general principles, in that its membership was limited to members of the Tazewell County Farm Bureau and that each member was beholden to pay his share of the other members' losses. As George Mecherle's idea began to take shape he gave considerable thought to the various farmers' mutuals throughout the state, wondering if, perhaps, they might not form a nucleus for the statewide mutual company that was beginning to be the objective of his researches. But all his ideas, in the spring and summer of 1921, were diffuse. All, that is, except one. He had made up his mind definitely, somehow and soon, to enter the automobile insurance business.*

Always a blunt-spoken man, when the occasion warranted it, George Mecherle made no bones about what he had in mind to do. By the summer of 1921 he was telling everyone he met that he would soon be organizing an "honest insurance company." Years later he was to write that, after giving up farming, "I cast about for something to do and I believed that the building of a business as an off fall of one of the biggest industries in the country, which at that time was the third largest industry in the United States, was the thing to do." This terse statement

---

authorized the organization of town, county, and district farmers' mutuals, and required a minimum of $50,000 of risks for a company in either of the first two classes, and $100,000 in the case of a district company. The designation of a company by the words "town," "township," or "county" no longer meant that it was limited to a single unit of such area, but rather that the territory permitted was a given number of townships or counties, as the case might be. Valgren, p. 32.

* It has been impossible to trace the exact chronology of the development of George Mecherle's "idea," or even to isolate its exact origin. His older brother, Willis F. Mecherle, who was closely associated with him in the earliest days of the State Farm company, is said to have put the idea in his mind. According to one reliable source, Willis one day read a vigorous editorial in the *Prairie Farmer* condemning fly-by-night automobile inter-insurance exchanges and reciprocal companies which were "rooking" the farmers, and complaining about the high rates charged farmers by reliable companies which based their rates on city experience, where the frequency of accidents was much higher. Impressed by the farm paper's editorial, W.F.M. passed it on to his brother with the remark, "Why don't you look into this?" I have tried to locate this editorial, without success. The truth probably is that G.J.M. got the idea from a variety of sources—his talks with farmers, his own reading of farm papers, etc. He studied insurance in books, asked questions of his friends, and "played around" with the idea for many months, before he actually decided to do something serious about it. Even then he might not have gone ahead with it had it not been for the interest and encouragement of Mrs. Mecherle. He made many notes, working out his plans, and threw them away. Once she rescued his notes from the fireplace where he had thrown them (there was no fire going at the time) and returned them to him, urging him not to drop his idea or lose interest.

only partly explains his attitude. His researches had shown him, of course, the great size of the industry, but it does not seem to have influenced him greatly then. His horizon was still limited. What he definitely had in mind was a liability company based on mutual principles that could sell automobile insurance to the *farmers* of the *state of Illinois** at rates which they could afford. It was to be fundamentally an extension of the farmers' mutual idea to the automobile field, managed in such a way—he did not then know exactly how—as to return him a reasonable profit while keeping the rates as low as could possibly be justified.

He worked constantly toward this end. During the spring and summer of 1921 he put down several of his ideas on paper. Nights, when he found sleeping difficult, he would snap on the light and reach for the batch of cardboard inserts that had come from the laundry in his shirts and, with a stubby pencil, jot down on one of them his endless figures and his ideas. Days, he discussed his ideas with anyone who would listen. As one of his old friends recalled later, "George became sort of a pest in those days. You couldn't get through a game of cards or a street-corner conversation without his bringing up this insurance idea. Why, we got so we used to duck around corners whenever we saw him coming."

Among those whom he consulted was Minnie Jones. She not only understood what he was driving at, but she approved of its general tenor, and probably she helped him work out some of the early details. Herself a shrewd businesswoman, she was more than willing to be associated with a man of George Mecherle's caliber and character, especially now that she must have known that her future with the doomed Illinois Exchange was becoming more and more precarious. No matter how much George Mecherle was joshed about his "honest insurance company" there were few who did not believe that, once he got started on the right path, he would "make a go of it" and reach his avowed goal. From her knowledge of insurance practices Miss Jones must have known that, given the proper guidance, he was bound to succeed. Undoubtedly she encouraged him when he announced his intention of going to St. Louis in late September, 1921. Whether she did or not, he went; and the State Farm Mutual Automobile Insurance Company moved one step nearer creation. It was at St. Louis that the transformation of George Mecherle from Merna farmer to active businessman was completed.

* Hence the name eventually chosen by George Mecherle—State Farm.

4

FIRST GROWTH

Warren Gamaliel Harding had been in the White House for six months when George Mecherle boarded the Alton express for St. Louis. The depression that had come in the wake of the Armistice was working itself out. In Washington, the "great debate" over the Paris Peace Treaty and the League of Nations was drawing to a sorry close. There was a subdued air of optimism in business circles as that "Normalcy" which Mr. Harding had predicted in Boston several months before seemed about to arrive. Things were looking up a little, business was going to be better very soon—so they said in the smoking car on the way to St. Louis, and so it turned out to be.

Quietly puffing his inevitable panatella, George Mecherle considered the general situation as reported in the *Chicago Tribune*, wondered if he were not a little crazy to be thinking of starting an insurance company, and then put such doubts out of his mind. Many of his friends had seriously told him he was off on the wrong track. "Look at what's happening to poor Larison," they said. But he had back of him something more substantial than such well-intentioned doubts. He had, and this was what counted most of all, the faith and encouragement of his wife. All along she had believed in him and in his idea, and he knew her insistence was not just compensation on her part for having got him to give up the farm. Farming was done for, now; he would be forty-five years old in less than a year; he had made his choice and now he was in for it. He would find out at St. Louis just how crazy he was.

St. Louis was the place to go for the answer, for on his train and all the other trains pulling into the city were the men who ought to be able to tell him. Meeting there that warm week, to discuss all aspects of their mutual problems, were three national groups of insurance men. There were delegates to the Federation of Mutual Fire Insurance Companies, men who insured lumber yards, hardware risks, grain mills. With these George Mecherle had little in common. Nor was he greatly interested in the problems of the National Association of Mutual Casualty Companies, for these were then mostly concerned with workmen's compensation acts that had recently opened up a whole new field of business. He was looking forward to the sessions of the National Association of Mutual Insurance Companies.

This association, which had been organized in 1898, had originated with the farmers' mutuals and, although other mutual companies of all classes were members, the farmers' mutuals still predominated. It served as a legislative watchdog, or lobby, for the interests of the mutuals in Washington, and as a clearing-house for all kinds of information and advice to the officers of the state associations as well as to officers of the local mutuals. George Mecherle was not an officer of the Illinois State Association of Mutual Insurance Companies, but his close friend, S. B. Mason, of Bloomington, was the state secretary and a member of the National Association. Mr. Mecherle's Old Town mutual was a member of both organizations, but since he was only a member and not an officer of this farmers' group his presence at the St. Louis meeting was strictly unofficial. He was, however, among friends. Here he could talk and argue and sell his idea. Here, too, he could listen and absorb pointers that came right from the horse's mouth. He was adept in both roles.

It was at this convention—perhaps the most important of the hundreds of gatherings of insurance men he was to attend in the next thirty years—that he got the "inside" story of the Tazewell County Farm Bureau setup that had then been in operation just about five months. This was significant, for the information he obtained from the president

of the Tazewell County Farm Bureau, who was running the new automobile insurance association, helped crystallize his own ideas. But in the
final analysis it was not so important as the fact that, in making his gregarious way among the delegates, he met a slim, bemustached, spec-
tacled little man named George E. Beedle.

This meeting may have been deliberate on George Mecherle's part, for
then, as later, he had an uncanny way of finding his way to the right
place and spotting the right person. George Beedle himself was not the
right person, but he worked for him. By now Mr. Mecherle had learned
that if he were to start an insurance company he would need expert legal
advice, for no business can be set up without the aid of a competent
lawyer, one who knows the intricacies of the particular business involved.
All his life, when he acquired anything, whether it was a team of draft
horses, a tractor, or a planting of seed corn, George Mecherle had always
gone after the best. Now that he had come to the point where he felt
his idea should be set down on paper he wanted the best insurance attorney he could find to make the arrangements. Everyone whose judgment he valued told him that Herman Ekern of Chicago was that man.
When they told him that Ekern was the best, but that he probably
would be too busy to bother with a "downstate farmer" with nothing
more tangible to offer than some scribbled notes, Ekern became, in
George Mecherle's mind, the only lawyer who would do for the job. But
he did not see him now. Instead he saw George Beedle, who was Ekern's
man.

Because they were general counsel for the three organizations meeting that week in St. Louis, Herman Ekern and his younger partner, Erwin Aaron Meyers, were two of the busiest men present. George Mecherle did not meet either of them for any extended conversation at this
time. But he had a long talk with George Beedle, who had a wide knowledge of insurance problems of all kinds. Mr. Beedle had been an insurance commissioner for the state of Wisconsin from 1907 to 1911, and
he had also been a member of that state's legislature. At this time he
was assistant secretary of the Federation of Mutual Fire Insurance Companies. He was also office manager for the law firm of Ekern, Meyers &
Janisch, where his wide knowledge of the technical aspects of insurance
made him invaluable. He was a quiet, precise sort of man, with a neat
and orderly mind which made up for his apparent lack of aggressiveness.
George Mecherle laid his proposition before him and George Beedle
was sufficiently impressed to urge him to come to Chicago and talk with

the majestic Ekern as soon as possible after the convention had adjourned. This George Mecherle promised to do. If, as seems probable, Beedle promptly forgot about it, he made a great mistake. For George Mecherle always did what he said he would do and he was now in deadly seriousness about founding and financing a statewide farmers' mutual automobile insurance company.

Mr. Mecherle came back from St. Louis fired with enthusiasm. In the big, sprawling house on South Main street Mae Mecherle, now a semi-invalid from arthritis, greeted him with her usual encouragement. He then had a long business session with Miss Jones, who agreed then to become his partner in the new company and even to help finance it. It is possible that at this time he drove to Pekin and made a personal examination of the Tazewell association, gathering facts and figures from Chester G. Starr, the farm advisor for the county and the attorney-in-fact for the association. On October 5, 1921, he and Miss Jones composed their first letter to Ekern, Meyers & Janisch, Attorneys at Law and Insurance Counsel, 208 South LaSalle Street, Chicago, Illinois. It read as follows:

Gentlemen:
Relative to the proposition which we had under advisement in St. Louis, during the Convention of the National Association of Mutual Insurance Companies, will say,
That I have been handicapped considerably in obtaining information relative to this proposition on account of the death in our family to which my time and attention have been given.
We have succeeded in framing a policy which I hope will meet with your approval, but it may be necessary to make some changes in order to cover the ground necessary to conform with the mutual laws of the state of Illinois.
I will be with you Friday morning and at that time hope to be able to finish this matter up in a satisfactory manner to all concerned.
With kindest regards, I am
Respectfully yours,
George J. Mecherle.

George Mecherle was unable to keep his date in Chicago "on Friday" because "the lady who is to accompany us"—undoubtedly Miss Jones—could not get to the city on that day. In spite of the delay he kept busy. In a brief note to the law firm, still addressed to no individual member, he reported that "everything is progressing nicely with us" and that he still "hoped to be able to make some satisfactory arrangement regarding policies and applications." He was, in fact, so sanguine of starting his business almost at once that he took a room at the Illinois Hotel in Bloomington for use as a temporary office. Unfortunately he forgot to give this address in his letter to the law firm and the letter setting up another appointment was delayed; but the confusion was soon straightened out and George Mecherle went off to Chicago to see the great lawyer. His hope of being able "to finish up this matter in a satisfactory manner to all concerned," however, was to be rudely shattered.

George Mecherle, the farmer from downstate, armed with his notes and his checkbook, was not kept waiting or given a "run-around" by the big city lawyer, as the legend familiar in Bloomington has it. They met as agreed and they had a long and businesslike, if not warmhearted, talk, in which Mr. Mecherle outlined his scheme, which was frankly based on the Tazewell County operation. He stressed the fact that what he wanted to establish was a farmers' automobile insurance company on a statewide basis which would sell good insurance at the lowest cost possible. He thought he knew how to do this.

Herman Ekern, a man of wide experience, who quite probably until this moment had never heard of the Farmers Automobile Insurance Association of Pekin, Illinois, was not impressed. He pointed out, one by one, the flaws he immediately saw in the proposition and did his best to discourage Mr. Mecherle's enthusiasm for this particular scheme. He was impressed by Mr. Mecherle's manner, his stubborn conviction that he was right, his obvious honesty, and his over-all conception of the desperate need for "an honest insurance company." There is no question but that George Mecherle was shocked by this realistic reception and that he was, as he later told many friends, "pretty damned mad" when he left the law office on South LaSalle Street.

He may have been mad, but he was not convinced that he was as wrong as Ekern had implied. Within a week he wrote a remarkable letter. Because more than anything else it shows the temper of his mind and the true tenor of his thoughts at this most crucial period in his life, it is worth giving in full.

In this letter I hope to be able to give you some figures that will prove to your satisfaction that I have been in the right at all times regarding the cost of the insurance we have had under consideration. I will submit figures to you for the cost of the insurance for a period of six months in the Farmers Automobile Insurance Association of Pekin of which Mr. Chester G. Starr, Farm Advisor of Tazwell [*sic*] County, is the attorney in fact.

We must make allowance for the cost of office rent, stenographers hire and probably a few other small charges which are not taken in consideration in this organization as the work is done in connection with the Farm Bureau, the stenographer and Mr. Starr being paid by the Farm Bureau and their services up to the present time have been paid from the Farm Bureau fund. The cost of printing policies, application blanks, and all other literature necessary to the conduct of this business has been paid for out of the assessment of the association. There has never been any allowance made as yet for Mr. Starr's remuneration as attorney in fact. So the figures I will submit will be the actual cost of the insurance less the cost of the items I have mentioned.

This organization has been running some time over six months. As you know it was necessary to obtain two hundred applications before they could obtain a charter. They had considerably more than two hundred applications at the time they began business. At the present time they have six hundred seventeen policies in force and levied their first assessment a short time ago. The six months average loss per car was $2.31 which included 67¢ per car of office expense namely, printing bills and other items which were necessary to the business. The cost per car for fire during the period of six months was zero. The cost for theft per car was 2¢. The cost for property damage per car was 13¢, and the cost of collision per car was $1.49, leaving the 67¢ office expense to make up the required $2.31 of business operation. This, Mr. Ekern, bears out my argument in every way. I have contended at all times that the cost of this class of insurance, insuring the class of risks which come under this class of insurance, would be astoundingly low.

The members of this association are all members of the Farm Bureau and the application makes provision that unless they continue members of the Farm Bureau, their connection with the Insurance Association becomes void. The class of risks in this association are identical with the class of risks I intended interesting in my organization, and I am still satisfied that these risks will result in an exceptionally low cost insurance to the men that are connected with that kind of an organization. You can take the cost of $2.31 per car as a six months cost; that can be doubled and tripled and then will be lower than anything that is offered in the way of a real sound automobile insurance company. As far as the office work is concerned the care of these six hundred seventeen policies is in the hands of the one stenographer in Mr. Starr's office. Mr. Starr spends Saturday in his office and the young lady stated that the matter of taking care of the business amounts to practically nothing after he had once got started. She says it just passes along with the regular line of business and they don't notice it.

I am satisfied that my idea is right and more than ever convinced that the plan under which you would expect me to operate in regard to the collection of an abnormal premium cost in the incipiency of the association is absolutely wrong and cannot be sold in competition with the class of insurance being sold at the present time. I am firmly convinced that the plan under which I have arranged to operate together with the collection of one per cent of the face of the policies at the time of delivery of the policies would be ample for a six months period. Further than that, if we would be able to sell three or four thousand applications for insurance prior to the organization, it would accumulate a fund of thirty to forty thousand dollars which I would gladly place in a position so it would be available for the payment of losses until such time as assessment could be levied. It will be necessary to sell this business on a loss [low?] cost basis and in no other way, which the figures from Mr. Starr's organization prove can be done.

The matter of organizing a company of this class seems a very simple matter as Mr. Starr and the stenographer in his office were not acquainted in any way with the insurance proposition prior to the beginning of this company, and after laying my proposition before you in a clear, concise, candid, matter of fact manner, with the intention of operating in justice and fairness to every person we could interest in this kind of a proposition, I feel that I am entitled to every cooperation that you men might be able to give me from your office. I realize the responsibility you take in passing on this proposition, but you must remember that my interests and my connection with this company I consider of just as much importance as the connection that your organization might have with the company, and if this organization resulted in a failure it would reflect on me in a manner which would be very distasteful and would be the last thing I would wish to happen in case this matter is continued. I feel that this project is too good and means too much to every car owner in the State of Illinois to abandon it without an attempt at organization.

I am willing to do anything that your office might suggest in the way of protection to policyholders, but if it is impossible for you people to take any other viewpoint of the proposition than the collection of what I call an abnormal premium deposit in the beginning of the company, it will be necessary for me to either abandon the project or else attempt to perfect the organization without your assistance. Please let me hear from you at your earliest possible convenience as I have a proposition which I must pass on by the last of the week, which, if this matter of insurance is abandoned, I expect to take up.

I am inclosing a sample policy and application from Mr. Starr's company, which policy I consider one of the fairest policies which would be written in an organization of this kind. Although, there are a few minor changes I might suggest and which I think you will see when you look these papers over.

Hoping this letter will be the means of giving you a different viewpoint as to the possibilities of cost in an organization of this kind, I beg to remain,

Very respectfully yours,
George J. Mecherle.

The letter was a revealing combination of shrewdness and naïveté, injured pride and dogged determination, and plain, old-fashioned bluff. George Mecherle had, as far as anyone knows, no other "proposition" in mind, but was trying to hurry Ekern into giving approval to his plan. At that time he had already conceived one of his real strokes of genius, which he had laid before Ekern in his conversations. This was the idea of making the Farm Mutuals throughout the state the nucleus of his agencies. He had impressed Ekern with the breadth of his vision in this respect, and, indeed, the Chicago lawyer had no intention of letting Mecherle escape him. But he knew more than Mecherle about the "esoterics of insurance," as his partner Erwin Meyers called the intricacies of this complex business, and he knew that Mecherle, a proud and honest man, had to be humbled a little. Mecherle, on the other hand, seems to have been trying to goad the lawyer into giving him the best advice available, hoping, of course, that it would jibe with his own conceptions. Ekern's answer, which was sent out by return mail on October 20th, was as frank as it was prompt. And it shows that he had a clear conception of the broad principles of the determined farmer downstate.

My dear Mr. Mecherle [Ekern wrote]:—
I have your letter of October 18th addressed to our firm for my attention, and I am very much interested in the figures you submit and the idea generally.
It does not seem to me that you should seriously consider going to work on the basis of an experience of six months for such a limited number of policies as mentioned in your letter. It is obvious from these figures that these cannot in any way represent an average. It is also plain that this does not take into account any cost for losses which may have been unascertained or unsettled. Even if it did, there has not a sufficient length of time expired to give an insurance average. It is just this kind of data which misleads people and starts insurance companies on a wrong basis.
There is no question in my mind that you could start a company on a very low cost basis and that you could finance it yourself out of the membership fees collected and such additional money as you might put in yourself. In this way you might build up quite a membership to begin with, and you could then figure on taking your chances on being able to carry these along at a low cost, raising your price later on. That is, of course, the way it is done in a great many cases. This would mean that you would do your work for nothing, or less than nothing, for a considerable time. If things went well you probably would repay yourself what you put in and possibly get back a little something at some time in the future for the time and effort you put in without any compensation.
It has not been my idea that you wanted to do this, and it is not my

idea that it is necessary to do it, and I want to be very frank in stating that the figures you submit rather confirm my views than otherwise. I am certain from the experience that we have had that if you could look five or six years into the experience of this organization you would find entirely different results.*

You do not say whether or not you have submitted this to Miss Jones or whether she has changed her mind about going on with the organization on some different plan. There is, of course, nothing final in the plan we discussed and there may be other plans as good or better, and my only suggestion would be that if you can work out another plan with Miss Jones which she approves of heartily and would be willing to join you in, I should be very pleased to go over it with you. It seems to me, however, futile to discuss plans for which you would not be able to get the approval of some person who has considerable familiarity with the insurance business, the manner of keeping accounts, setting up reserves, and doing all the work that is necessary to conduct the business in accordance with the requirements of the Insurance Departments.

You must keep in mind in this connection that you are not contemplating the organization of a purely local company where it would be possible to take a chance on getting a heavy loss at some particular time and getting the members to pay it because they know about it. Even this is very precarious and we frequently have cases in our mutual farm companies insuring fire, where the companies are obliged to wind up because these farmers find the assessment to pay a single loss heavier than they want to bear. Your plan, as I understand it, contemplated establishing a state-wide company. For this purpose it is absolutely necessary that it should be on a fully adequate basis.

I am going to Washington tonight and will be gone most of the coming week. But I take it this will make no difference as it would be necessary for you to take up your plan with different secretaries or some committee of the secretaries of the state association, and this will take some days. I will be pleased to take this up with you when I return, in case you conclude to go on with it.

Yours very truly,
Herman L. Ekern.

The weeks following the receipt of this letter were a period of extreme uncertainty for George Mecherle. He had listened carefully to Ekern's arguments against his proposal and also to the lawyer's ideas on how the plan could be salvaged. Nothing was settled in his own mind. But no matter how tempted he was to throw the whole thing overboard he stuck to it, greatly encouraged by Mae Mecherle's unswerving belief in his destiny. On November 16 he wrote to "My dear Mr. Ekern" informing

* In 1930 the F.A.I.A. of Pekin had 6,583 subscribers; in 1952 it had 50,100 subscribers. See Best's *Reports,* 1930 and 1952.

him boldly that "I am now satisfied in my own mind that your plan is the better plan to insure permanency in the business venture which I have contemplated.

"I am not in the position just at present to tell you definitely what my future plans are," he went on, "but believe that in the near future I will ask you to complete the program according to the plan outlined." He insisted that there were several minor changes that would have to be made, but "after due deliberation, I have come to agree with you as to the feasibility of your plan."

He sought a further conference with the attorney, adding, with typical determination as well as sound prophecy, "I am still confident that this proposition is right and still feel that I am able to put it over in good shape. I have not lost confidence in myself or in my proposition, although I have been resting my case until conditions get better, and believe that conditions will get better as a result of the Peace Conference and the reduction of railroad rates which will make it possible to do business with this class of trade more easily in the near future."

Nothing happened at once. George Mecherle continued to study the situation carefully, and a few weeks later he again wrote to Chicago asking for an appointment, because he now had a plan "which is workable and which," he believed, "would meet with your approval. I have one very interesting proposition which I will submit to you when I am in Chicago." Ekern, however, had other matters on his mind than the farmer who would be an insurance man, and reported that he would not be in the office until mid-December. George Mecherle was not to be put off. He came to Chicago anyway, and this time he met Ekern's partner, Erwin A. Meyers. From then on, things began to move.

George Jacob Mecherle

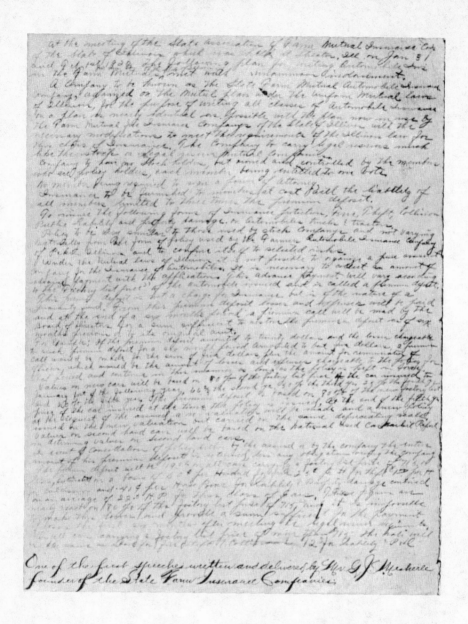

One of the first speeches written and delivered by Mr G J Mecherle, founder of the State Farm Insurance Companies.

Manuscript of G. J. Mecherle's notes

Durley Building

McLean County Farm Bureau Building

Handwritten rate sheet

Original home office building

Present home office building

State Farm Fire and Casualty Company building

G. J. Mecherle beside Model T Ford

Branch office building

G. J. Mecherle family

Berkeley office building

Ramond P. Mecherle

Adlai H. Rust

5

THE PLANT IS NURTURED

If he had tried, George Mecherle could not have found a person who was more of a contrast to himself than Erwin A. Meyers. About the only thing these two men had in common, when they first met, was the fact that both were country boys. In all other respects (except, of course, their mutual interest in the insurance business) they were opposites. George Mecherle had not gone through high school: Erwin Meyers had been graduated from college when he was twenty-three years old and had acquired his law degree three years later. The closest George Mecherle had ever come to politics was as a road commissioner of a rural township; Erwin Meyers had been interested in politics since his university days in Bob LaFollette's Wisconsin and then in Woodrow Wilson's Washington. George Mecherle was a steady reader of newspapers, farm publications, and magazines, a pragmatic searcher after the usable fact; Erwin Meyers was a lifelong student of history, economics and political science in the abstract. Eleven years George Mecherle's junior, Meyers had already acquired a wealth of experience that had brought him a partnership in one of the most successful insurance law firms in the Middle West. Tall, slim, somewhat nervous in movement and careless in manner, he was a shrewd observer of the specialized world of business in which he operated.

Then just thirty-three years old, he had come to his present position through a series of unusual and interesting experiences. The son of a lumberman, he had been born in Verona Township, Daine County, not far from the state capital at Madison. His father, Herbert Oscar Meyers, did not see what good a college education would do him, but told him he might attend the University of Wisconsin at Madison if he were willing to work his own way. Young Meyers did this by acting for two years as research worker for the Wisconsin Tax Commission and the Wisconsin Revisor of Statutes. When the State Legislature was in session he acted as a bill draftsman, much to the annoyance of the law school, which had a rule that no law student should work while attending the school. Through this work he met many politically powerful individuals, not the least important of whom was Senator Robert M. LaFollette, the great insurgent Republican.

In the spring of 1914, just after Meyers had obtained his law degree, Senator LaFollette recommended him to Louis D. Brandeis, the brilliant Boston attorney who had been retained as special counsel in connection with the railroad rate case involving most of the railroads on the Atlantic seaboard and central states, which was then pending before the Interstate Commerce Commission. LaFollette was responsible for the ICC investigation and was following it closely in the Senate. Young Meyers went to Washington and for several weeks worked with the great enemy of the "curse of bigness," Brandeis. But shortly thereafter LaFollette became seriously ill with arthritis and borrowed Meyers from Brandeis to help him with legal and economic research in connection with his legislative matters, including the history-making rate case. Meyers stayed with LaFollette for nearly a year.

During this period he had one adventure which was to be of great value to him in his later work as counsel for various insurance companies and organizations, work which was to bring him continually before various lawmaking and regulating bodies. Brandeis discovered that a powerful railroad lobby was at work seeking to stymie his efforts before the Commission by inducing that body to decide the proposed rate increase in favor of the railroads. Thousands of letters, telegrams and other messages flooded the offices of the members of the commission, streaming in from all parts of the country, from bankers, businessmen and other persons presumably with influence in their communities. Brandeis reported this state of affairs, which he believed far exceeded the constitutional right of petition, to LaFollette, who introduced a resolution demanding the delivery of these lobbying messages to the Senate. He won his point and the Commission sent a drayload or more of letters and telegrams up to his office on Capitol Hill.

To young Meyers fell the laborious task of sorting them and tracing them back to their origin. He finally followed the trail to a dinner given by the railroad industry in Atlantic City. With this damning knowledge, buttressed by convincing evidence and charts showing the lines of force followed by the lobby, Senator LaFollette, although still ailing, exposed the affair in a powerful speech from the floor of the Senate. The result of this publicity was that the pressure on the unhappy Commission was lifted and the rate case decided against the railroads.

Soon thereafter President Wilson nominated Louis D. Brandeis an Associate Justice of the United States Supreme Court. This unloosed a barrage of criticism from conservative and reactionary quarters and started one of the bitterest of Senate battles for his confirmation. It was a personal blow to Meyers, for it meant the removal of his friend and employer from public life. Ironically he was assigned by LaFollette, one of Brandeis's staunchest supporters, to prepare an elaborate brief on the Boston lawyer's record for use in his behalf before the Senate. When Brandeis's appointment was confirmed, Meyers was, of course, at loose ends. The great jurist offered him a job in his Boston law firm, but with Brandeis's departure from the firm he lost interest and decided to return to the Middle West where he had grown up and had friends. Senator LaFollette then offered him a junior partnership in his Madison law office, with a promise of political support should he later decide to seek public office. After a great deal of thought Meyers rejected the offer because he was convinced that there would be too much politics and too little law.

Erwin Meyers had met Herman Ekern when the latter was a deputy Insurance Commissioner of Wisconsin and Meyers was drafting legislative bills while studying law. Mr. Ekern, who had practiced law for twenty years in Whitehall and Madison, now offered him a partnership, having decided to leave the insurance commission and return to private practice. The two started their law office in Chicago toward the end of 1916 with the intention of specializing in insurance law. Shortly after the beginning of this venture the United States entered the World War. Un-married, in good physical condition, and of the proper age, Meyers, it became evident, would be a good candidate for A-1 in the draft. His own recollection of what happened is worth telling:

Knowing this I began looking around for life insurance which would not be voided in the event of service in the army or navy. I succeeded in buying a little insurance but found it rough going. So one evening in the office, I pointed out to Mr. Ekern my difficulty, which would be even more pronounced to those in the service who knew less about insurance than I did. I suggested some form of insurance to protect service men. The more we pursued this the more we got interested, with the result that Mr. Ekern drafted the first bill providing for war risk insurance for soldiers and sailors.

We went down to Washington and finally sold the idea to the Insurance Commissioner of the District of Columbia, to Mr. Joseph Davies, who was then chairman to the Federal Trade Commission, and to William Gibbs McAdoo, Secretary of the Treasury and son-in-law of Woodrow Wilson. The result was that President Wilson endorsed the plan which, with various changes, was finally enacted into law and became the Soldiers and Sailors Insurance Act.

Federal Judge Julian Mack of Cincinnati took great interest in the bill and, I think, was author of the final draft which I honestly believe was not as good as the one we had. Our bill provided for permanent insurance on a whole life basis whereas Judge Mack's bill called for straight term insurance. Our theory was that if the soldier or sailor had whole life insurance he would have a reserve value which would keep the policy in force while he was getting adjusted to civilian life. The trouble with the term plan was that it lapsed the moment the ex-soldier or ex-sailor stopped paying premiums, since he had no credit to fall back upon.

After passage of the act Commissioner Nesbitt of the District of Columbia was appointed Commissioner of the Bureau of War Risk Insurance in the United States Treasury Department. He tried to induce Ekern to join him but the latter was unable to do so. Instead, Meyers went to Washington as administrative assistant to the commissioner, where he remained for several months. He then entered the Army, which he was to leave with the rank of Captain. Since the end of the war he had practiced insurance law with Ekern and Harold F. Janisch in the office where George Mecherle now faced him for the first time.

Once again Mecherle presented his plan, which, in essence, was as follows: He would insure an automobile for $1.00 per $100 of the physical valuation of the car that was to be insured. Since the prevailing stock company rate for insuring an automobile averaged $40, the difference between the two rates was astounding, and, as both Ekern and Meyers pointed out, it was, for this and other reasons, far too low. For one thing Mecherle's plan provided nothing for an agent's commission, beyond the $1.00 flat fee which he proposed to pay at the time the policy was sold. It was his belief that he could sell enough policies this way to do business. As they talked Meyers agreed with Mecherle that the stock company rate, especially as it applied to rural areas, was far too high; but he was equally insistent that Mecherle's proposed rate was far too low.

"The stock company figures *can't* be *that* wrong," he said, pointing to Mecherle's figures, "and you can never win at your rates."

The two men argued back and forth for several minutes. Meyers was deeply impressed by Mecherle's stubborn determination and his natural salesmanship and Mecherle must have been impressed by Meyer's obvious knowledge of the mathematical intricacies of the business they were discussing.

After a while Meyers offered to make a study of the whole situation, starting with Mecherle's basic proposal, and to see what could be worked out that would meet the economics and the legal necessities involved. Up to this time no money had passed between George Mecherle and the lawyers, and no mention had been made of any retainer. Mecherle now reached for his checkbook and, sitting across the desk from Meyers, wrote out a check for $500, to pay the costs of the investigation and research. Still not completely convinced that the relationship between himself and the lawyers was a friendly one, he said, "If you don't think it's any good, call up the bank." Meyers looked at him a minute and said, "If it's no good we wouldn't want your kind of business, anyway." He gave Mecherle back his check, saying, "We have never asked you for a check. But you've got a partner. I'll do the law work and you'll do the selling. We'll get up the plan for you. If it goes, we will get paid. If it doesn't, neither of us gets anything."

Mecherle looked closely at the younger man, and reached out his large, farm-hardened hand. "Son," he said, "you're on." *

* This version differs from other versions, notably Williamson, *American Story*, pp. 44-6, which indicate that Ekern, Meyers & Janisch would not do business with Mecherle until he paid a $500 fee. The firm of Ekern, Meyers & Janisch received no money for its work in organizing State Farm until several months after the company was organized. The agreement between Ekern, Meyers & Janisch and State Farm is explained later in the text. Prior to the meeting described above Mecherle dealt with Ekern; from now on almost all the firm's affairs were handled by E. A. Meyers, as the

While Meyers was doing his "paper work" George Mecherle was busy with his end of the bargain. There was a great deal of preliminary salesmanship to exercise before the proposed company was ready to do business. Basic to the entire idea was the new company's similarity to the farm mutual companies. At that time it was thought that the greater part of the new company's strength would come from these organizations, of which there were 216 then operating in the state of Illinois. Further strength was expected from the farm bureaus, but members of these, of course, fully understood the operation of farm mutuals. It was this aspect of the new plan which Mecherle and Meyers decided to stress. In most instances these farmers' mutuals were operated by the best-known and most highly respected farmers in their communities, and it was felt that if these gentlemen could be made to be interested and shown that this new company was no fly-by-night reciprocal or attorney-in-fact company its immediate success would be assured.

Early in January a prospectus was prepared in which it was made plain that the plan of operation was as similar to that used by the farm mutuals as was then permitted under Illinois insurance laws. This was sent to a selected group of farmers, all secretaries of farm mutuals. Thus the way was paved for the next important step.

On January 31, 1922, the Illinois State Association of Mutual Insurance Companies opened its annual two-day meeting in Streator. George Mecherle went up by train, with his old friend William Lausterer, a director of the Old Town Mutual and a neighbor of his since boyhood, and S. B. Mason of Bloomington, who was secretary of the State Association and vice president of the Illinois Farmers' Institute. Also on the train was J. W. Coale, a farmer from Holder, and secretary of the Old Town Mutual. If these gentlemen were not already fully aware of George's plan, they were by the time they got off the train at Streator

---

correspondence between the firm and the law firm indicates. Williamson erroneously puts the meetings with E.A.M. after the Streator meeting (February, 1922). They took place in November and December 1921. In 1923 G.J.M. stated publicly: "During the year 1921 I called on 25 or 30 secretaries of Farm Mutual Insurance Companies in this State, and asked them what would be their opinion of organizing a Mutual Automobile Insurance Company on the same plan as we are now operating fire mutuals, and all went to Mr. Gregory [editor-in-chief] of the *Prairie Farmer*. He had written many articles concerning mutual insurance. He said, 'I think you are on the right track. . . .' With the assistance of Mr. Meyers of Ekern, Meyers & Janisch a plan was worked out, and it was laid before the meeting [of the Illinois State Association of Mutual Insurance Companies] at Streator, and was unanimously endorsed at that meeting."

Junction. Hard-headed farmers, who knew the value of a dollar, they liked the idea; shrewd when it came to buying anything, from a second-hand harrow to a brand-new idea, they thought it was sound as a nut.

When the time came, George Mecherle was introduced to the gathering by Mr. Mason and Mr. Lausterer. His sales talk was succinct and to the point. There were no oratorical flourishes, no nonsense, just "plain talk." "I will take up this proposition without preamble," he said, and proceeded to tell why, up to now, farm mutuals had not been able successfully to write full coverage for automobiles. First, they weren't big enough; second, they couldn't stand the overhead; third, they had no organization for the recovery of stolen cars. But, in spite of these and various other handicaps, "there is no reason why you should not enjoy the benefits of an insurance written by your local secretary and directors, in which you have an interest identical with your interest in your local fire organization, but with all the advantages of a company with sufficient volume of business to insure a very low cost of insurance with a minimum of hazard."

He then pointed out how, in spite of the fact that the stock companies had worked out a classification system which supposedly set rates "in proportion to the losses in each territory," it didn't always work out to the advantage of the insured. "This has been some improvement," he admitted, "but as the business has been written by agents interested solely in the commission paid, the result has been that many cars are insured in which the moral hazard is very pronounced.

"Investigations show," he went on, stressing what he had always meant by "an honest insurance company," "that by the elimination of the moral hazard, losses are decreased very materially—and that is the point I wish to make very pronounced in connection with the organization for which, with your assistance, I expect to stand sponsor.

"The representatives of the Farm Mutuals are the representative citizens of the communities in which they reside. The fact of their being members of such organization stamps them as men of high character and good business judgment. The automobiles owned by these men are as much a part of their every day lives as their coats, their hats, or their shoes. It is a necessity in their every day business and when one has outlived its usefulness it is replaced by another.

"This class of risk has no more reason for carrying their automobile insurance in a company insuring mortgaged cars, cars purchased on the time payment plan, commercial trucks, cars used for hire, taxi cabs, or any car used for purposes in which the hazard is abnormal, than they would have reason for cancelling their present policies in the Farm Mutuals and buying insurance in any of the stock companies. This organization will be as distinct and separate from any other organizations writing this class of insurance as sunshine is from shadow. All members must necessarily be men of some property, and no application will be accepted from any but members of Farm Bureaus, members of Farm Mutuals, their immediate families, or those eligible to membership in such organizations."

George Mecherle proceeded then to give a general outline of the organization as he and Meyers had worked it out, explaining how its rates would be arrived at, how the membership fee would be good during the life of the company, the proposed method of having no agents except Farm Mutual secretaries and a few special agents from the home office to show them how to operate, and how adjustments would, whenever feasible, be settled at once by local agents. He summed it up as follows:

"You will carry your insurance in a company in which all members are the same stamp of men as yourselves. You will not be paying losses for those who have cars insured that may become a liability on their hands. Your company will have every benefit the same as though you were conducting your own company, with the added benefit of a larger company in reducing the amount of liability in the first instance. The business will be written by men with direct responsibility to the company and who know the men they insure by their first names—as against the average agent whose sole aim is securing the commission regardless of the nature of the risk. Losses will be adjusted by your local agents. You will pay no more than the actual cost of the insurance plus the small amount of remuneration to officers as against a 50% profit in most stock companies and 30% to 50% of the premium calls in all reciprocal companies. It will be the policy of our company to build membership by straight forward business methods, conducted honorably and fairly so that no one connected with it will ever need to make apology. The Farm Mutuals require no apology and this organization must be absolutely on a par with their high class methods. Furthermore, every dollar put into this organization purchases something; the premium deposit may be withdrawn on cancellation of the policy; and the only expense above the actual cost of insurance is the small charge for service rendered. In my opinion the plan is ideal, and I wish an expression of this meeting as to the feasibility of the plan."

If George Mecherle had had any forebodings of failure when he took the train for Streator, they now evaporated. Without a dissenting vote the members of the State Association gave their endorsement to the State Farm Mutual Automobile Insurance Company.

This freely given endorsement was a red feather in George Mecherle's cap, for, above all, it meant that the top men among those people from whom he expected to get his business approved without equivocation of himself and his plan for "an honest insurance company."

George Mecherle must have been the busiest man at this busy convention that bright January day. He not only made his speech, but he signed up twenty-two men who agreed to serve as sponsors of the company. Their signatures were necessary for the articles of incorporation soon to be filed with the state. He also collected the signatures of the six farmer mutual secretaries who agreed to serve with him as a temporary board of directors until the first membership meeting could be called. All were farmers, or ex-farmers like himself. Besides himself they included J. J. Prater, president of the State Association of Mutual Insurance Companies, from Vandalia, the seat of Fayette County in the south central part of the state; W. B. McFarland of Hoopeston, Vermillion County, over near the Indiana border; Charles B. Holz, secretary of the Farmers Pioneer Mutual Fire and Lightning Company, whose charter went back to 1874 and which then boasted 1,960 policies in force, amounting to $7,000,000 in value. These all were men of substance, whose willingness to support George Mecherle and the little company in the making was something not to be taken lightly.

The winter must have passed slowly for George Mecherle and Minnie Jones, the two people most involved in this little project. Even in their minds there was no conception of anything tremendous to come, although Mr. Mecherle had revised his estimate of doing business on the small scale of the Tazewell association. An idea of the size and importance of this operation can be found in the fact that when an investigator from the State Insurance Commissioner's office came to Bloomington he found that nobody had heard of the State Farm company and he had difficulty in locating either of the partners. The application for a charter had been filed with the Director of Trade and Commerce, immediately after the Streator meeting, in which it was set forth that the purpose of the company was "to insure against loss, expense and liability resulting from the ownership, maintenance or use of any automobile or other vehicle." No difficulty in obtaining it was anticipated, but before the articles of association could be approved by Director George A. Barr, certain technical requirements had to be met.

The state certificate of approval of the articles of association was forthcoming on March 29, and then it was necessary to acquire a license. In order to do this a "certificate of deposit" for $25,000 had to be deposited with the insurance commission and a minimum of 200 applications for insurance policies had to be received. The laws of all states require domestic insurance companies to maintain a deposit of cash or government bonds for the protection of policyholders, the deposit being made either with the insurance commissioner or the state treasurer. As evidence of this deposit the company receives a certificate. Without this it cannot operate. But this money is not to be used for operational purposes. Funds for these had to be obtained elsewhere before the State Farm company could start business.

A stock company, of course, would collect this operating money from its stockholders, but this was to be a mutual company, owned by its policyholders. Until there were policyholders there would be no money. This had to be furnished by management through what is known as a surplus note, a form whereby management lends to the new company the necessary amount. This obligation of the company is to be paid back to the lender only at such time as the company has excess surplus funds available for that purpose.

But who was to be management? The obvious answer to that was George Mecherle and Minnie Jones. The means were accomplished by businesslike methods. The firm of G. J. Mecherle, Inc., was set up, with George Mecherle, Minnie A. Jones, and her sister, Susie E. Jones, as incorporators. The stock value of this corporation was set at $5 a share. George Mecherle held 60% of this, Minnie Jones held 30%, and her sister held 10%. The amount of the authorized stock was $20,000. The board of directors consisted of Mr. Mecherle, Miss Jones, and Erwin Meyers. Thus there was brought into being a business organization to conduct the affairs of the State Farm Mutual Automobile Insurance Company, which thus far existed only on paper.

The money for the certificate of deposit and the surplus note had to be raised by the partners. One of Bloomington's leading bankers turned a cold and fishy eye upon George Mecherle when he laid his proposition before him. He is reported to have said to him: "How do you expect to build an insurance company in these difficult and highly competitive times in Bloomington where we have just had one of the biggest failures in the country? Why, you do not know anything about the business."

But George Mecherle was a man of substance and a man of determination. As he often told the story in later years, he was pretty mad as he walked down the street and pushed his way through the revolving doors of a rival bank. He had no difficulty in approaching the president, who greeted him affably as one good neighbor to another.

"I've never had an account here," he blurted out. "I've never cashed a check here, as far as I know. I've never tried to borrow your money. But I'm going to start a little business in this town and, by golly, *you're* going to lend me the money I need to get started."

It took him only a few minutes to outline his proposition and state his financial needs. The banker listened in silence. He knew the man he was talking to and the good reputation the name Mecherle of Merna bore in the community. When Mecherle walked out of the bank, less than half an hour later, he had the money.

Thus he was able to meet the state's requirement. Miss Jones also contributed to this fund and together they loaned the new company the money for the surplus note—$4,000 at 6% interest for five years. And so, when the new company began to conduct business officially in June, there was sufficient capital—but not much more—for all immediate operating expenses.

In the meantime Meyers was busy in Chicago. He consulted Raymond T. Smith of the Alfred M. Best Company, New York publisher of *Best's Reports*, who was enthusiastic about the new company because he felt that if it succeeded it would set a pattern for other sound automobile insurance ventures. As western representative of Alfred M. Best, whose insurance reports were the Bibles of the industry, he was in a position to know how many unsound companies were in the field. Equally well informed in this matter was William T. Davis, manager of the Protective Union, a service department of the *Prairie Farmer*. At first Davis looked askance at the embryo company. His weekly paper, then published by Burridge T. Butler, maintained high standards regarding those to whom it opened its advertising columns. Believing that "farmers do not get what they are entitled for their money" from attorney-in-fact companies, the *Prairie Farmer* consistently refused to accept their advertisements. The *Prairie Farmer* hesitated before it accepted the first public announcement of the State Farm Mutual Automobile Insurance Company. But the interest in it of such men as Meyers and Smith showed it was no fly-by-night. Mr. Davis went down to Bloomington that spring to make a personal investigation. He put Miss Jones "through the third degree," as she expressed it, visited available applicants, and interviewed George Mecherle. Satisfied, the *Prairie Farmer* printed the first advertisement in its issue of April 29, 1922.

Sometime in the early spring the little company took a single room in the Durley Building in Bloomington as an office. There was a partition at the back of the room to make a separate office for George Mecherle. In the front office were two desks, one for Miss Jones, who assumed the duties of office manager, and the other for the staff, which consisted of a stenographer, a young lady named Verna Crusius. Besides rent and Miss Crusius's modest salary about the only other expenses were the printing of a rate card and application blanks.

Now for the first time George Mecherle had a chance to show his genius as a salesman. He had to get 200 applications for insurance before the state would grant the license to do business. As the first agent of the State Farm Mutual Automobile Insurance Company he took to the road with a will. It was then that he established his lifelong belief that the backbone of an insurance company is its agency force. He never tired of preaching this to the agents of State Farm or of impressing this philosophy of his business upon his fellow executives. In the early spring of 1922 he alone was the agency force. But April was hardly a good month to begin seeking applications from the members of the Farm Bureau, for most of them lived on roads that were all but impassable at this season because of the prairie mud.* And, of course, he could not sell his insurance to his friends among the merchants and professional men of Bloomington, for few of them were eligible to become members. The start was slow and even discouraging. In mid-April Miss Jones reported to Meyers that "business has not come in as fast as expected."

Probably the main reason was a minor tragedy which occurred at this time in the rambling Mecherle house on South Main street, Nor-

---

* The building of durable hard-surface roads in Illinois did not begin until about 1917, when the legislature appropriated $60,000,000 to modernize the highways connecting the principal cities of the state. The bonds were approved at the next general election, in spite of bitter opposition from the rural districts. The road from Chicago to Bloomington was opened to traffic the same year State Farm was founded. See Brigham, *McLean County* . . . , p. 26. In spite of the lack of good roads the total number of deaths from automobile accidents between 1918 and 1922 in the United States was 12,720, or 13.9 per 10,000 motor vehicles on the roads. The total number of nonfatal injuries was 445,000. The figures for Illinois in this period are not available. *Accident Facts*, Chicago, 1948, p. 60.

mal. Mildred, then thirteen, and Hubert and Herbert, the twins, then eleven, came down with the mumps. This in itself would have been annoyance enough for any one to bear at so crucial a moment in his career. Then, toward the end of April, George Mecherle himself was stricken by this juvenile disease and he was not allowed out of confinement until May 10, less than a month before his forty-fifth birthday.

On May 1 an important development in the establishment of the company occurred. Charles Wonderlin started work as the first agent. Mr. Wonderlin had retired from his farm between Colfax and Cooksville to live in Bloomington so that his daughter could more easily attend high school. He was supplementing his income from the rental of his farm by selling insurance for the Northwestern Mutual Life Insurance Company and for several farm fire insurance companies. He and George Mecherle were fellow members of the Bloomington Club, and there one afternoon the two men sat for several hours going over Mecherle's plan. Wonderlin thought it looked pretty good; when Mecherle asked him to become an agent for State Farm they shook hands and now, on May 1, he was ready for business.

Soon after Wonderlin joined the company—he did not resign his other insurance connections for two years—other salesmen were hired.* In mid-May there were, as Miss Jones gleefully reported to Meyers, "four special salesmen out all of the time," although, unfortunately, rain had held them up somewhat. She fully expected that they would have their necessary 200 applications, "by the end of the week." As of May 16 they already had 140 names signed up.

Meanwhile George Mecherle, confined to his house, had worked up a list of fourteen leading questions which was mailed to the secretaries of farmers' mutuals throughout the entire state. This mimeographed letter was the first direct advertising of State Farm. What it lacked in sophistication it made up in the directness of the questions asked. Judging by some of the answers received (and almost all the secretaries returned them) the management of the little company was able to determine pretty accurately how the idea was being received around the state.

Some of those questioned tossed the proposition off with such a comprehensive and terse answer as that from J. C. Reardon, who replied: "Gentlemen: I am not able to serve you or your company; at present, as a fool farmer, I am doing only a small part of the work allotted to me."

* The first agents after Wonderlin were Willis F. Mecherle, brother of George Mecherle, William Barthel, and Owen R. McDonald.

And J. J. Garman of Brookville, Illinois, replied, "I could positively not be interested in taking on another line of insurance i am sick and tired of writing insurance and want to be relieved of what i have got thanking you for your kind offer and to remain your truly . . ." But most of them gave it serious attention. A typical reply was that which came from Franklin Porter, secretary of the Appanoose and Sonora Mutual Insurance Company:

Don't you think our proposition the best Insurance Plan for Farmers that you have seen? *I think it all right for those that want it.*

What did your board of directors think of it? *Have not met since I received your circulars.*

Would you like to save your friends and the members of your Farm Mutual Ins. Co. some money? *Yes.*

Would you like to make some money for yourself? *Yes if honorable.*

Are your Farm Mutual members satisfied with Old Line or Reciprocal rates and their method of settling claims? *I think not.*

Would you endorse our proposition if you found, after a thorough investigation, that it was worthy of your endorsement? *Yes.*

Will you write to Mr. S. B. Mason of Bloomington, Secy. of the State Association of Mutual Insurance Companies, for his opinion of our proposition? *I think I have read it.*

Will you write to Mr. H. Fahrnkopf of the McLean County Farm Bureau, of Bloomington, for information concerning us? *Don't think it necessary.*

Will you write to the *Prairie Farmer* about our proposition? *I read it.*

Did you see our advertisement in the April 29th issue of the *Prairie Farmer?* *If so I do not remember it.*

How does the fact that Mr. J. W. Coale, Secy. of the Old Town Farm Mutual at Holder, Ill., wrote 32 applications in two and one-half days, appeal to you? *I think he must be quite windy.*

If you had the time to devote to our proposition, could you do as well or better than Mr. Coale? *I don't think so.*

How much time could you devote to selling our insurance? *Perhaps one half of my time if convinced it would prove satisfactory.*

How soon would you like to have our Special man spend a few days with you to explain the plan to your neighbors? *I am an old man and intend to quit the business at the end of the year and do not care to take up anything new any more. However, some younger man will take my place and it may be you can interest him. I am opposed to theft insurance for the reason that the lakes and ponds are not all full yet.*

From Golconda, away down in Pope County near the Kentucky border, came this succinct criticism: "I cain tell wether it would do any more good or not I do not understane all about your plane as the most of the people like to pay at one thime the money so they no the cost of it I work for the Union Automobile Association of Bloomington and the ass was every six months the same." The majority, however, expressed interest and enthusiasm for the plan, as outlined in the prospectus that accompanied the questionnaire.*

As the end of May approached, an air of optimism filled the small office in the Durley Building in Bloomington. From Chicago came word that all the legal requirements had been met and the license to operate had been issued by the state. Meanwhile Erwin Meyers, after many consultations with George Mecherle and Minnie Jones, had prepared a set of proposed by-laws for the new company. The agents sped through the country, led by Mecherle, and more than 400 applications for coverage were on file in the "home office." It was with a sense of accomplishment and satisfaction that George Mecherle, toward the end of the month, called a meeting to elect permanent directors and set the wheels in motion for his "honest insurance company."

* A few replies to this questionnaire were quite sarcastic. Many had fun with Mr. Coale's record—"a pretty hot coale," as more than one remarked. One said he did *not* want to make money for him or his friends. Another said, of the latter, "They will look out for saving their own money."

6

FIRST FRUITS

Long before ten o'clock on the warm, sunny morning of June 8, about a dozen persons gathered in the small room of the Durley Building at 102 East Jefferson Street in Bloomington which was the "home office" of the State Farm Mutual Automobile Insurance Company. It is quite probable that most of them were a little excited, but is unlikely that many of them had any deep appreciation then of the historical significance of the meeting. Enough chairs had been borrowed for the group, which grew to more than twenty before the morning was over. Four hundred persons might have attended, if they had felt it important enough, for this was the first meeting of the incorporators and the applicants for membership in the new insurance company.

It was, of course, the most important day in George Mecherle's life. There had been other days he would never forget: the day he started farming "on his own farm," the day he married Mae Edith Perry, the day he moved from the farm forever, and the day he quit as a tractor salesman to face an uncertain future. The day before had been an important day, also. It was his forty-fifth birthday.*

If he felt that he was getting a rather late start on a new career, whose success or failure would depend almost entirely upon himself, he showed no outward signs of inner qualms. He exuded confidence. He was in complete command of the situation. Yesterday he had worked out the agenda for today's meeting and he knew nothing could go amiss. By mid-afternoon the business he had dreamed of, his own little part of the third largest industry in the United States, would be a reality. After that, it would be up to him.

He still looked like the farmer he essentially was. His large, muscular frame strained at his clothes and his necktie never seemed to be in the right place. But his big hands, that seemed more used to plow handles than to a pencil, were steady, and his hazel eyes twinkled with fun. As the time for the meeting approached he singled out his star agent, Charley Wonderlin, who was responsible for sixty or more applications, and chuckled, "Charley, you and I had better go over and get slicked up." Together they let the barber down the street "give them the works" and, like a boy all scrubbed and shined for his first day at school, George Mecherle climbed the stairs to the already crowded room and a future that even he, for all his optimism, could not then visualize.

He was all business as he called the meeting to order. Rapidly, as had been planned beforehand, dignified S. B. Mason, the experienced secretary of the Illinois Association of Mutual Insurance Companies, was elected chairman of the meeting. As he stepped down from the

---

* The legend is that George Mecherle started State Farm on his forty-fifth birthday. His birthday was the 7th of June, and this is the date on the license for the new company, but the founding meeting was the 8th. Inasmuch as he had to send announcements to the applicants and directors in advance, he could just as easily have had the meeting on the 7th as the 8th, had he been so sentimentally inclined. There is nothing in the correspondence files to indicate he had this in mind. He was, however, sentimental about anniversary dates, and he was also somewhat superstitious. At least, he had some superstitious habits, such as throwing salt over his left shoulder before starting a meal; and one old friend, who knew him for fifty or more years, insists he was fascinated by the figure eight and its multiples—this, his friend has said, is why he had eight stories in the first State Farm building, among other instances. Perhaps this is why he chose the 8th of June, but I think it was because Meyers could more easily come down from Chicago on the 8th than on the 7th. In any event, it is not too important. After the success of the company, George Mecherle allowed the legend of the birthday to become fixed. He had a sense of the dramatic at all times and never missed a bet when it came to making a good story better.

chair George Mecherle saw that everyone who should be present was there: his brother Willis, who was to serve him faithfully for many years to come at every board meeting until his death; Miss Jones, whose exactitude may already have begun to irritate him; Henry Stubblefield, to whom he had sold the first application and who was to have policy number one; A. J. King, a farmer from Carlock and an incorporator; P. N. Jones, who was not related to Minnie Jones but who was slated to be a director; kindly and dignified W. B. McFarland from Hoopeston; his friend Charley Holz; and there in the corner with his brief case, Erwin "Hank" Meyers. Her notebook primly open on her lap, Miss Jones served as secretary.

George Mecherle then sketched for the gathering the history of the company from the Streator meeting to the present, and Meyers filled in on the legal and technical steps that had been taken. Then came the presentation of the by-laws, which were fully explained and discussed before they were unanimously adopted.

In the history of State Farm the by-laws as approved that day are an important document for they set forth completely the idea of an automobile insurance company for farmers as conceived by George Mecherle and put into practical form during the months that had passed between his first meeting with Herman Ekern and the actual organization of the company. Although the purpose of the corporation is identical with that set forth in the articles of association, the real "farm flavor" of the company, as it was at the start, is most fully captured in the dry legal wording of this paper. It had always been George Mecherle's belief that the stability of an insurance company would depend in great measure upon the character of those men and women whom it insured. He believed that farmers were good risks, even if none of the large stock companies had ever realized this and had treated them scornfully by subjecting them to rates based upon urban experience, where the ratio of losses was, he insisted, bound to be higher than in the country. He believed, also, that the farm mutual companies and the Farm Bureaus of Illinois were the most fertile field of operation and the potential source of a far-flung agency setup that could not then be improved upon. For these reasons the by-laws restricted membership in State Farm to

. . . members of Farm Bureaus, Farm Mutual Insurance Companies, their immediate families and those eligible for membership in such organizations. . . .

But it went even further, in its insistence upon living up to its ideal of a strictly farmer-owned and farmer-operated company, by stating that persons

> . . . residing in the Counties of Cook [*where the great metropolis of Chicago is located*], DuPage [*into which the Chicago metropolitan area overflows*], St. Clair [*which is adjacent to the industrial region of St. Louis and East St. Louis*], and Madison [*which is adjacent to St. Clair*] . . . and applicants residing in such other territory as may, from time to time be named, shall not be eligible. . . .

Since the plan was, to a large extent, based upon the mutual system of insurance, provision was made in the by-laws to perpetuate State Farm as a mutual company. Each member was therefore entitled to one vote at all meetings of the membership, in person or by proxy. The "general control" of the company, however, was vested in a nine-man board of directors to be elected by the membership. They were given authority to amend the by-laws, to make "all rules and regulations," and to delegate such powers as they deemed "expedient and proper" to an executive committee. All officers, who also might serve as directors, must be members of the corporation, and the "chief executive officer" was to be the president, elected by the directors. All were to serve without compensation or salary.

These provisions, however, did not designate who was actually to conduct the business affairs, the day-to-day running of the company, the selling of insurance, the payment of commissions, the handling of the complex details of the office. Members of mutual insurance organizations theoretically run their own business, just as stockholders theoretically run corporations. But in each instance there has to be a management. In mutual companies there are two ways of creating management; by hiring salaried executives, or by signing a contract with an agency which, for a percentage of the income, will conduct the business. The by-laws left the way open for either by stipulating that the board of directors "shall contract for a general manager . . . for such term and with such power and duties as they may deem for the best interests of the corporation."

Three of these provisions were fundamental foundation-stones of State Farm. They were diametrically opposed to the standard methods of automobile insurance. The clauses setting up the membership fee, the premium deposit, and the six-month term of insurance, which were adopted that day, were so different from the methods then in general use that in insurance history this day became of a lasting historical importance.

The "membership fee" provision was duly set forth in the by-laws as follows: "The membership fee shall be such amount and graded on such scale as shall, from time to time be stipulated in the application for insurance and approved by the board of directors. A membership fee paid by any member for any class of insurance shall exempt him from further membership fee for such class on any one automobile."

That which provided for the "premium deposit" and the six-month term features said: "A premium deposit, in such amount approved by the Board of Directors as set out in each application for insurance . . . shall be collected when the application is taken and the premium deposit shall be for an insurance expiring six months from the date the policy becomes effective and for the successive six months' periods for which the premium deposit is restored. If, for the purpose of restoring the premium deposit, the member insured shall pay his share of the losses, expenses and liabilities, as required by the Board of Directors, the insurance shall be renewed automatically for the six months' period from the expiration of the preceding six months' period. Such premium deposit shall be treated as earned pro rata during each six months' period. The Board of Directors may require additional payments to meet losses, expenses and liabilities in excess of the earned premium deposit, but no such payments shall be required in excess of an amount equal and in addition to the premium deposit. No member insured shall be liable for the losses, expenses and liabilities except those incurred during the period for which he was insured."

Once these important matters were out of the way the group resolved itself into an organization meeting of the applicants and proceeded to elect the permanent directors. Henry Stubblefield, Charles Wonderlin, and A. J. King, retiring from the room as a nominating committee, returned with the following board, which was approved by the membership and duly elected:

J. J. Prater, William B. McFarland, and W. F. Mecherle, to serve one year; Minnie A. Jones, S. B. Mason, and Charles Holz, to serve two years; and G. J. Mecherle, J. W. Coale, and P. N. Jones, to serve three years. With this the first membership meeting of the State Farm Mutual Automobile Insurance Company came to a close. It seemed then as if the members had selected a sound and a durable group to guide the destiny of the new corporation. It was a conservative board, made up of men trained in the marts of agriculture, each of them close to the problems of the farmer. They had carefully studied the plan they were now to operate within its self-imposed restrictions. Only a short time before George Mecherle had declared that if he could sell one policy he could sell a million. Even with all his confidence, it was only a figure of speech. Not one of these nine men, including George Mecherle, took such a goal seriously as they left the smoky room for lunch at the Illinois Hotel, and there were some in the group who were, in a surprisingly short time, to stand in the way of its achievement. Now, they were just a group of farmer-businessmen who had started a small company to sell automobile insurance to their friends and neighbors up the back roads of the prairie state.

The first thing the directors did, when they met in the Durley Building office after lunch, was to amend the by-laws, cutting in half their own per diem for attending directors' meetings—down to $5 each. They were well advised, for the company was then operating, as they say, on a shoestring—although it was a good, strong shoestring. They then proceeded to elect S. B. Mason president, P. N. Jones vice president, Charles Holz secretary, and Minnie Jones treasurer. These officers proceeded to thrash over thoroughly the matter of a general manager's contract, which George Mecherle had previously submitted to them. With the two partners abstaining from voting the contract was accepted. Then the surplus note for $4,000 for five years at 6% interest was executed. The First National Bank of Bloomington was named as the depository of the company's funds. The bonding of the officers responsible for handling the funds was approved. The payment of the expenses of organization, other than legal expenses, was authorized. Then a contract with Ekern, Meyers & Janisch—who thus far had received no payment for their services—was discussed but not then accepted. The officers and one other director were named as the executive committee with all powers, except the amending of by-laws, of the full board.

By mid-afternoon these dreary but necessary affairs were attended to. Then, by prearrangement, President Mason and Secretary Holz, whose terms officially were for three and two years respectively, tendered their resignations and George J. Mecherle and Minnie Jones were unanimously elected to fill their unexpired terms. And that brought the meeting to a close. The warm June sun was shining brightly down on Court House Square, the same Court House Square that had welcomed the two brothers from Germany just sixty-five years ago, as the little group dispersed. It was with a profound sense of achievement—and, no doubt, with many misgivings—that George Mecherle drove north along Main Street to the rambling house in Normal, to report the day's doings to patient, courageous Mae Mecherle, whose fortitude and foresight had helped make this day possible for the farmer from Merna whose dreams of an honest insurance company she had once rescued from the ashes of his despair.

One of the most important accomplishments of the day, for everyone involved, was the signing of the general manager's contract between G. J. Mecherle, Inc., and the State Farm company. It was this document that, in the final analysis, furnished the incentive which eventually made State Farm the largest automobile insurance company in the United States, if not in the world.

The contract adjured the general manager to "exert every reasonable effort to build up and honestly and efficiently conduct the affairs of the company." It gave to the manager the task of solicitation of members. As "general agent" he was to select and appoint the special and local agents and fix their compensation and commissions. These costs were to be paid by G. J. Mecherle, Inc. The manager further agreed to supervise underwriting, accounting, correspondence, collection of premiums, and the adjusting of losses. The company was to bear the expense of losses to policyholders, expenses of adjusting losses, legal expenses, all taxes, salaries of clerks and stenographers, directors' expenses, printing, postage, telephone and supplies.

For the work performed by G. J. Mecherle, Inc., the company was to pay "the sum of one dollar from each renewal premium, such payment to be made when the company receives the renewal premium necessary to restore the premium deposit on each policy to its original amount, and . . . the membership fee received from each applicant as soon as the applicant is accepted for membership." * By these terms management had its own funds to operate the business of selling insurance and seeing that those once "sold" remained active insurers in State Farm.†

---

* The original contract was for fifteen years, with a renewal option.
† The contract with Ekern, Meyers & Janisch was not signed at this meeting. The company agreed to pay them $500 for organizational work already done—within one year. This, however, was paid by October 14, 1922, at which time the law firm was hired, for a term of three years, to take care of all legal services (except adjustment of claims and liabilities), for which it was to receive 1% of the gross income, payable monthly. It also had an option stating that should the company expand "to

Never did George Mecherle need an incentive to "exert every reasonable effort." After all, it was *his* project, now, as it had been from its conception. There were those who worked with him then who sometimes thought he was making them exert unreasonable efforts in his drive for success. But since he worked harder than they did, and exuded such confidence and such joy in accomplishment, they did not complain.

George Mecherle and his little group of "special salesmen" took to the road at once. They went after the farmers with a will. Their first mode of operation was to contact the secretaries of the farmers' mutuals and induce them to take the State Farm man with them on a tour of the locality. The State Farm agent's task was twofold—to sell applications for policies and to train the farm mutual man to become a permanent agent after the initial drive was over. This procedure worked well from the beginning, and within a few weeks of intensive effort the foundation of an agency force was laid.

The first policies issued by State Farm provided for insurance protection against loss or damage to an automobile by fire, theft, or by collision with a movable object, and insurance protection to the policyholder for any liability which might be incurred because of personal injury to some other person, or damage to another person's property. Under the theft and movable object collision clauses there was a provision that the policyholder himself should bear any loss up to $10, but if the loss were over $10 it would be paid by the State Farm company. This was George Mecherle's ingenious invention, placed in the contract because it was his theory that if a farmer had to pay for minor repairs he would be more careful with his automobile. It also would save the company from a flood of petty claims each time a member scraped a fender or dented a mudguard. Liability limits were placed at $2,500 for one person and $5,000 for two or more persons involved in one accident. Property damage was limited to $500 for any one accident. This full coverage cost the insured $15 for the life membership fee and $19 for the premium. As Charles Wonderlin, reminiscing eighteen years later, said: "You had to be a real salesman in those days to take $34 away from a farmer with those provisions."

---

other states" (the first documented intimation that such a move was contemplated) the same arrangement would hold. Over the years the terms of the contract have been altered, but the law firm—now Meyers & Matthias—is still general counsel for State Farm.

The restriction of the coverage to "movable objects" was made at the determination of George Mecherle. He had some old-fashioned ideas that stemmed from his farming days that were hard to shake. It was his firm belief that anyone who hit a stationary object, such as a curb-stone, or a hydrant, or a building, had no right to be driving a car and therefore should not be insured. He could see how anyone might hit a movable object—from another car to a cow crossing the highway—but for anyone to drive his car into something that was fixed solidly to the ground or pavement was beyond his understanding. Of course, Mr. Mecherle's ideas on this were not as "ornery" as they may seem today. When the company was starting, the speed of automobiles was less than today, there were fewer cars in use, and the mileage of improved highways and streets was considerably less. Nor was the automobile the all-weather vehicle it is today. Many cars were stored away as soon as the first snow fell.

The term "movable object collision" gave rise to one of the State Farm legends. Rather than use the cumbersome phrase, movable object collision, everyone in the field and in the office began calling it MOC, which, of course, was soon translated from the initials to the word "mock." When, some years later, "stationary object collision" was added to State Farm coverage, this became known as SOC, or "sock." Thus "mock and sock" became familiar phrases among the old-timers at State Farm and persisted in usage for many years. Often an agent, used to referring to these provisions in these terms, would use it before a poten-tial member during his sales talk, much to the bewilderment of the automobile owner who did not know what "mock and sock" could possibly mean.

In a letter written less than a year after the company was started, Mecherle gives a vivid picture of the way he and his salesmen worked and the problems he faced as the organizer of a statewide sales force:

> The question of salesmen is the thing of greatest moment at present in our organization. The result of my work the past season has established us in so many different mutual fire companies in the state that we could handle a good number of salesmen who are qualified to sell this insurance without too much coaching.
>
> I find there are many so-called salesmen who are little more than order takers, and as you know, the selling of our insurance requires a man of ability to create a demand, sell the insurance, take the application and complete the whole deal in one call if he expects to make a success of this business. These men seem to be a rare article, but with the standing we

have with the Mutual Fire Companies it seems as though the average sales-man could qualify.

As a result of our last week's work in Cass County we wrote 96 applica-tions on cars in four and a half days, also an amount between $75,000 and $100,000 of fire insurance for their local mutual. I am satisfied that we wrote 70 per cent of our calls for automobile insurance; at least I know that Mr. McDonald and myself wrote a higher percentage than this, but I have no means of checking up on the other boys to find out just what percentage of calls they wrote; but I believe at least 40 or 50 per cent. This of course was well planned and the territory was well developed by circularizing the members of the Farm Bureau before the drive. Everyone was acquainted with the fact that the drive for Mutual insurance was the most valuable asset we had. . . .

The next week they invaded Edgar County, where they organized another farm fire mutual, thus widening their territory. "What we want to do," George Mecherle told the Township and County Mutual Asso-ciation a few months later, "is to spread the gospel of mutual insurance and increase every mutual company's business all that it is possible to do. Mr. Mason states that his company has increased $200,000 this year and gives our company credit for part of it. Mr. Beekman's mutual in Menard County increased their business from approximately $500,000 to something over $980,000. Our home mutual increased its business $73,000. It is impossible for us to say a word about the State Farm Mutual Automobile Insurance Company without talking farm mutual fire insurance. This company is dedicated to the farm mutual companies and intends to give the same protection that you have had for over 50 years in your Farm Mutual Companies."

The success of this system soon showed itself. Before the first year was through Mecherle and his salesmen had covered most of rural Illinois. They had policies placed in forty-six counties through ninety mutual com-panies. They ran up a lot of mileage on their automobiles and had tested the beds and food in every kind of hotel or boarding-house the small towns and county seats afforded.

It was their habit to return to Bloomington at the end of each week, to square up accounts, turn in their applications, collect their commis-sions, and lay their strategy for the next week. How well they did can be seen from the figures totaled up at the end of 1922, a little more than six months after they started their operations. There were 1,300 policies in force. Income was $29,222.10; assets stood at $27,444.87; reserves were $19,686.75, and surplus was $7,758.12. A breakdown of these figures might not have revealed as healthy a picture as they seem to do today at first glance but, however looked at, they were an answer to those who had laughed at George Mecherle less than a year earlier.

The "home office" was a plain, dreary room on the second floor of one of the oldest buildings in Bloomington, on East Jefferson Street, a few steps from Court House Square. George Mecherle had a cubbyhole office at the rear of the room. Miss Jones and Miss Crusius had desks in the larger space. The office equipment, besides the desks and chairs, consisted of one or two cardboard files, a typewriter, and a telephone. In this drab setting the "staff" was busy six long days a week, "processing" the applications as they were received and issuing the policies. If Miss Jones had ever believed her partner's assumption that this could be done on Saturdays, as it was over Tazewell way, she was quickly disabused of the thought. Most of the office work fell on her, in her capacity as secretary and treasurer, and as partner in the general managership. During most of the week George Mecherle was out on the road and they had little time to get together, discuss policy matters, and co-ordinate the work of what actually were two departments.

The first acquisition to the meager office was a fireproof safe. Then there had to be a corporation seal, record books, and a minute book for the keeping of the corporate history. But getting these was easy compared to the major problem that beset Miss Jones at this time. That was, as Mr. Mecherle had explained to the farmers at Streator, the matter of acquiring proper reinsurance. Reinsurance is a standard practice of the industry, the process whereby one insurance company transfers to another risks which are of a greater size than the first company wants to bear alone. Miss Jones and Erwin Meyers did a lot of shopping around before they found what they considered a good "deal" on reinsurance. After much argument they finally wrote a contract with the Integrity Mutual Casualty Company of Chicago, an organization that then had assets of nearly $2,000,000 and was considered a sound company. This provided that in case of personal injury or death Integrity would assume half of all losses under $2,500 and the entire amount of losses in excess of $2,500. The cost of this reinsurance was higher than State Farm wanted to pay and eventually other arrangements were made.*

---

* Other matters that took time and effort in these confusing early days was the bonding of Mr. Mecherle and Miss Jones for $10,000 each; taking out insurance against forgery and check alteration; and the insuring of Mr. Mecherle's life for the protection of the company. When this last-named matter came up before the board

The days passed quickly and, a great deal of the time, in confusion, for this was a new sort of venture for almost all concerned. The board of directors took their part seriously, giving their time and attention to a variety of matters. Most of these gentlemen were of a conservative nature and were undoubtedly a little frightened at the quick success of the company and, in certain instances, at the powerful drive of George Mecherle. Although he was too wise ever to admit it, in writing at least, there are indications in his correspondence at this time that he, too, was somewhat afraid of the speed with which the little company was forging ahead. A close friend of his said that at this time he really did not know just what kind of animal he had by the tail.

---

of directors toward the end of January, 1923, it was decided that the company was in strong enough financial condition so that this insurance was not necessary. Later, however, such insurance was taken out and kept in force until his death in 1951.

7

SUCCESS IN SIGHT

The busy year had passed. Anyone examining the books of this little insurance company would have to admit that, on the whole, it had been an extraordinarily good year. The membership had grown from the original 400 to about 2,200, thanks to the untiring efforts of George Mecherle and his small group of salesmen. By June of 1923 the tidy figures in the ledger showed that the gross income added up to $44,839. Losses and adjustments had run to $8,111, but $457 had been recovered in salvage. Salaries had amounted to $1,634 and rent had been $508. There had been, also, the matter of the $25,000 certificate of deposit to satisfy the state of Illinois. All this, of course, was hardly a drop in the bucket of what was the third largest industry, but it was a pretty good beginning, and it showed that the farmer from Merna had been right, as even his most severe critics were beginning to admit.

All had not been plain sailing, however. As with any new and unproved business, the State Farm Mutual Automobile Insurance Company had its difficulties and its moments of crisis. While George Mecherle had been pushing his Model T up and down the dusty and muddy roads, exhorting the presidents and secretaries of the farmers' mutuals, the difficult affairs of the "home office" had been borne by the slender but capable shoulders of Minnie Jones. Except for Verna Crusius, her assistant, she *was* the "home office." It was around her shoulders that the first storm clouds gathered.

Minnie A. Jones was a determined, ambitious, shrewd businesswoman. A spinster in her middle years, she lived with her father, a crusty old Yankee, and her sister, a schoolteacher. She was a pleasant lady, with a certain amount of charm to her manner, who had been well trained in office routine. She knew most of the "tricks of the trade," having been schooled in the Illinois Automobile Insurance Exchange. Such seemingly mysterious matters as legal requirements as to reserves were no mystery to her, and she quickly understood the plan of operation of the new company. Understanding it as she did, she was able to set up a good office record system, without which the little company might well have floundered in confusion.

Her advice on matters of policy was sought and often accepted. It was Minnie Jones, however, who was as much responsible as anyone for the method used in making out the first premium calls—an error that was later to cause trouble for the company. This was accomplished by dividing the losses and expenses for a six months' period by the number of policies in force at the end of the period. The proper way would have been to arrive at the premium call figure by a mean of the number of policies in force at both the beginning and end of the period. Whether this came about because her mathematics were wrong or because, as seems more likely, she felt that by keeping costs low sales would be higher, there is no way of knowing. George Mecherle, busy with selling policies, impatient with office details, and then unversed in many of the technical aspects of insurance which he later came to understand thoroughly, saw no fault with this method. It remained the company's way of doing things for ten years; and later, as we shall see, caused the company some uneasy moments.

It was not around this mathematically unsound method that the storm broke. There was, indeed, no one thing that went wrong. She had for example a bitter argument with her partner over the proper system of determining the valuation of the automobiles the company insured. Out on the road Mecherle or Wonderlin or Barthel, anxious to please a prospective customer, would set the valuation of the farmer's Ford at

80% of the cost of the car. Back in the office Miss Jones cut this to 80% of the "list price" as stated in the current National Used Car Market Report which she received each month from Chicago. There were some directors, too, who began to wonder if the frequent bickering between the two "managers" did not screen a struggle for control of the company. The situation that existed can best be described by a letter which Charles Holz, the director who had been associated with them both almost from the beginning, wrote jointly to Miss Jones and Mr. Mecherle at the time matters were coming to a head:

Dear Friends:
    Since coming back from our meeting the other day I have been thinking about the situation in your office. I am of the opinion that it is lack of understanding between both of you. Now, do try to be more congenial. Let the past be past. Try and talk matters over between yourselves, get a thorough understanding. Perhaps I take the wrong stand but it seems to me it is the duty of the one in the office to manage that end of the business and the one in the field to take care of that end of it. However, at the end of the week or perhaps oftener just have a conference and go over the week's business together. Give and take. Neither of you can afford to be arbitrary in the matter. Think it over. Now, I want both of you to read this letter, ponder it well. My wish is for the good of this little company which I have taken a small part in, in getting it started. Let's keep it going. Kindest regards . . .

The kindly intervention of Mr. Holz did not work. The rift apparently was too wide. George Mecherle's suspicion that Miss Jones and certain members of the board of directors and even some of the salesmen were engaged in intrigue would not be kept down. There could be no "thorough understanding," and Miss Jones knew this. She realized that most of the directors, whose power was not just on paper, sided with George Mecherle. A fortnight after Mr. Holz's joint appeal she handed in her resignation as director, secretary, and treasurer and as a member of the executive committee. In the meantime she had sold back to Mr. Mecherle her own and her sister's shares in G. J. Mecherle, Inc. Her association with State Farm was ended.

Miss Jones's departure left the company without a manager for the office work. Verna Crusius by now had been joined by her sister Edna. While they were highly efficient women and fully capable of carrying on the routine affairs of the cramped office, they had no business experience. To help out in the crisis George E. Beedle was sent on from the office of Ekern, Meyers & Janisch as a "loan" for a few weeks, until a successor for Miss Jones could be found. The successor turned out to be himself. George Mecherle liked the way he ran the office and appreciated his knowledgeable background. He was named secretary and treasurer and in 1925 was elected a director. He remained with State Farm until his death.

The following January Mr. Holz resigned from the board of directors, and two months later S. B. Mason and P. N. Jones also handed in their resignations. Although these were undoubtedly connected with the "Miss Jones affair" they came about primarily as a result of differences of opinion over methods of running the business. The Messrs. Mason and Jones, for one thing, did not think the treasurer of the company should also be a member of the management company, and they were disturbed at suggestions of expanding the company beyond the restricted boundaries staked out in the original charter.

George Mecherle went to this March meeting in no conciliatory mood. He had already seen the vision of his "honest little insurance company" growing into one much larger than he had originally conceived and he was convinced that its proved merits would make it even larger as time went by. When he was met with opposition from these members of the board he was determined to fight for what he felt was the right policy. To their objections that expansion would entail many difficult if not insurmountable problems of procedure, he replied by saying that he thought the objecting members were merely confessing their own inadequacy to meet the challenge. Having said that in plain language, he dared them either to raise their sights or resign, since there was nothing to fear by branching out, as the State Farm principle was sound and if it worked in Illinois it would work anywhere in the country. Directors like W. B. McFarland stood by him, as they were to do for many years. Those whom he had accused of myopia withdrew.

Ironically enough it had been Miss Jones who had first suggested enlarging the company's fields of endeavor. In a letter to E. A. Meyers written in March, 1923, she asked, "What would you think about writing a policy for automobile insurance for merchants, professional men, and other city residents who are not eligible for membership in the State Farm?" This, of course, was far different from a 100% farm company, and would have entailed revising the by-laws; and probably even then it could not have been done easily under the insurance laws of the state. Nothing further was attempted in this direction at this time.

It was not until the next year that George Mecherle took the suggestion seriously. "Our agents," he said, "are clamoring for the opportunity to write business in the cities and small towns," and he added sorrowfully that he had to turn down seven applications in two days that had come in unsolicited. He asked Meyers to "devise a plan" for writing this additional business. None was devised for two years, however. Messrs. Jones and Mason wanted no part of this city business and they felt that George Mecherle was trying to get too much power in the business that, after all, was his original idea. After their departure there was no further dissension in the ranks of the directors. Expansion was the word.

In the meantime the company had moved in October, 1922 to the McLean County Farm Bureau Building. Later, needing larger quarters, it had moved in the autumn of 1924 again to the Durley Building. Then it found "permanent" quarters in 1925 in the somewhat newer, but still far from modern, Odd Fellows Building, where it was to remain until 1929. In 1924-5 there were only five employees of the company. The Crusius sisters were the accountants of the firm and they also took care of the major part of the office work. Most of the correspondence was handled by Mr. Mecherle or Mr. Beedle. These two were also the company's "claims department." Such losses as could be adjusted in the office were handled by Mr. Beedle, while Mr. Mecherle took care of the more difficult "outside" claims. A Mrs. Erickson was the office stenographer.

As business increased other young people came to work in the office. Ramond Mecherle, George Mecherle's oldest son, who had finished school and was working for a Chicago printing concern, returned to Bloomington in April, 1924, and joined the staff in a general capacity. He was then just twenty years old. A short time later he was placed in charge of commissions. Others who came to the company at this time were Elsie Morton, Lucille Staley, and Marguerite Henderson. Miss Henderson was the first switchboard operator and information clerk. Later she became a general assistant to George Mecherle.

In 1925 it became apparent that the settling of claims and adjustment of losses would have to be handled separately. The man chosen for this position was E. J. Carmody. Like George Mecherle, Mr. Carmody had been a farmer "out Merna way" most of his life and had had little, if any, business experience. His father had come from Ireland and, like the Mecherle brothers, had acquired farmland when the prairie was being opened up. George Mecherle had known him for most of his life and realized that he had all the capacities of a good claim adjuster. In his derby hat he looked somewhat like Al Smith, then Governor of New York.

Mr. Carmody had been closely associated with State Farm almost from the beginning. At the first annual meeting in 1923 he had been made a member of a special advisory committee which was created at this time and which included J. J. Prater of Vandalia, A. T. Strange of Hillsboro, J. Colby Beekman of Petersburg, Howard Jokisch of Virginia, W. H. Bean of Blue Mound, D. E. Turner of Rockford, and John Turnbull of Sparland. In this capacity he attended the special meeting of the directors in October, 1923, at which the difficulties with Miss Jones, then coming to a head, were threshed out. When her resignation was accepted later that month Mr. Carmody was elected to the board of directors as her successor.*

Mr. Carmody had, as Mr. Beedle once put it, "a peculiar ability in ferreting out those who were attempting to defraud the company." His "ability to locate the proper persons in order to secure correct information [was] pronounced and his God-given sense of right and wrong and justice to all [was] wonderfully developed." From the beginning of his active association with State Farm he was a key man in the organization. He quickly built his department into a state of high efficiency, coordinating it with the work of the office force and the field staff. Although, at the start, he did most of the work himself, he added adjusters as business increased.

Mr. Carmody's greatest handicap as superintendent of claims was his lack of legal training. Such claims against the company as eventually worked their way into court were the concern of a young Bloomington attorney named Adlai H. Rust, who, like most of those responsible for the growth of State Farm, was the personal choice of George Mecherle.

Adlai Rust's family had been located in McLean County since the 1830's. The first of that name to migrate to the prairie had started life there as a hired man for the Funks of Funk's Grove. Adlai Rust's father, Francis M. Rust, was a farmer and stockman and a raiser of draft horses. He died when Adlai was five years old. Adlai's mother, the former Julia Hollis, had then run the store and post office at Randolph, Illinois, to support the family. Later they had moved to Bloomington,

---

* At this same meeting George Mecherle was elected treasurer and Mr. Beedle was elected secretary. Mr. Carmody was elected to a full three-year term at the annual meeting in June, 1924. He remained as a director until 1936.

where Adlai attended the public schools. After being graduated from the Bloomington High School he worked his way through Illinois Wesleyan University, where he had received his law degree in 1914. In high school and college he was an outstanding basketball player—a member of the championship high school team in 1910 and of the two-time state championship winners while in college.

Although the Rusts had known the Mecherles through the Orendorff family, the first business connection came some years before George Mecherle had left the farm. With other members of the Old Town Mutual, Mecherle came in one day to see the senior members of the firm, Barry & Morrissey, where Mr. Rust first practiced law, seeking legal ways of paying a farm neighbor for the loss of his barn. Rust was the only one in the office and took on the chore. Now, whenever there was legal work to be done locally, not of a nature to be assigned to Ekern, Meyers & Janisch, it was turned over to him. By 1927 there was to be so much of this business that Mr. Rust was forced to stop taking on new clients. In 1929 he was to give up his private law practice entirely and devote his full time to State Farm.

Within five years of its founding, the home office staff of State Farm was to grow to 183 employees.* Those who joined the company in 1925, the year in which the small staff nearly doubled, were Pauline Schmidt, claims; Mary Herder, assistant treasurer; Bertha Powell, x-cards and correspondence; Sylvia Caldwell, policy-writer; Ermond Mecherle; Zelma Dunn, commissions; Alice Smith and Marie Fogel, valuations; Lois Beedle, Minnie McMillion, and Minnie Huffman. With about three exceptions these first employees remained with State Farm for many years. Some of them are still in its employ.

During this period of rapid expansion events of momentous interest in the life of the company crowded one upon the other. Two were of the greatest significance, for they opened the way to the wide future. One was the invitation from the Indiana Farm Bureau to operate under its auspices across the Wabash and the other was the establishment of the City and Village Automobile Insurance Company. While negotiations toward both these developments were going on other changes were taking place. Early in 1924, for instance, the directors voted to change the coverages for fire and loss to cover all damages in excess of $1.00, and the following year it was decided to increase the movable object

---

* Employees as of the 1st of the year: 1924, 5; 1925, 9; 1926, 21; 1927, 34; 1928, 69; 1929, 183.

collision coverage to cover all losses of $1.00 or more up to 80% of the loss, if the total loss, thus computed, did not exceed the amount of insurance provided by the policy.

On June 19, 1926, a new coverage was provided, known as stationary object collision—or SOC (sock) in State Farm parlance—which also included insurance for glass damage. With these provisions in effect complete coverage for collision was made available to all State Farm policyholders.

Later, between 1927 and 1930, other features were introduced, such as wind coverage, loaned-car protection, and insurance for buses or private cars used for transporting children to and from school.

In the beginning almost all the agents sold insurance only in their spare time. Except for the special salesmen working out of the home office, they were generally secretaries or other officials of the farm mutual companies. The great majority of the early policies were sold through the efforts of these gentlemen, some of whom were exceedingly active in their territories. Few if any of them, however, were able to devote their full time to the work of selling policies, and for this and other reasons the plan to restrict agents to mutual officials did not work out as well as had been expected. As early as the spring of 1923 George Mecherle who, from the very beginning, believed that his agency force was the heart of the company, realized that he would have to find men who would be "more than order takers," for the "selling of our insurance requires a man of ability to create a demand, sell the insurance, take the application, and complete the whole deal in one call if he hopes to make a success of this business. These men seem to be a rare article." It was in search of this "rare article" that George Mecherle first considered the local Farm Bureaus as a source of business. He also sought agents among high school principals in the small towns on the theory that these underpaid public servants would be glad of an opportunity to add to their income through an honest and legitimate business. One type that George Mecherle steered clear of, however, was the lightning-rod salesman. These glib gentlemen of the road were too much of the "high-pressure variety" to suit his taste.

The fact that Mr. Mecherle's plan was a decided success, and was so considered by all observers within two years of the founding of State Farm, is proved by certain negotiations that took place in 1924. In that year the powerful Illinois Agricultural Association began paying serious attention to the farm automobile insurance situation in the state of Illinois. Among its leaders were some who thought the Association itself should enter this business. Others, after due consideration, were of the opinion that an alliance should be made with that up-and-coming little company in Bloomington. The Association made the first gesture by suggesting that it take over control of State Farm. George Mecherle saw certain virtues in this but was not entirely convinced that such an arrangement would be mutually beneficial. His counter-offer was to make an agency arrangement with the Association and its farm advisors throughout the state. In the meantime the Association gave serious consideration to the establishment of its own automobile insurance company. This, however, was not done at this time. Instead a loose arrangement was made whereby State Farm did not surrender its identity and become the creature of the I.A.A. It did appoint farm bureau advisors as agents for State Farm on the same commission basis it had with the farm mutual agents. Thus the rural scope of State Farm influence was widened.

The suggestion for broadening the eligibility rules for membership in State Farm, first raised, as we have seen, before the company was fully a year old, came to fruition in its fourth year. After mature consideration it was decided that, instead of amending the by-laws and revising the charter, a separate company, owned and controlled by State Farm, and known as the City and Village Mutual Automobile Insurance Company, would be established. This was done on April 5, 1926. State Farm agents were thus allowed to write insurance for persons who were not eligible for insurance in the original company.

This separate company, operating under a management contract similar to that of the parent company, brought a measure of new business to the company, but there were various reasons why it was not so successful as it might have been. Toward the end of November, 1927, a special meeting of the board of directors was called, and Mr. Mecherle explained why it was thought best to merge the separate company with State Farm. By then State Farm's expansion had, as we will see, burst out beyond the borders of Illinois. In order to expand alongside of the parent company, the City & Village Mutual Automobile Insurance Company would have to acquire separate licenses in all the states where business was being done, or where it was anticipated. Unfortunately, this was impractical for the reasons that the smaller company's assets and surplus were not always sufficient to meet requirements for many of these licenses. Another practical reason was that it had not become large enough to meet competition from other companies, even if other, longer-established companies were beginning to feel State Farm rivalry in the rural areas.

At this meeting directors McFarland and Asplund sponsored the following amendment to the by-laws, which was unanimously adopted by the eight directors present:

> All persons, partnerships, public or private corporations, boards or associations, insured by this corporation shall be members. Members shall be limited to such persons and be divided into such classes as determined by the Board of Directors. Each class of members shall bear its own equitable proportion of the losses, expenses and liabilities of the company. The Board of Directors shall determine or may delegate to the executive committee the duty of determining the territory in which the company shall operate and territory from which members shall not be taken.

To meet the provisions of this amendment the directors then established two classes. Class (1) was the Farm Department. This included all policyholders who were members of Farm Bureaus, farm mutual insurance companies, their immediate families, or those eligible to membership in such organizations. Class (2) was to be known as the City & Village Department. (Later it was known as the Metropolitan Department.) This was to "include all policyholders not eligible to membership in the Farm Department or Class." Thus town and country became one under the name of State Farm as the little company began to spread in all directions almost at once.

Sometime in the summer of 1924, a State Farm policyholder put a bee in the bonnet of the progressive-minded officials of the Indiana Farm Bureau Federation, which had then a membership of some 60,000 farmers. He was sufficiently versed in the operation of the State Farm company to become its advocate along the banks of the Wabash. As a result of the talk engendered by this propagandist's glowing accounts of what was going on over in Illinois, the Farm Bureau decided to investigate. It appointed a committee to cross into Illinois and find out the facts. Its inquiries brought satisfactory answers and soon negotiations were initiated by representatives of the Farm Bureau with George Mecherle.

There were some obstacles to overcome. One or two members of the Board of Directors, being men of conservative bent, looked with disfavor upon the proposal. They felt the time had not yet come to expand beyond the borders of Illinois. But they soon found themselves persuaded by the eloquence of George Mecherle's arguments, and on November 22, 1924, a contract was signed making the Indiana Farm Bureau Federation of Indianapolis, Indiana, the first state agent for the State Farm Mutual Automobile Insurance Company of Bloomington, Illinois.

Working for the Indiana Farm Bureau at this time was a forty-one-year-old organization director named Harold R. Nevins. He was a man of engaging personality. By birth and upbringing he was a farmer and, although his job with the bureau took most of his time, he still operated a working farm profitably near his birthplace, Rockville, Indiana. At one time he had been an undertaker. He knew the people of his state, their wants and needs, and he was as enthusiastic about the State Farm deal as George Mecherle was about naming him the Indiana state director.

The first five years of the alliance proved that George Mecherle once again had chosen an associate with that unerring instinct for which he was famous. By the end of 1930 the Indiana Farm Bureau had sold 44,252 policies. Twenty years later this had more than doubled, despite the grueling years of agricultural depression that had intervened, and at the end of 1954 there were 136,740 policies in force in Indiana. Although the alliance between State Farm and the Farm Bureau had lapsed in the meantime, Harold R. Nevins was still state director—as well as a member of the board of directors of State Farm—and, under his leadership as the dean of state agents, Indiana was still one of State Farm's most important states in volume of policies and underwriting experience.

With the "invasion" of Indiana in 1924 began a trend that in less than thirty years was to make the name State Farm known in every state of the union and an actuality in all but the New England states. State Farm began selling insurance in Indiana on April 9, 1925. Within a few months other states were entered by the company, with the State Farm Bureau Federation inevitably acting as its contractual sponsor.*

Once State Farm really got going, its growth seemingly could not be stopped. The stark figures best show its amazing progress. At the end of its first calendar year its 1,339 members had given it an income of $22,000. During its fifth year this figure had increased to $773,000. The year of 1927, its sixth year of operation, was to exceed all expectations. When they added up the income to report to the policyholders

---

* See Chapter Nine for the story of State Farm's state-by-state expansion and its early alliance with the Farm Bureau Federations.

in June, six years after the little group headed by George Mecherle had met in the stuffy room in the Durley Building, the figure was $1,568,000. Thus in 1927 for the first time the annual income of George Mecherle's "honest insurance company" exceeded one million dollars.

To handle this business, which amounted to 69,345 policies in force, State Farm now had 73 employees on its payroll, a far cry from the little handful which had kept the books and records six years before. Already these workers were becoming as cramped as the original staff had been before the offices had been moved to the Odd Fellows Building. The expansion of territory and the broadening of the rules of membership meant that the company needed more space and in a hurry. It did not take George Mecherle long to realize that Bloomington, busy county seat and growing city though it was, offered no usable quarters. He acted with characteristic decision and early in 1928 bluntly told the board of directors that State Farm must have its own building. Four years earlier some of them might have thought George Mecherle was getting too big for his boots and objected to such a move. But one look at the company of their creation convinced them that he was right. They approved plans for a building to be built on East Washington Street.

On September 15, 1928, the company bought, for $55,000, a tract of land with an area of 7,590 square feet, on East Washington Street, half a city block from the courthouse where the Mecherle brothers first met their patron, John R. Benjamin, nearly three-quarters of a century before. Within two months construction was started from plans drawn by the Bloomington architectural firm of Schaefer & Hooton, and by August, 1929, just two months before the stock market crash that was to usher in the Great Depression, the eight-story structure was ready for occupancy.

This building had cost a little more than $400,000, and the State Farm directors thought they might retrieve some of this expenditure by renting the first two floors for offices and stores and using merely the upper six stories. They never did. Within four years every inch of the entire eight floors was in use and more space was needed. In 1935 five full floors were added, at a cost of $220,000, and once again the State Farm officials thought they had provided well for the future. But within two years more space was needed.

This time the company bought a lot that was the same length as the original but separated from the first building by a narrow alley. It was occupied by an office building. It cost $70,000. The alley was vacated by the City of Bloomington, the standing structure was razed, and another eight-story building adjoining, and becoming a part of, the original structure was erected. This was completed in 1942 at a cost of nearly $1,500,-000. And once again it did not prove to be large enough to house the home office staff of the "little insurance company."

Six years later five stories were piled on top of the "new" building, making the dual home-office structure uniformly thirteen stories in height, a handsome tan brick pile that towered high above all the other buildings in Bloomington, looking in all directions across the prairies George Mecherle had known and loved all his life.*

Besides the building of the first permanent home office, two other major events occurred before the State Farm company was ten years old. One, which perhaps more than anything else signified the increasingly national nature of State Farm, was the opening, on September 24, 1928, of the company's first branch office. This was located across the continent in Berkeley, California. Another event was the organization in January, 1929, of the State Farm Life Insurance Company, owned by and under the management of the State Farm Mutual Automobile Insurance Company.†

* As this book was about to go to press the board of directors (March 14, 1955) announced plans for a new million-dollar office building to be erected during 1957 in Bloomington on a nine-acre plot on East Oakland Avenue, between Mercer Avenue and Route 66. The principal function of the new structure was to house the operating divisions of the automobile company and the operating units of the life and fire companies. The Home Office building was to continue to be general headquarters, housing the general and executive departments.

Here is perhaps as good a place as any to give in detail the exact chronology of the company's various moves in Bloomington. Its very first "office" was in a room in the Illinois Hotel. [See Ch. IV.] Its official "birthplace" was in a single room in the Durley Building, 102 East Jefferson Street, where the founding meeting was held on June 8, 1922. Within six months the company moved to the McLean County Farm Bureau Building at 109-11 West Monroe Street. In 1924-5 it returned briefly to the Durley Building and in the autumn of 1925 moved to the Odd Fellows Building, where it remained until its own eight-story structure was ready for occupancy on August 31, 1929.

† A suggestion that State Farm acquire ownership of a small Chicago fire insurance company, with a premium income of about $14,000 annually, was made to George Mecherle in 1926. He and Meyers and Beedle, then busy organizing the City & Village Company, discussed the idea thoroughly but turned it down. "We have decided that our time will be fully occupied with our new activity," Mr. Mecherle wrote, "and it is best for us not to divide our activity at the present time. It is getting to the point where there are not enough hours in the day or days in the week to finish what we have to do. . . ."

When the investigators for the Alfred M. Best Company finished their report of State Farm in 1931, on the eve of its tenth anniversary, they remarked, "Its growth has been phenomenal." They reported that its aggregate volume of premium income from 1924 through 1930 was $17,190,688. George Mecherle was particularly proud of the fact that, after the Best Company's qualified experts had spent eleven weeks examining the company's books and going into every detail of management, their estimate of the company's reserves differed from the company's estimate by only six-tenths of one per cent.

At the end of the fiscal year of 1931 the State Farm company was able to present the following statement to its membership:

Income	$7,450,891
Assets	6,603,746
Reserves	5,576,894
Surplus	1,026,852

There were, at this time, 370,045 policies in force. Three hundred and thirty-four persons were employed by the automobile company and twenty-two persons were on the payroll of the life company. All this in a decade! No matter how you looked at it, State Farm was a success. And not just a success in its own originally limited bailiwick but on the national scene. The honest little automobile insurance company for farmers had spread in all directions over the United States. It had a branch office in California and it had branch claims offices in strategic centers throughout the country. Wherever there were automobiles, except in the northeastern section of the nation, you could see the emblem of State Farm on old jalopies and brand-new Cadillacs, on the old back roads and on the new boulevards. Within ten years State Farm had moved from an idea scratched on the cardboard laundry insert to the very edge of Big Business. George Mecherle's crazy idea had almost run away with itself.

8

HOW IT ALL WORKED

During the years of its growth to the commanding position of the largest automobile insurance company in the United States, the secret of State Farm's success was a continual source of puzzlement to the insurance fraternity. The incontrovertible figures of its annual statements proved that it was a financial success, and the findings of the examiners for the insurance departments of the various states in which it was licensed to operate revealed no flaws in its method of doing business. But questions were forever being asked. What was the secret formula that allowed this company, almost alone of all automobile insurance companies, to undersell the market and still show such amazingly large figures on the right side of the ledgers? How did it actually work?

One obvious answer to the first question was the organizational genius of the "super-salesman" who was at the head of all its operations. In George Mecherle, who had come to the business at a time in life when most men have long since reached the peak of their ability, State Farm owned a chief executive of exceptional talents. He had been at the forefront of every progressive move the company had made, and as the years went by he had chosen those capable associates who had worked so well under his all-seeing direction. Especially in the early years was it true in his case, as Emerson once said in a rather larger conception, that "an institution is the lengthened shadow of one man." * But there was really more to it than that. There was, for one thing, the philosophy underlying the institution that was his lengthened shadow.

In order to see just what did make State Farm tick it is necessary to go back to the beginning and examine the structure on which the company was established. In many ways it was different from anything that had preceded it, and yet, paradoxically, there was little that was original in its plan. It was a distinctive plan but, although it enabled the company to sell policies at a lower rate than its competitors, and to do so on a sound basis, there was nothing in it that was new to the field of insurance economics. Some who have studied it believe that perhaps it would not have worked without the guiding genius of George Mecherle, or someone like him, who was willing to go ahead regardless of the fact that he himself did not fully understand all its complications.

In the 1920's, when George Mecherle first got the idea of an insurance company for farmers, the bulk of automobile insurance was written by the capital stock insurance companies. Because most of these companies—they were then immune to the antitrust laws—set their own uniform premium rates by agreement among themselves, there was little or no actual rate competition. With very few exceptions the stock companies used the annual premium payment plan, paying an average 25% of cash premiums as commissions to agents. New policies were issued annually, which meant that every year the agent received this 25% commission. The policies were issued by the agents, who also collected the premiums, which they remitted to the company on a monthly basis. Premiums for January, for example, were not due at the

---

* Emerson said, in *Essays, First Series*, "Self-Reliance": "Every true man is a cause, a country, and an age; requires infinite spaces and numbers and time fully to accomplish his design:—and posterity seem to follow his steps as a train of clients. A man Caesar is born, and for ages after we have a Roman Empire. Christ is born, and millions so grow and cleave to his genius that he is confounded with virtue and the possible of man. An institution is the lengthened shadow of one man; as, Monarchism, of the Hermit Anthony; the Reformation, of Luther; Quakerism, of Fox; Methodism, of Wesley; Abolition, of Clarkson. Scipio, Milton called the height of Rome; and all history resolves itself into the biography of a few stout and earnest persons."

He also said, "No institution will be better than the institutor." *Essays, Second Series*, "Character."

home office until March and agents were free to extend credit as they might see fit. There were some variations to this plan and schedule, but, on the whole, stock companies and their agents followed this general rule.

Some mutual companies also wrote automobile insurance, but the number was few and their business small. Most mutual companies also collected the annual premium in advance and generally charged the same rate as the stock companies. At the end of the policy's term they would declare a dividend to the policyholder. Most of these companies paid little or no renewal commissions to agents, and the cost of the declared dividends came from the money thus saved. Both mutual and stock companies charged high rates; there was little if any differential between urban and rural territorial rates; and none of the companies made any attempt at establishing a basis for selective risks.

The plan sweated out by George Mecherle, E. A. Meyers and Herman Ekern possessed a combination of somewhat novel features and unusual elements that set it apart from the stock companies and other mutual companies and enabled State Farm to do business for nearly 40% less than its stock company competitors. One of the outstanding features of the State Farm plan was the method of collecting premiums.

Here State Farm departed radically from normal insurance procedure, although it was not actually the first company to collect in this manner. The little Farmers' Automobile Association at Pekin was probably the first automobile company to collect premiums semiannually rather than annually. It was, in effect, an application of the installment payment plan that became so definite a part of the American economy in the Coolidge era. The practice of paying twice a year instead of once had several advantages both to the customer and the company. For one thing, it was easier to sell, for it required less cash from the customer at the outset (although, as Mr. Wonderlin has pointed out, the outlay of the starting premium plus the membership fee, a total of $34, at first scared away a good many thrifty farmers). But it did make the payment of renewal premiums much easier for the policyholders, most of whom, in those days, were farmers who operated on a small cash economy. They often paid original premiums with "time checks," dated to coincide with the time they expected to have crop money in the bank. State Farm was geared to the prairie from the start.

As far as the company was concerned, this semiannual system was beneficial, for it made it more difficult to "twist" the business, because

most of State Farm's competitors required payment of an annual premium, whereas the renewal cost of State Farm for a six-month period
was less than half the cost of the stock company annual premium.
Furthermore, it required a smaller unearned premium reserve. This
could be figured at one-half of the six months' premium, rather than at
one-half of the one-year premium. And an inadequate, or excessive rate
could be corrected at the end of six months rather than waiting until
the end of the year.

Another feature that contributed to operational economy was the
issuing of policies by the home office rather than by the agent in the
field. Relieved of this clerical work, or of the expensive necessity of
hiring someone to do the work for him, the agent could concentrate on
selling. Since his income depended on sales, he could afford to work for
less than the agent who had to keep an office force. State Farm policies,
once written, were not rewritten and replaced each policy term. This
greatly saved expense, work, and time. The same policy remained outstanding until the policyholder bought a new car—and, in those days
of agricultural uncertainty, the farmer did not turn in his old Ford or
Chevrolet for a new car each year, by any means—or made a major move
or change of coverage. This feature was borrowed from the standard
practice of life and accident companies; but it had never previously been
tried out in automobile insurance until adapted by State Farm.

Also borrowed—this time from the mail-order houses—was another
feature, one never before used in automobile insurance but one that
had been found efficient in the operation of many accident and health
and several life companies. This was the system of billing and collecting
renewal premiums by the home office, or by branch offices after they
were established. This relieved the agent of the task of collecting renewals, and thus obviated the necessity of compensating him for such
collections. This, of course, resulted in a material saving in expense for
State Farm, which was passed on to the policyholders. Agents were,
however, paid fees and expenses for adjusting losses. This, at first, was
on a *per diem* and mileage basis, but later was changed to a percentage
of the premiums, largely for ease of administration. The system of home-
office renewal and collection, with the agent receiving a commission
only for the initial sale, with all its saving to the benefit of the policyholder, is still in force. Furthermore, since all premiums had to be paid
in cash in advance, the expenses of a credit system of operation were
avoided. In contrast to the usual stock company agency operation,

State Farm agents had no credit losses, no books to keep, and no bills to mail. All of this expensive time-consuming detail was eliminated. As a further advantage the company was able to earn more money on assets than under the stock company plan, where the agent held the premium from forty-five to seventy-five days. It also eliminated the necessity of employing special agents to collect premiums from delinquent agents.

The most novel feature of the State Farm plan was the life membership fee system. Any person who joined State Farm did so for life, or at least for as long a part of his life as he remained a "good risk." His membership did not cease even if he should allow a policy to lapse for a time.

Then, as now, a new member insuring an automobile with State Farm for the first time had two separate items to pay—a membership fee and a premium (then known as a "premium deposit"). The membership fee covered the cost of solicitation and sale of the insurance policy. In ordinary insurance parlance this is the "acquisition cost." Under the standard insurance practice of that time, and in most companies today, the acquisition cost was a part of the premium and was paid by the policyholder both at the inception of the policy and at each subsequent renewal. State Farm's advantage lay in the fact that it charged the member this cost once and only once. Since State Farm renewal policies contained no provision for new business costs this factor alone provided a large part of the price advantage which State Farm enjoyed over its competitors.

This membership fee, it is interesting to note, was not a premium. It was, instead, an admission and inspection fee. It was not returnable. For this reason no unearned premium reserve was set up on it. The premium, or premium deposit, was a separate item. The reserve was set up only on that item. Much of the expansion of State Farm, especially in the early days, when the company was operating on Mr. Mecherle's surplus note, was traceable to this, since the company was not burdened with reserves.

One of the most burdensome problems for fire and casualty insurance companies operating on the ordinary, routine basis was that of meeting new business costs and setting up adequate unearned premium reserves on new business. It is an axiom of the business that all growth in premium volume creates a drain on surplus, to be absorbed out of earnings on business previously written. The amount of earnings and surplus available to finance additions to premium volume has always determined the ceiling which management must erect over its plans for expansion. The plan evolved by George Mecherle and Erwin Meyers solved this basic problem by the simple expedient of an extra collection from new members to meet new business costs. The phenomenal growth of State Farm Mutual could not have been realized without this innovation, and yet the very plan that made growth possible also provided a price advantage to create this growth.

There were other distinctive features in State Farm policies. Some were borrowed from old ideas hitherto applied to other types of insurance. The so-called "eighty-twenty" plan of collision insurance was, in reality, an adaptation of the ancient principle of co-insurance, where the policyholder assumes a part of the risk, in this instance 20% as compared to the company's share of 80%. The sound psychology of this lay in the fact that it gave the policyholder an interest in keeping his losses to a minimum. The classification of risks also was distinctive. At the time the company started, in 1922, there were more than one hundred different makes of automobiles on the market. The stock companies had separate rates for each car and even for various models of the same make. George Mecherle devised the system of classing all automobiles by list price into seven classes, from A to G in the simplified State Farm rate manual. This was easy to understand and to apply. In the first agent's manual—a masterpiece of simplicity—there was an uncomplicated formula by which anyone could readily determine the amount of insurance that could be written on any car, whether new or old.

Another saving for the policyholder came about through lower average losses resulting from the careful selection of business. The restriction of those eligible to membership in State Farm, and such clauses as the drunken driver clause, not only appealed to farmers, with their more rigid code of morals, but also saved the company money. All of these economies, acting together, enabled State Farm to do business in the early days for nearly 40% less than the stock companies.

After Minnie Jones's departure from State Farm, there were no insurance experts on the staff. George Mecherle, in all truth, was an amateur when he started the little company on the road to its tremendous success. Quick to understand, shrewd in his interpretations of new and complex situations, and mathematically minded though he was, he was not a skilled accountant. In fact, in the first four or five years, there were no skilled accountants connected with the company. It is more for this reason than for any other that the original system of premium charges, cancellations and renewals did not work as perfectly as it should have and almost led the company to grief, as later developments were to show. The utter integrity of George Mecherle and the men associated with him in those striving years, those years of inevitable growing pains, was more important than expert mathematical knowledge or a graduate degree in insurance accounting.

How and why this system led to eventual complications makes an interesting exercise in the esoterics of insurance.

The first policy contracts issued by State Farm consisted of the policy itself and the application which was attached to it and which formed a part of the agreement. The fee for the membership and the amount of the original premium deposit were written out in the application. There were, as we have seen, seven classifications of automobiles, ranging from Class A for a car with a list price up to and including $699 to Class G for a car with a list price from $2,200 to $2,500. Charges were the same for any car in a given class regardless of its age.

The application blank set forth that the original premium deposit was for the first six months' term of insurance. The premium deposit, according to the contract, was earned *pro rata* during the policy term, and at the end of the period was entirely earned. Should the member then terminate his insurance he had no legal claim for the return of any portion of the premium deposit. The membership fee was not returnable in any case.

Thirty days before the policy's term was due to end the company sent the policyholder a notice of the amount the insurance had cost (or would cost) in losses and expenses during the expiring term. If the policyholder paid this amount before the term expired his account was credited with an amount equal to the original premium deposit. Although the original premium was fully earned at the end of the six months' term, it was restored by his payment plus what was, in effect, the automatic declaration of a dividend equal to the unused portion of the original premium deposit.

Thus, if the premium deposit was $19—which was the average—and if the policyholder's share of the cost to be absorbed from this for losses and expenses was $10, then the policyholder was credited with $9 as a dividend. This $9 credit, plus a new payment of $10, restored the premium deposit to the original amount. The same process was repeated at every renewal period.

There existed no contractual obligation on the part of the company to pay any dividend to the policyholder at the end of the term. This system had the merit of favoring the continuing policyholders and discouraging lapses, much after the system of surrender charges generally in use in life insurance companies.

Under this plan the State Farm company set up a *pro rata* unearned premium reserve on deposit premiums.

In the case of the $19 deposit premium, this was $9.50. There was no reserve on the membership fee—for the simple reason that this was not premium and was not returnable, membership being for life. In insurance accounting, the purpose of the unearned premium reserve is to set aside funds to meet losses and expenses during the term of the policy, to reinsure the risk if necessary, or for the return of a part of the premium in the event of cancellation during the policy term. The 50% method is based on the mathematical assumption that at any given date one-half of the premiums in force are earned and the other half are unearned.

In the first several years in which State Farm was operating, the mathematics of this system seem not to have been understood fully by the management. At any event, it was not completely followed. Because of these deviations, several problems arose as time went by. As we have seen, back when Miss Jones was in charge of the home office the premium calls were set at a figure which was too low to restore wholly the premium deposits for renewal. As a result, dividends allowed on renewals were excessive and amounted to more than actually should have been paid.

When cancellations took place, during these early years, the method of refunding unearned premiums was one which did not follow the contract and was unduly liberal to canceling policyholders. Refunds were computed on the basis of the original deposit less only current costs, instead of *pro rata* (if canceled by the company) or short rate (if canceled by the policyholder) of the premium deposit. Once again it was a matter of the wrong mathematics. If the premium deposit was $12 and the current cost for insurance during the six months' term was $4 and, for instance, the policy was canceled by the company after three months, the refund was $12 less one-half of $4, or $2. On this basis the insured got back $10, even though under the terms of the policy he was entitled only to a *pro rata* return of the $12 premium deposit, or $6. The net result was that, in many cases, the company returned more than the unearned premium which had been set up. This excess payment had to come from surplus. As insurance department examiners were later to point out, if the company wanted to treat as unearned all except that part of the premium deposit needed for current loss and expense costs, a larger sum should have been set aside as unearned premiums. Fortunately, cancellations were not so numerous as to cause much difficulty, but the arithmetic was wrong.

Luckily for State Farm the company grew so rapidly under George Mecherle's driving salesmanship that there was always plenty of income on hand to meet these unduly liberal payments, as well as losses and expenses. But the truth is that the early policyholders were actually carried at a slight loss. Later policyholders made up this difference. And the erroneous system did not, in the long run, cause any serious difficulty.

The errors involved in the foregoing were not discovered and corrected for nearly eight years. A few former agents of the company found the system of refunding the premium deposit less the cost of current call during the last term of insurance to their advantage. Some of them began to encourage lapsations of policies, so that policyholders might collect this cash windfall to apply toward insurance in competing companies. To counter this, the management ceased refunding the premium deposit remainders, crediting them to the policyholders, and making these sums available to members on subsequent insurance carried with the company. Again this was a liberality not required by the contract, but was done nevertheless, the company taking the view that it was unfair to forfeit the balance of premium deposits for members who wanted to get back in good standing. This practice also made it easier to reinstate lapsed policyholders.

Management shifted by degrees from the premium deposit plan to the net premium plan. It established a fixed, net premium graded according to the risk in each case, with the premium entirely earned at the end of the term. The automatic dividend was abolished. Within a few years all policies, old and new, were switched to this more stable system. The old premium deposit method went into the discard, where it has since remained.

The older plan, of course, could have been continued, and fully adequate reserves could have been maintained, had the premium calls been adequate. Interest earnings alone would largely have solved the problem, even with reserves set up on the 100% basis, less credit for the absorbed parts of the deposits at any time. This same plan was not new. It had been in use by the Factory Mutual Fire Insurance Companies of New England for more than a century at this time. But it would work only when the current calls from policyholders were always sufficient to meet losses, expenses and reserve requirements.

As time passed and the business forged ahead with such phenomenal strides, with the home office increasing its staff tremendously year by year, competent actuaries and skilled insurance accountants were brought into the organization. Some of the best in the business came to work for State Farm. Members of the original company were learning more and more about the intricacies of the industry. Although he always remained dominant as a salesman and stressed the importance of the agency force, George Mecherle absorbed the lore of insurance and took a more active part in this end of the business than he had in the days when he was bringing the business to the company. Secretary Beedle, whose duties from the start of his association with State Farm included handling the accounting, was not a trained accountant, although his knowledge of insurance problems was wide. When in 1929 he went to the West Coast to establish the branch office in Berkeley, California, his close connection with this phase of State Farm ceased and these du-ties were taken up by men trained in this field.

Such were the real growing pains of State Farm. The fundamental soundness of the company, and the practicality of the plan originated by the farmer from Merna, proved themselves over the years. In spite of miscalculation there was never any real question of the firmness at the core.

9

WESTWARD IT SPREAD

Born in the heart of the Middle West and nurtured in the soil of the great Corn Belt, State Farm Mutual looked mainly westward in the late 1920's as the course of its empire spread. Thus it followed the history of its country and the tradition of the people. Within ten years of its meager, back-roads beginning it had penetrated twenty-nine of the forty-eight states. Except for Arizona and Louisiana it had state offices and agents in every state west of the Mississippi River. Its one branch office was on the West Coast. It had nine claims offices—ranging from Lansing, Michigan, to Yakima, Washington. Through the merger of the City & Village Company with the parent institution it was serving every type of citizen, although the greater part of its business was still with farmers or with those who lived away from the great urban centers. It owned its own life insurance company and was soon to own its own fire insurance company. Already its eight-story building in Bloomington was too small to house the 350 employees who struggled vainly to keep their bulging files and heavily laden desks in order.

Pushing westward was not always as easy a task as it might seem. There were obstacles in the way. Some were to be expected, others arose unexpectedly. Most of them were overcome without too wearing an expenditure of the resources of State Farm and almost always the results were worth the effort. Each state presented its own problems, both in the early days when state regulations were not, as a rule, too arduous, and after the advent of the New Deal, when the legislative passion for stricter regulation of private enterprise spread from Washington to the state capitals.

In most instances the state Farm Bureau Federation, as sponsor for the growing insurance company, was able to pave its way into the new states. Coming from an organization potent, for the most part, in the politics of those states where agricultural interests were uppermost, the Farm Bureau sponsorship was a decided asset to the company. Occasionally there had to be minor changes made either in the state insurance law or in the insurance department's strictures before the State Farm Mutual system of operation was considered acceptable. In several instances the stock companies would lobby vigorously against revisions which they felt would favor the mutual from Bloomington. This was particularly true in the South, where a great portion of the insurance business was held by family-controlled stock companies, which had sprung up rapidly after the Civil War.

George Mecherle often found it difficult to "sell" the story of State Farm in new territory. That is, he found organized opposition set up in advance of his arrival. But once he had broken down the initial barriers and was able to approach the agricultural leaders of a community, in the same candid way he had approached the farm mutual leadership a few years before at Streator, he invariably found a receptive audience. He often was surprised to learn that the story he had to tell had gone before him. One of the great virtues of the company under his leadership was the utter fealty of its employees to the company. Especially in the days when it was a small and growing company, those who worked in the expanding home office thought of themselves as part of a family. George Mecherle headed this family and guided it with benevolence. This same feeling of loyalty was also held by thousands of its policyholders, who proudly bore the State Farm Insurance medallion on their automobiles, as if it were the symbol of a fraternal organization. Many policyholders in Illinois would write to friends or relatives on farms farther west telling them about State Farm, although they were not its agents and had nothing to gain by spreading the word. They felt they were getting a fair deal and wanted others to share it with them. Sometimes people who did not own cars sought membership—just for the sake of feeling they, too, belonged to the same "club" as their friends and neighbors.

But often, especially after the company's phenomenal growth had become a matter of record, enemies arose to block its progress. In one state in the Far West an agent for a number of insurance companies took a full-page advertisement in a newspaper to attack the State Farm plan. Instead of sticking to sound competitive sales arguments the agent wrote an ad that was compounded mostly of lies. Ordinarily George Mecherle took little notice, publicly at least, of these attacks on his company, but this particular one was so flagrant that he authorized the State Farm agent in whose territory it was published to take legal action. The result was that the State Insurance Commission ordered the agent to publish a retraction of all the falsehoods, using the same space and the same style of type as in the original ad. It was a costly venture for the misguided salesman.

In *An American Story*, A. R. Williamson tells how Mr. Mecherle forced a rough Western newspaper editor to quit "rawhiding my agents out here every week" in his newspaper. Such attacks were not infrequent; sometimes they were in the nature of blackmail, inspired with the hope of forcing State Farm to buy the editor off through advertising. George Mecherle always refused to do this. He went on the theory that the product he was selling would win in the end on its own merits —and it usually did.

During the 1930's State Farm was plagued by a series of anonymous letters and pamphlets which were sent to policyholders and agents in different parts of the country, especially in the West. They were obviously the work of some outdistanced rival who found the competition of State Farm greater than it could bear. Many of them were mimeographed, some were even semiliterate, and most were so transparently inspired by jealousy that State Farm chose to ignore them, or to answer them by personal letter when—as was often the case—some faithful and satisfied policyholder sent them to George Mecherle out of a sense of fidelity and outraged justice. There were, however, one or two instances of "unfair and contemptible propaganda against State Farm" that had to be answered publicly.

One was a widely distributed circular which purported to be a copy of a letter from a Minnesota attorney in which it was claimed that State Farm denied liability and refused to defend a policyholder who had injured four persons while driving his car. Justifiably angered by what, if true, would have been a damaging attack on the company's reputation for a quick and fair-minded settlement of all claims, George Mecherle carefully prepared a statement.

"The facts are," he wrote with a restraint he did not feel, "that the Company has definite proof that the driver was intoxicated at the time of the accident. The company denied liability because our policy plainly and specifically provided that we assumed no liability for automobile accidents sustained by our policyholder while intoxicated. This company does not insure intoxicated drivers and we are not willing that our policyholders should be called upon to pay losses occurring while our policyholders are intoxicated. This policyholder—if he believes that this company is liable—has a perfect right to sue us and we stand ready and willing to defend our company and its policyholders on the above grounds at any time and without apology to anyone." *

This forthright answer not only was further evidence of George Mecherle's deep understanding of the Midwestern mind, which would see at once that the moral right was entirely on his side, but further proof of the rightness of the policy he was forever dinning into his agents' ears —that it was their duty to the company always to exercise the utmost care in selecting potential policyholders.

On the whole these attacks did the company more good than harm. None of them ever managed to contain any really damaging information. Even an eleven-page assault on the corporate structure of the company, which first appeared in the *Insurance Examiner* and was reprinted in the *Northwest Agency Bulletin*, failed to stand up against analysis. At the end of one letter answering a widely broadcast attack, George Mecherle showed how to turn the tables on his tormentors:

This Company is going steadily forward—increasing its business, assets, loss reserves and surplus. This sort of propaganda always arouses interest in our company. It gives us further opportunity to advertise and increase our business. Like previous efforts of this kind, it will soon wear itself out. The obvious course of action for our agents is to take full advantage immediately of the new interest aroused, and go after business harder than ever.

---

* The intoxication clause was eliminated from State Farm policies early in 1934.

In 1933, he and his son Ermond—who had joined the company in 1928—went on a tour of several states, in an effort to get State Farm licensed to do business in them. One state which the company had not penetrated was Maryland. For reasons that are now obscure, Mr. Mecherle discovered on arriving in Baltimore that the Maryland Farm Bureau had filed a petition with the insurance department, objecting to the company's entrance into that state. The two Mecherles stayed in the city several days until the hearing on the matter was called. They found that certain witnesses had come on from another state in which the company was not then doing business, and that two unfriendly Farm Bureau agents from Virginia also were on hand to give reasons why State Farm should not have a license. The two Mecherles from Bloomington sat quietly while these witnesses gave their testimony, and then George Mecherle told his story.

"Inasmuch as I was not represented by counsel," he wrote to Erwin Meyers, "it was necessary that I assume the duties of a counselor, and I feel that I exploded all the questions of their petition, as in my opinion they amounted to very little. . . . I feel satisfied that we will be licensed in Maryland within the next week or ten days."

They were.

In Pennsylvania they found that the use of the word "State" in the title of State Farm was against the long-standing policy of the Pennsylvania commission. The commissioner hinted that if they changed the name they might have less difficulty.

"I told him that the good will and traditions and romance that had grown up around the name 'State Farm Mutual' would not justify us in making any change in our name to secure admission to any state— as the value of the name, due to the success of the organization, was of greater worth than the admission into any state."

The good will and traditions and romance! Those words, as nearly as any that could be chosen, summed up what George Mecherle carried in his battered brief case along with the indisputable figures that showed the phenomenal growth of the ten-year-old company. In making these rounds George Mecherle was the diplomat as well as the salesman. "The thing that concerns me most," he wrote, "is the fact that our plan is eternally under question." But although it concerned him it did not overwhelm him. Indeed, he thought, "maybe it is a good thing." It kept him, and all his associates, on their toes.

In some instances the unwillingness of a state commissioner to license

State Farm to operate within his jurisdiction could be traced directly to a competitor. This was the case in one of the Far Western states, where a license was refused because the State Farm application provided for a policy fee. A rival company—incorporated in an adjacent state but doing business in the state in question—was able to keep this provision in the insurance code for many years, and temporarily delay State Farm's admission to the state, although the Bloomington company did business in all the five surrounding states. When a similar restriction kept State Farm out of an Eastern state, George Mecherle told the state commissioner that the rule would probably force him into "some form of subterfuge"—perhaps establishing a separate organization in the state and then reinsuring the business 100% in State Farm Mutual. But this, he added, "is a thing we do not desire to do."

In 1933, the first year of the New Deal, there were thirty-five state legislatures in session. Perhaps it was because of a zeal for reform, born of the New Deal, that there was more radical and novel legislation affecting insurance introduced that year than for many years previously. In these legislatures there were nearly one hundred bills which would, in some way or another, affect the mutual companies. Some may have embodied needed reforms. But, in one state at least, the source of the proposed measure was apparent.

There State Farm's competitors sought to amend the insurance law to make it mandatory for reserves to be carried on membership fees, a direct slap at State Farm procedure. In another state proposed amendments to the Uniform Mutual Law would forbid management and general agency contracts for terms of longer than one year, unless approved by the policyholders and by the insurance director, and in no event for longer than five years. This amendment, actually written by the lobbyist of an organization that had recently founded an insurance company in direct competition with State Farm, would also have made the complete list of policyholders—their names and addresses—open to inspection by all policyholders, including agents of its rivals! The management and agency provision, of course, was a direct slap at State Farm which, since its founding, had been operated under the fifteen-year contract with G. J. Mecherle, Inc., with unusually successful results.

These were just some of the headaches for the State Farm Mutual in the years of expansion. As the company moved westward it also moved southward and, as early as 1928, it came to the border of Louisiana. It came to the border—but it did not get beyond.

For many years the stock companies had had their way in the state where Huey Long had just become Governor. The Insurance Law of 1918 was written in their favor. It allowed stock companies to transact all kinds of insurance business but it restricted mutuals to transacting only one kind. Under this onesided law State Farm was welcome to sell theft insurance, or fire insurance, or accident insurance, but not all three. It was forbidden by this law to sell a "full coverage" policy.

At just the time State Farm began its first southern campaign (it was also knocking at the borders of other states in the Deep South at this time) the American Mutual Alliance, which represented most of the nation's mutual insurance companies, was girding its loins to fight the continuance of this discriminatory act. Its ultimate aim was the enactment of a Uniform Mutual Law. In 1928, however, an investigation of the situation in the politically turbulent state of Louisiana had shown that the time was not yet ripe to go that far. Instead, it was agreed to seek the passage of a "short bill" which would do no more than remove the prohibition against mutual companies transacting more than one kind of business and place them at long last on an equal competitive footing with the stock companies.

Such a simple revision would not, of course, remove all the difficulties that would face State Farm—such technical matters as surplus and reserves, for instance—but it would allow the company to sell "complete coverage" without resorting to an alliance with another company or to some other legal subterfuge, such as would be necessary under the 1918 law. It agreed to go along with the Alliance and, indeed, led the way into the arena at Baton Rouge. A bill was written by E. A. Meyers— counsel for both State Farm and the Mutual Alliance—and it was introduced as "an Act to authorize Mutual Insurance Companies to transact the various kinds of insurance as is now provided by law for Insurance Companies organized under the stock plan." The battle was on.

Perry Crane, superintendent of agents, a young and able executive who had come to State Farm from Indiana a few years earlier to be George Mecherle's right-hand man, went with Mr. Meyers to Louisiana. Although he found "dealing with these Southern gentlemen . . . quite a little different from dealing with most of the people with whom we have contact," he and J. M. Eaton—the able lobbyist for the Alliance— lined up the lumber and hardware interests, cotton growers and cotton ginners, as well as farmers, behind the bill.

They found the political situation "terribly mixed up," as well they might. Huey Long had just taken office and was busy firing his enemies right and left and generally raising political hell as he started that Messianic career which was to lead the Kingfish in front of an assassin's bullets within a few wild years. After a preliminary canvassing of the situation Meyers and Crane returned north to the comparative political calm of McLean and Cook counties, leaving Mr. Eaton in charge of the bill. He knew how to treat with Southern gentlemen, apparently, for the bill passed both Houses. It was an empty victory. Huey Long, who had admittedly favored the bill on its merits, had quarreled bitterly with the sponsoring Senator between the bill's filing and its passage. He now vetoed it, out of personal pique. An attempt to revive the measure at a special session called later in the summer failed. It was not until 1935, after the state's entire insurance code had been overhauled, that State Farm entered Louisiana on a par with the stock companies.

The barriers which State Farm had to overcome were not always political. In some instances they were purely technical, as in Iowa. This rich farming state was ripe for the type of insurance offered by State Farm and, in 1927, the Iowa State Farm Bureau Federation approached the Bloomington company, much as Indiana had two years before. An agreement was easily reached for the Farm Bureau to act as the company's state agent. But then the Iowa insurance commission raised the question of unearned premium reserves and the minimum surplus of the company. The Iowa commission made the point—as did some other states—that reserves should be carried on both the membership fees and the premiums. It felt, for example, that if the premium was $19 and the membership fee was $15—as it then was—then the total on which reserves should be carried would be $34. Iowa at that time was the one state which required only a 40% reserve. Other states required 50%. Thus Iowa required $13.60 as the reserve on premium and membership, instead of the $9.50 which the State Farm system considered adequate. From the Iowa standpoint, raising the reserve had the effect of reducing the surplus. Therefore, Iowa demanded a stipulation from State Farm to the effect that the company would always maintain a sufficient surplus to equal the Iowa minimum surplus of $100,000—after charging reserves on the Iowa basis. For several years—or until the Iowa requirements were changed—State Farm had to submit any change in its by-laws to the Iowa commission for approval.

In the majority of cases, however, no major obstacles—political or otherwise—arose to beleaguer State Farm. The formula which had been worked out during the negotiations with the Farm Bureau Federation of Indiana, in the summer of 1924, furnished a pattern which was to prove eminently successful in state after state, as State Farm swept westward and southward.

George Mecherle was ever a strong advocate of standard and uniform practices and provisions. Although sometimes even he had to admit that exigencies called for unusual measures, he sought to avoid them whenever possible. He did not believe in making special "deals" or arrangements. It was his well-proven theory that uniformity and an inflexible standard made for fewer errors, eliminated confusion between the home office and the field, and promoted better understanding and good will all around.

The original ten-year contract with the Indiana Farm Bureau Federation at first provided that the Bureau, as general agent for State Farm Mutual, was to receive on all business written by the Bureau, or by sub-agents of its choosing, 80% of all membership fees collected and 25 cents for each policy that was renewed. This contract was revised twice during the first year until it finally provided that the Indiana Farm Bureau was to receive 86⅔% of all membership fees and—in lieu of the 25-cent renewal fee—was to receive 50 cents for each policy renewal as soon as 5,000 policyholders were attained in Indiana. Half of this 50 cents was to go to the district representatives or their agents. The Indiana agency was to pay, out of its receipts from State Farm, the compensations of the local and district agents.

The secret of the success of the Farm Bureau contracts in Indiana— and later in many other states—lay not only in the sound coverage offered by State Farm Mutual but also in the fact that George Mecherle exercised general supervision and motivation of the agency organizations in these states. Beginning with Indiana, each Farm Bureau that took advantage of the plan became the official state agent. In return, it received the state agent's commission and gave the plan general endorsement and sponsorship at Farm Bureau meetings of all types. The State Farm home office representatives were made welcome at farmers' meetings to "sell" the insurance idea, but the actual selling of policies was left to agents appointed through the Bureaus. However, George Mecherle personally approved all the state directors appointed by the Bureaus who gave their time to promoting the sales of State Farm policies. These directors were always Farm Bureau employees, being paid from the commissions earned by the Farm Bureau, but they received a considerable proportion of their promotional material, encouragement, and education in insurance salesmanship from Bloomington. This system worked to the mutual advantage of the company and the Bureaus and kept the agents much more on their toes than if they had been left entirely to themselves. The Farm Bureaus were not allowed to handle other automobile insurance or act as a "general agency" that would merely add State Farm to its lists in the hope of getting some business. George Mecherle was unwilling to place his company in this position, where he would be unable to maintain control of its business. Without defining it as such, he was operating everywhere on the life insurance system of selling through individual calls from individual agents, rather than through an "over-the-counter" general agency operation.

On December 5, 1925, the South Dakota Farm Bureau Federation was made state agent under a contract similar to that with Indiana, and three days later the Missouri Farm Bureau Federation entered the fold on the same terms.

The South Dakota arrangement, as well as many others that were to come along in the next few years, was salutary to all concerned in more ways than one. In 1924, a young man with a degree in animal husbandry from the State College of Agriculture and Mechanic Arts had become the executive secretary of the South Dakota Farm Bureau Federation. It was, in many respects, a precarious way of making a living. South Dakota had been particularly hard hit by the deflation in farm prices during the depression of the 1920's that spread havoc among the farmers on the eve of Normalcy. The Farm Bureau was facing financial difficulties that spelled disaster for the organization if some alleviation of its woes were not speedily found. There did not seem to be in the offing any quick way of getting cash to meet the Bureau's legal obligations or even to pay for operating expenses.

In the summer of 1925, A. W. Tompkins—the young secretary—happened across a brief item in one of the publications of the United States Department of Agriculture which told about the arrangement made between the Indiana Farm Bureau and "an insurance company in Bloomington, Illinois, headed by George J. Mecherle." This set him to thinking, and he passed the squib on to others in the Farm Bureau office. After talking it over, they decided no harm could come from dropping that Mecherle fellow a line. The letter was sent off, promptly answered, and in due time it was arranged for Mr. Mecherle to come west to tell his story.

George Mecherle arrived at Huron, South Dakota, in time for the annual meeting of the Farm Bureau. On that fateful day he sat around the office visiting, talking about his insurance plan, chatting about farm problems—in that easy, knowledgeable way he had when in the company of farmers. He and the young animal husbandry expert got along real well. Mr. Tompkins was a laconic young fellow but he knew what he was talking about, and both he and Mecherle sized each other up as men who understood what was on the farmer's mind.

It was not until late in the afternoon that Mr. Mecherle was asked in to the meeting to deliver his message. In his disarming way he told them that it would take him just about half an hour to tell them all he had to say about the State Farm Mutual and that when he was through he would take no more of their time—unless they wanted him to. His talk was as lucid and comprehensive as the historic presentation he had given the farmers at Streator three years before. The only difference now was that he could tell about accomplishments, with facts and figures, rather than what he hoped would happen. He was still answering questions at supper time. The delegates were convinced and showed their appreciation of his sales talk—his message, really—by passing a resolution authorizing the board of directors to take the steps necessary to set up the same kind of arrangement State Farm had with the Farm Bureau in Indiana. Mr. Mecherle stayed over the next day, going into details. He then moved on to Missouri to repeat the performance.

When he got to Jefferson City he found that the Farm Bureau there was no happier financially than the one in South Dakota. In fact, things were so bad that R. B. Brown—a farmer who lived many miles away—found it impossible to spend as much time as he should in the Bureau office taking care of his duties as president. He was at the farm when Mr. Mecherle showed up at the office. Mr. Mecherle put in a call for him. Mr. Brown was out in the field cultivating corn and did not want to be bothered with any insurance agent. But Mr. Mecherle's persuasiveness finally brought him to the telephone and, when he offered to pay Mr. Brown's expenses to come down to Jefferson City and talk over the proposition of becoming state agent for the State Farm Mutual, the busy man reluctantly agreed to do so.

On Mr. Brown's arrival, George Mecherle found him to be in a thoroughly skeptical frame of mind. Even when he pointed out that if the Farm Bureau became the state agent of the State Farm Mutual Mr. Brown would at long last be able to devote his full time to Federation affairs and be reasonably well compensated for doing so, Brown was hesitant. But few people could argue with Mr. Mecherle when his missionary zeal was at full force, and after a while Brown agreed to think it over. He thought it over for weeks, threshing the matter out in his mind in the clear hot sun of the corn field and discussing it thoroughly with his directors. At last he made his decision. A meeting was called, action was agreed upon, and the contract was signed. As had been the case in Indiana—and was to be the case in South Dakota and elsewhere —the arrangement turned out to be profitable for all concerned.

Almost all of the Farm Bureaus during the 1920's were no better off than those which had been already signed up by George Mecherle. He was now putting in the same long hours on the road, spending almost more time in sleepers and hotel rooms than he spent at home, as he had done in the days when he was badgering the secretaries of the farmers' mutuals in the back counties of Illinois. At this crucial period in agricultural history the Minnesota Farm Bureau Federation—one of the most progressive in the old Northwest Territory—was having its woes along with the rest. Its membership dues were not sufficient for it to carry on the broad program of services to the farmer to which it aspired, and its executive board was desperately casting about for some means to improve its precarious position. On the board, however, was a member who was an ardent protagonist of mutual insurance. His fervent pleas brought about the creation of a committee which was set up to inquire into the farm insurance situation in Minnesota, with an eye to possible revenues that might be available to the Federation from that service.

With typical Minnesotan thoroughness this group plowed into the subject until it came up with some startling conclusions. Among other facts it learned that less than 2% of the farmers of Minnesota carried any insurance of any kind on their automobiles, and that which they did carry was the least necessary—fire and theft. Further study showed that this was about all the casualty companies operating in the state offered. Having proved the necessity for a wider range of automobile insurance for farm people, the committee then came to the logical conclusion that the Federation ought to know more about insurance itself. The committee looked about for a company that was operating over a wide area on the sound theory that the losses incurred would be aver-aged over a wide area. State Farm Mutual seemed to fill the bill.

Many conferences were held with George Mecherle and George Beedle before a contract was drawn up. The Farm Bureau at last agreed to become the state agent or—as J. S. Jones, secretary of the committee of inquiry, put it—the "production agency." But it left the big headache of handling claims entirely to State Farm. It was a good deal all around. For one thing, it supplied the Federation with a much needed "service" to help attract membership at a time when this was all-important. From the start the Insurance Department of the Minnesota Bureau not only paid for itself but its revenues helped carry on the work of the entire organization, through many crucial months.

When the history of the American Farm Bureau Federation is written it will be incomplete without a chapter on its close relationship on the state level—especially in the 1920's and early 1930's—with State Farm Mutual. In the early days in Illinois George Mecherle and his little "gang" of mud-lane salesmen sought those who were members or eligible to be members of that far-flung organization. But it was not until the first out-of-state contract was signed by State Farm and the Indiana Farm Bureau Federation that the connection became, as it were, official. From then, as the company's expansion grew, it became so close that, in the eyes of many, State Farm and Farm Bureau were one and the same.

At no time, of course, in any of the states, did State Farm Mutual have anything to say about Farm Bureau policies or affairs—or vice versa. The association, from the beginning, did not extend beyond that of a business contract between two parties for the single and simple purpose of mutual advantage. It was a firm and friendly relationship but it was a business arrangement and nothing more. That it worked, as the Indiana pioneers had predicted and intended that it would, for the benefit of both, is a matter of history. That, in the early days, State Farm was of considerable economic help to the Farm Bureau, especially during the years of agricultural depression, is also a matter of history.

This was particularly true in Western states. At least two state Farm Bureaus were saved from temporary financial disaster in the 1920's through their alliance with State Farm Mutual. At the time of the signing of the contract between State Farm and the Minnesota Farm Bureau the latter was in grave financial difficulties. Its treasury had become depleted through nonpayment of dues by too many of the harried and depressed farmers of that state. Because of this situation it was on the verge of losing its voice in the national council of the Farm Bureau. As it turned out, the contract making the Minnesota Farm Bureau the state agency of State Farm became its most potent asset. When J. S. Jones, the

Bureau's executive secretary, went to the annual meeting of the national Bureau in Chicago in December, less than a year after the signing of the contract, he carried with him a check from State Farm Mutual. This was for the income earned by the Minnesota Bureau as state agency. Mr. Jones endorsed this check over to the Farm Bureau Federation—thereby paying the Minnesota organization's dues in full for the year and bringing that state back into good standing with the parent organization. The association between the Minnesota Farm Bureau and State Farm continued for more than a quarter of a century. At the end of that period 156,000 Minnesota autoists were protected by State Farm policies bought through the Farm Bureau.

In 1926 North Dakota was assigned to the South Dakota and Minnesota Farm Bureau Federations, which had contracts with State Farm as state agents. The North Dakota Farm Bureau was at that time in desperate financial straits. It was dead broke and in debt. In order to keep it going as even a paper organization the directors had been forced to advance personal funds to the Bureau as loans. The condition was so bad that North Dakota had, to all intents and purposes, been read out of the national organization. And it looked as if it might not be able to re-establish itself for years to come. As was the case with Minnesota, however, the money earned through the association with State Farm enabled it to pay off not only its dues but also the loans from its directors. It was re-established as a going branch of the parent body, rehabilitated by the sale of State Farm Mutual automobile insurance.

And so it went. From Minnesota and Michigan in 1926, the Farm Bureau Federation and State Farm Mutual alliance spread. In 1927, the states of Colorado, Iowa, Kansas, Kentucky and Nebraska joined the parade. The next year saw California, Mississippi, Montana, Nevada, Texas, Utah and Washington fall into line. Arizona, Idaho, New Mexico, West Virginia and Wyoming came in 1929. In 1930—with the Great Depression looming—North Carolina, Oklahoma, Oregon and Virginia became State Farm states.

In most instances, where entrance had been facilitated by Farm Bureau sponsorship and contract, the relationship lasted for ten or twenty years. Then many of these Farm Bureaus set up automobile insurance companies under their own control and supervision. Invariably they patterned their companies almost identically on the plan of operation of State Farm Mutual.

Nothing, perhaps, better symbolized the national expansion of the

State Farm Mutual than the decision of the board of directors, in 1928, to establish the first branch office on the West Coast. During that year the company was licensed to operate in California, Washington and Utah—all just about as far to the west of Bloomington as it was possible to go. It seemed a logical move to set up a headquarters nearer this scene of operation, and centrally located Berkeley, California, seemed a good place. As soon as the deal with the Farm Bureau was consummated, and the license to operate in California was obtained, a small crew from the home office was sent out to start things going.

To Edna Crusius—the sister of Verna, the first employee of the company, and herself a "veteran" of the "old days in the Durley building"— went the task of organizing the office. With her went another experienced employee, Fanny Bailey, who had helped organize the state office when Michigan was added in 1926. Later George Beedle, who was still secretary of the company, went out to take over-all charge of what was to be known as the Western Department.

Something of the spirit of the State Farm Mutual in those days when the company was growing fast, but before it had become the tremendous organization it is today, can be seen in excerpts from a letter Edna Crusius wrote George Mecherle a few weeks after her arrival. It was the same spirit that George Mecherle strove to maintain throughout his entire life with the organization of his creation. The letter reveals, between the lines, a great deal about George Mecherle's own character and his zealous concern for the institution:

> First of all, I want to thank you so much for my Christmas present, which I gratefully accepted although I really felt that I had had my Christmas before I came here—after getting that beautiful fitted traveling bag ——And the Christmas money came in very handy when I took a little trip to the southern part of the state. I took Saturday morning, Monday all day, and Wednesday all day (Tuesday was New Year's Day—a holiday), but I worked nights and Saturday afternoons to catch up before I went and I've been doing it since, so I really feel that I *played fair.* . . .
>
> Everything at the office is going nicely. We are trying to reach the place where we shall have all the applications received one week out of the way the next week. Haven't quite accomplished that *yet*, but WE WILL. The last bunch received from the Farm Bureau office yesterday number very close to 2,700. They are getting close to 150 per week. . . .
>
> Fanny and I are having Mr. and Mrs. Beedle and Mrs. B's mother over for dinner this evening. Have the chicken on—so bring Mrs. Mecherle and you can come over, too. . . .
>
> Assuring you that the Berkeley Branch of the State Farm Mutual shall

do all in their power to put California on the State Farm map and if there is anything we seem to be falling down on, we are willing to be corrected —yes, and maybe scolded. . . .

Business was so good in California that by summer they had to take more room in the Mercantile Bank Building for the office staff, which by then had grown to twenty-one persons; and even with this many employees it was difficult to keep up with the work of getting out policies and commissions on time. Washington, however, was a harder nut to crack. Miss Bailey was assigned to the Farm Bureau headquarters at Colfax—a small town with about 3,000 population—to handle the office there, while others concentrated on getting reliable district agents and training them in State Farm methods. This came close to pioneering, for the Farm Bureau in that state was not so well organized as it was in the Middle Western states.

In those days, even in the states where the Farm Bureau Federation was well established, all the men who spread the coverage of State Farm were pioneers. They were breaking new ground, even as George Mecherle's forebears had broken the rich soil of the Illinois prairie to bring it to productive heights. In the home office in Bloomington, beginning with the hiring of Charley Wonderlin, George Mecherle had shown remarkable aptitude in choosing the men to work under him. Once he had made his selection he firmly believed the men of his choice should carry out their heavy responsibilities without much further supervision from himself. If he had chosen them, then it had to follow that they owned the same courage, idealism, and over-all philosophy as his own. He made few mistakes in his exercise of human judgment in those pioneering days.

After the state agency contracts were made with the State Farm Bureaus it was up to them to carry out their responsibilities. George Mecherle was well aware this might not be done properly if he did not select the right leaders. The men who were to be charged with recruiting, training, and supervising the agency forces in the field had to be individuals of tremendous capacity. At the very beginning of the era of expansion he had set a high standard when he had approved the choice of H. R. Nevins as state director. Evidence of Mr. Nevins's ability can be best seen in the fact that he has been the only state director for Indiana in all the years that have passed since the first policy was sold across the banks of the Wabash in 1925. Many of the company's top field directors were trained under his firm but gentle hand.

Mr. Nevins has been on the board of directors of State Farm Mutual for many years.

In Missouri, the first to come into the State Farm family after Indiana, E. L. Corbin was the original director. He served there many years before becoming state director of Texas. He was followed in Missouri by Frank Stonner, who has held that position since 1930. A. W. Tompkins, now executive vice president in charge of all agencies, was, as we have seen, the first director in South Dakota. Like Mr. Tompkins most of these early directors were closely associated with the farmers and the farm movements in their states. Several of them had been county agents before joining State Farm Mutual.

Alfred Bentall had been a Farm Bureau organization director before he became state director in Michigan, the post he held for twenty-three years until his death in 1949. In Minnesota E. A. Tyler was the first director. He had previous experience in the insurance business in the predominantly agricultural states of Indiana and South Dakota, and during his many years with State Farm contributed a wealth of novel ideas, many of which were adopted by the company. After serving in Minnesota he took over the state directorship in Nebraska. Upon his death in 1944 he was succeeded by his stepson, Virgil R. Hoover, who holds that position today.

Louis Kelehan, a county agent in Minnesota, succeeded Mr. Tyler as state director there. Six years later he went to Iowa, where he still supervises State Farm affairs in that vast region of corn and hogs. In California A. M. Stanley moved from his post as an organization director for the California Farm Bureau Federation to the state directorship in 1928. He served there until his death in 1950. A former newspaper editor in a small town, Mr. Stanley had a fertile and creative mind from which flowed many a brilliant promotion idea, scintillatingly expressed, to become a part of the State Farm tradition.

Virginia, first of the old Southern states to be entered by State Farm, took as its state director a young man experienced in the insurance field, H. E. Baumberger. That was in 1930. He is still state director, but now his territory includes Delaware, Maryland and the District of Columbia. That same year M. S. Judy took charge of West Virginia, where he is still state director. K. A. McCaskill, another county agent, took over the Colorado territory. He is now retired. M. B. Nugent, still another county agent, moved from Indiana to become assistant state director in Kentucky in 1929, then in a year or two became the state director, where he remained until his recent retirement. Ed A. Mack, who had been a rancher, became a local agent in 1928 but within a year had become the state director in Montana, where he remained in charge until his retirement a few years ago. And A. W. Palm, a former county agent in South Dakota, took over the North and South Dakota territories in 1930 and is still active.

Like George Mecherle, these early leaders were, with two exceptions, men with little or no experience with insurance when they joined the company. But, like the man who chose them, they knew the land and the people whence they came; and, as one of them put it, they knew a good thing when they saw it—an opportunity for themselves but one equally good for the people with whom they lived and worked.

Another symbol of the spread of State Farm far and wide across the country was the establishment, in 1927, of the *Reflector*. Even this early in the development of the company the need for some means of keeping the company's increasingly far-flung agency force in touch with developments of the home office was keenly felt. There were frequent changes in policy, and even in the policies, that had to be explained. This mimeographed publication was the ideal way to get this information regularly to the agents. It was not directed to the office staffs so much as it was aimed directly at the agents. It sent them the company message, the news of what the various state agencies were doing, the pertinent facts, figures, and news of the entire organization. It was also a medium for the expression of George Mecherle's messages—his inspiring talks. Later, when it was enlarged, it attained a reputation in the insurance industry as one of the best publications of its kind.

In 1925, the first convention of agents had been held in Bloomington. For two bright, cold February days those who had been selling State Farm policies throughout Illinois flocked to Bloomington as guests of the company. A group picture taken at the time is still one of the prized possessions of the company. Here—more than in any of the old papers or documents in the files—can be seen the truly Midwestern agricultural character of the company in its early days. Most of the agents were working farmers and looked it: rough, ready, hard-headed men from the prairie. Some were bewhiskered, old-fashioned, horny-handed. A few of the younger men were dapper in their appearance, but even their snappy ties and clothes had something of the true country flavor about them. Looking at the picture today, one can realize how close to the days of the prairie pioneers most of these men were.

These annual conventions became a sort of goal for the agents. Those who had the best records in their localities came as guests of the company, often accompanied by their wives. To many of them this was their real vacation. They looked forward to this meeting throughout the year and they enjoyed every minute of it. Food and entertainment were plentiful. The home office did its best to give them a good time. Several hours were consumed with serious matters—ranging from sales "pep talks" to more or less learned dissertations on the technical workings of the business. Through them the company was able to instill that spirit of co-operation and loyalty which meant so much to the growth of the company. When they got too big to be handled properly in Blooming-ton—where the Tilden Hall Hotel, the Illinois Hotel, and the Rogers Hotel combined were not large enough to house them—the conventions were moved to Chicago. Later, because of the size of the organization, they became impractical and had to be abandoned. Regional meetings, however, took their place. Special meetings of state directors began in 1932, when they gathered at Signal Mountain, Tennessee, on July 14. These afforded an exchange of ideas between the state directors and the company's executives and were very helpful all around.

During the years of early growth several changes were effected in the coverage offered by State Farm Mutual. In 1927, coverage for damage from windstorm was made available. The following year the standard liability coverage was increased to $10,000 for one person and $20,000 for two or more persons—twice that standard in the industry today—and the property damage maximum was increased to $2,000. Later, liability and property damage was offered for a driver operating a loaned (but not hired or leased) private passenger vehicle. In 1931, coverage of school buses and private cars used to transport schoolchildren in rural areas brought new and profitable business to the company. And in 1932 an operator's policy, covering liability and property damage while driving any automobile not owned by the assured, was added.

In 1934 an entirely new policy form was prepared. This was for "omnibus coverage." Stationary object collision—hitherto issued separately— was made a part of the general coverage. Standard property damage was increased to $5,000. After thus combining all under one policy, the number of policies in force was not so large as heretofore, but from all points of view this was a more economical and efficient way to conduct the business.

On May 4, 1935, two important decisions were taken by the board of directors at a special meeting at the home office. One was to revise the by-laws so that the company might write lines of casualty insurance other than those provided for by the original articles of incorporation. The other was to establish the State Farm Fire Insurance Company. The Fire Insurance company was organized with a paid-in capital of $200,000, consisting of 2,000 shares of a par value of $100 each, to be sold for $200 each without promotion expense. Except for directors' qualifying shares, all were to be purchased with the assets of the State Farm Mutual Automobile Insurance Company.

The revision of the charter gave State Farm Mutual far greater leeway in the insurance business than it had heretofore enjoyed. There were nine general objects in the revised Articles of Incorporation, which were approved by the State of Illinois on May 22, 1935. These were:

1. Insurance against loss, expense, liability of every nature from or incident to ownership, maintenance or use of an automobile.

2. Insurance against loss, expense, or liability, by reason of bodily injury, death, or accident, suffered by employees or others for which insured may be liable.

3. Insurance against accident, sickness, old age, and funeral expenses.

4. Insurance of person or property against explosion or accident to boilers, containers, pipes, engines, fly-wheels, elevators, and machinery in connection thereto.

5. Insurance against loss from interruption of trade or business as a result of accident.

6. Insurance against loss or damage by burglary, theft, larceny, robbery, fraud, or otherwise.

7. Insurance against loss or damage to glass.

8. Guarantee the fidelity of persons.

9. Any other lawful casualty or insurance hazard except life or fire.

With these provisions State Farm Mutual was empowered to step forward to conquer new fields at such later date as it might choose. As the year 1935 ended, the "little insurance company" of Bloomington—despite the depression and the economic revolution that had been taking place during the early days of the New Deal—faced the future with confidence.

10

SERVICE AND THE SQUARE DEAL

"Those who were given the management of this new organization," George Mecherle told the assembled agents of State Farm Mutual in 1929, that year so fateful in the economic history of the nation, "were instructed to keep before them the principles of service and square-dealing, giving to each member equal and just consideration; and to build the organization grounded on the principles of true equality and right-dealing as between men. These principles have been religiously adhered to from the beginning and have been almost wholly responsible for the success and growth of the organization."

From the small beginnings of 1922, he continued, the company had grown to an organization with 225 employees in the home office, 22 state agencies, 175 district agents, and more than 4,500 local agents. The business had grown from 1,338 applications received in the first year of operation until—as he said—"it is not an uncommon occurrence to receive 5,000 applications as a weekly production." By that time State Farm had in force a total of 280,000 policies and it had assets of over three and one-half million dollars. Mr. Mecherle then added these significant words:

"In the territory in which the company operates there are potential prospects of over 15,000,000 automobile owners. And, judging future action by past performance, we have a glorious future before us."

Within a few months had come the stock market crash. State Farm continued to grow. Then the depression of the last years of the Hoover Administration spread over the entire nation. State Farm sold more insurance than ever before. The dire days of the banking holiday that ushered in the New Deal found State Farm functioning as always—paying its claims on the dot and being forced to foreclose not one mortgage on its farm land loans.* Other states came under the State Farm aegis and the figures under income, assets, reserves and surplus showed, year after year, a steady increase.

Six years after his prediction of a "glorious future," George Mecherle sat down at his desk in his always-open office in the State Farm building and wrote for the *Reflector*:

"The past few years have taught us that a new philosophy of life is in the making. Old standards have been swept away. Success and attainment is no longer measured by material acquirement. We have truly learned that what we really keep is what we give and that the returns are immediate. Therefore, under this new philosophy, the standard of success will eventually be the measure of service given."

---

* At the annual meeting on June 12, 1933, Adlai Rust stated that "the action taken by the company at the time of the national banking moratorium was the most generous of any company of which he had knowledge; that the company was able, even willing, to forego a month's income, and that during this time it could pay all claims and other obligations and was not required to dispose of any securities." He stated that "another progressive step was the fact that we had invested approximately one-half million dollars in farm loans, which was a new departure. None of these loans had been made since October of last year. On December 31st all had paid their interest. On the morning of the annual meeting there were only 7 who had not paid, but all had been in asking for a little extension and all would be cleared by June 30th." He stated that the company had a fine list of farm loans and that he was glad the farmer was receiving higher prices for his commodities; that all this will be of advantage to the company and that "since better days are ahead there is no telling how far this company may go."

At the same meeting Willis F. Mecherle said that "as far as life insurance and automobile insurance is concerned the Roosevelt Administration will be a good thing. He said that now that there will be good times and consequently more money to pay for life insurance and he thought that in five years' time the company will be about twice the size and that we should get our feet on the ground, ready for the prosperity that is coming."

In this same thoughtful article Mr. Mecherle also said:

"It is clearly evident that business practices are in transition. Apparently we are entering a new era, as determining factors which heretofore have been in evidence appear to no longer exist and in the natural process of any business we must be ready at all times to meet a new condition. . . . Our companies passed through the trying year of 1934 and emerged with their stability unquestioned. However . . ."

There was a note of ominous determination in that "however." Having seen his "honest little company" come this far from such obscure beginnings, George Mecherle was not going to let anything interfere with its future greatness. In the little black loose-leaf notebook which he carried with him at all times—and in which, in black and red, he kept an almost daily accounting of the status of every aspect of the business from the Yakima, Washington, claims office to the final overall accounting of assets and liabilities—there were some figures that did not satisfy him. One at which he looked hard and long showed that, in the six years which had passed since he predicted a glorious future, the actual gain in new automobile policies sold was just 103,152. And that— for a man who had once boasted if he could sell one policy he could sell a million—was not enough. In the first seven years they had sold 280,000 policies. Something had to be done.

But there were other problems in the early 1930's that had to be considered before the matter of sales could be given exclusive attention. During 1934 especially, the loss experience of the company jumped at an alarming rate. George Mecherle, addressing the annual membership meeting in 1934, gave a graphic description of the reasons why the company was experiencing a greater loss frequency than ever before. Cars, he said, were all being built for higher speed. This caused more accidents, and accidents called for repairs. New and different construction made these repairs more expensive. The National Recovery Act of the New Deal had eliminated discounts on parts. The increased wages demanded by the NRA codes added to the cost of repairs. Garages were no longer interested in making competitive bids and there was "some measure of collusion, where one garage will not make a lower bid than any other garage in that locality." However, he added, for the last few months this condition had been better and, anyway, "as long as the agency force is bringing in a satisfactory volume of business, then we have nothing to fear." For these reasons—in spite of his optimism—the situation called for a close examination by all the executives in the home office. With Mr. Mecherle they put their minds to the problem and within a few months were able to overcome the vexing situation and report a decided improvement. This is how it happened.

From the beginning—as we have seen—one of the cardinal principles of State Farm Mutual had been the "preferred risk." As T. F. Campbell, then the assistant secretary, once defined him, a State Farm "preferred risk" was "the average citizen of normal habits." But, the world and automobilists being what they are, "we must carefully examine every application that comes into the office in order to be certain that it is the right type of risk."

Once a person became a member of State Farm his individual record was carefully followed, especially in regard to the frequency of his losses. If, at the outset, an applicant's known record did not seem to measure up to standard, his application was rejected; and if, after acceptance, the insured was an undesirable risk, his policy was canceled. Special attention was given to the territories in which losses were the most frequent, and on this knowledge—in great measure—the rates for that territory were predicated.

During this period of national economic depression it began to be apparent that certain territories were showing higher loss records than the company felt were warranted. A state-by-state study was made under the direction of Ramond P. Mecherle, then vice president, which included a careful analysis of premium income, losses paid, losses incurred, and loss expenses paid to every agent. This led to the discovery that some territories* were unprofitable. After much discussion it was decided to exclude from the company's territory those regions which this analysis had shown were exceptionally hazardous; and, in some instances, to cancel policies which had already been issued in those areas. At the same time a number of agents who were originally responsible for the bad risks were dropped from the company's lists.

This discovery, which necessitated such drastic action, led to several procedural reforms within the company. Ermond Mecherle, Theodore F. Campbell and other executives began them by making an extensive and intensive study of methods used in other large insurance companies. They visited the home offices of a number of the largest casualty companies where business had grown to such a volume—as it was rapidly doing at State Farm—that they had been forced to decentralize. These companies had found it necessary to set up branch offices strategically

* Mainly parts of Oklahoma, West Virginia, and Mississippi.

throughout their territory, not only to serve policyholders more quickly and more efficiently, but in order to have closer knowledge of local conditions and more personal supervision of the agents.

As a result of this study, State Farm decided to divide the general underwriting department into eight separate geographical units. These were not set up in the territories themselves (the Berkeley office remained the only detached branch office until 1947, when the Minneapolis-St. Paul Branch Office was established) but were organized as underwriting bureaus within the home office in Bloomington. Men whom the company trained for this purpose were placed in charge. The agents in the field immediately approved of this scheme, for it made their relationship with the company much easier. State agents had their own geographically decentralized bureau to turn to at any time. Furthermore, this system appeared to save the company expense, as, for a time at least, its operation called for fewer employees.

The second major "reform" made at this time was also aimed at the more careful selection of policyholders. It was a part of a general revision of agents' compensation. During the early years of the State Farm Mutual the local agents received as commission 40% of the membership fee. This was paid to compensate them not only for the writing of new business, but also for the adjustment of losses. A few years after the founding of the company a change was made whereby the agent was paid—in addition to his share of the membership fee—at the rate of 50 cents an hour and 10 cents a mile for the adjustment of losses in his district. This plan gave the agents some needed extra compensation, but it had the shortcoming of providing agent's earnings only as he had losses to adjust. This defect produced some occasional abuses.

There was, for example, one district agent whose rural territory covered an unusually large area. He would go to a distant point, write a handful of automobile applications, leave some blanks with the local garageman. Then, when a loss occurred, even of the most minor nature, he would hop in his car and drive across his territory to the distant point to handle the claim. While there he would spend two or three days writing more applications, and then—upon return to his headquarters—send in a time and transportation bill for the entire jaunt. Another agent used to make it a regular practice to drive to a city 140 miles from his home almost every time a loss occurred in his district—in search of witnesses to the accident.

In 1932, A. W. Tompkins, the agency vice president, reached the conclusion that the company should find a way to provide agents with stable and continuing compensation. His reasoning—as he outlined the plan to George Mecherle—was that this compensation would assure the policyholder more prompt and efficient service. At Mr. Mecherle's direction an analysis was made of the per diem and transportation cost to the company, and it was discovered that this came to 76 cents per policy per year. Mr. Mecherle did some rapid calculation and came up with the suggestion that 49 cents be added to this figure. This was to be paid to the local agent as a "service fee compensation" at the rate of 62½ cents for each policy renewal. Since each policy ran for six months this meant the agent would receive $1.25 each year the policy was in force. Two years later—in 1934—the rate per policy was changed to 17½ cents for each section, which raised the rate to a maximum of 70 cents for each renewal of a four-section, or complete coverage, policy.

The 40% commission on a $5 membership per section prevailed until the autumn of 1933, when the Board of Directors voted, at Mr. Mecherle's suggestion, an increased schedule of membership fees. Under this new system the membership fees ranged up to $9 for liability and property damage coverage in metropolitan areas and, in addition, provided that 100% of the excess above $5 be paid to the writing agent.

Now, in 1935, two other important changes were brought about. These were:

(1) the payment of the service fee compensation on the basis of a percentage of premium renewals collected, rather than a flat amount for each policy renewal, and

(2) the initiation of the service fee bonus.

The agents everywhere hailed the new method of computing monthly service fee compensation, not only because it enabled them to increase their income by writing additional coverages but, as premium rates were raised, their compensation automatically increased through no additional effort on their part. It was an equitable adjustment.*

---

* "The importance of this . . . is more readily appreciated when we realize that in 1950 service fee compensation totaled $6,442,459.51—$2,589,895 more than would have taken place had the original method of 67½ cents per policy renewal been operative. In 1950, the average policy provided $4.04 in service fee compensation as contrasted to $1.25 in 1932—an increase of 223 per cent. In other words, based on 1,000 policies of average company premium, an agent in 1950 received $4,041 as compared to $1,250 in 1932—a ratio of 323 per cent."—A. W. Tompkins, "Landmarks in Agents' Compensation," *Reflector*, December, 1951.

The service fee bonus gave each agent an opportunity to participate in that underwriting profit in his respective state in an amount not exceeding 25% of his annual service fee compensation, provided his own business was also profitable. It not only augmented the agents' income but also provided an incentive for each agent to use care in the selection of drivers to be insured and to render efficient claim service.

As Ramond Mecherle put it, in discussing the changes before the annual meeting of policyholders in June, 1935, "In placing a bonus fee along with the service fee it makes every agent careful of his record; if an agent secures unprofitable business it puts him on the spot as far as the rest of the agents in that state are concerned.*

The policy of careful advance selection of policyholders, stressed at this time, was never to be relaxed. During the next few years the underwriting department, on which the screening of applicants naturally fell, played an increasingly important part in the organization. On the theory that the underwriters could perform their duties better if they were more closely aware of the problems confronting the agents, and that the agents would be more selective if they more clearly understood the problems of the underwriters, the latter, beginning in 1936, were frequently sent into the territories for conferences. These meetings were beneficial to both the home office and to the agency force.

The conferences between the underwriters and the agents were successfully directed toward a better understanding, on the agents' part, of these standards and resulted in conserving the agents' time and energy hitherto spent in going after prohibited risks and persons of questionable character. They saved the agent and the applicant much embarrassment. Accordingly, they helped build up the good will of State Farm. All this—along with the close and continuing scrutiny of the policyholders—combined to have a decidedly good effect upon the company's underwriting experience.

As a result of these "reforms," the loss frequency and the loss ratio of State Farm Mutual began to show a definite improvement. At the same time the claim department began an intensive campaign. Fletcher B. Coleman, who was then superintendent of claims, attended agency meetings in sixteen states. Nine new claims offices were opened. There were 44 traveling claims adjusters in the various states and in one year

---

* In 1952 the bonus was merged with service fee compensation so as to maintain the agent's rate of compensation but eliminate all contingencies based on underwriting profit.

(1935) they traveled 1,217,521 miles adjusting claims and servicing the policyholders. Claims department forms were revised and brought up to date and new record files were established—all of which were designed to promote economy in adjustment costs. As a result, the average expense of a paid claim for the company as a whole, and for all types of cars, fell during the first four months of 1935 from the 1934 average of $56.50 to $51.62; and this was at a time when the records of other automobile liability companies showed their loss records to be considerably worse than in the preceding year.

At the same time the company was busy solving these problems it was improving the coverages of its policyholders. In 1928, as we have seen, the standard policy limits on liability had been increased to twice the usual amount, and the limits on property damage had been increased from $500 to $2,000. In 1934, the property damage limit was increased again to $5,000. In 1935, automatic protection for ten days was extended on a new automobile, pending a transfer of the policy, and collision damage was extended to tires.

The fire, wind and theft protection was extended in 1936 to a comprehensive coverage which was very broad in its terms—covering all loss or damage to the automobile due to practically any cause except collision or upset. Some of the hazards listed under this new coverage were fire, lightning, transportation, theft, robbery, pilferage, chemicals, tornado, cyclone, windstorm, hail, earthquake, explosion, falling trees, water damage, glass breakage, strikes and riots, flood or rising water, malicious damage, falling aircraft and building collapse.

When this new protection was announced the agents were told: "The company desires to give this liberalized coverage to its policyholders in lieu of the present section one—ordinarily known as fire, wind and theft coverage. Effective July 1, 1936, this added protection will be given on all future applications and on all transfers . . . at the rates specified in the agent's manual for the fire, wind and theft coverage. . . . As to existing policies having section one, the basis of loss settlement from June 1st will be as though the outstanding policy was the comprehensive form."

Many a State Farm policyholder was grateful for these new provisions when the Ohio River floods of 1937 caused great property damage throughout the Ohio and lower Mississippi valleys.

This same policy of extending insurance policy benefits to existing policies—regardless of the limitations of the policy contract—continued to apply through the years. Benefits were extended to include the actual value of the car in 1937; making all policies nonassessable in 1938; and extending the liability and property damage protection for the policy-holder when he drove other cars, theft rental reimbursement, and an amended 80% collision provision—all in 1939.

On all fronts the company continued to forge ahead in this period of transition. When the fifteenth annual meeting of the policyholders and the board of directors was held in the home office on June 14, 1937, George Mecherle was able to report that "the company is in just as 'sweet' a condition as we could hope to have it." He was referring mainly to the financial condition, but the same word could be applied to the organization itself. Over the years he had gathered around him an able and loyal staff of administrators and executives who had worked closely with him in pushing the company toward the goal he had set. These included Adlai Rust, George Beedle, A. W. Tompkins, T. F. Campbell, and G. B. Brown—and his two sons, Ramond and G. Ermond Mecherle—among the executives; and Henry Gerdes, C. A. Asplund, J. Colby Beekman, W. B. McFarland, and A. J. King, among the veteran directors.

During the past few months George Mecherle had been giving the company—its past and its future, but particularly its future—much serious study and attention, and had at last made a major decision. Throughout all these formative years he had been, as it were, "on the top of" almost every one of the company's activities. He had spent grueling hours on the road from the very beginning and he had spent equally long and wearing hours in the office attending to the most minute details of management. This does not mean that he had insisted upon running everything himself—he was adept at picking executives and delegating authority—but the extremely personal nature of the business at the time of its founding had almost naturally tended to funnel the affairs of every department toward his desk. He had—as someone once said—"invented the company" and, as both general manager and president of his own invention, it was inevitable that he should be the focus of attention. With this system he had no fundamental quarrel. His whole life being wrapped up in the company as it was, he had no distaste for the many burdens he had assumed. But, after much study, he at last reached the conclusion that perhaps he was shouldering too much and that his absorption in detail was restricting him from a broader and more imaginative role. His fertile mind was already toying with the possibilities of an even grander design.

George Mecherle made his plans and carried them out at the fifteenth annual meeting. In order to relieve himself of the heavy administrative duties he had been carrying and at the same time gain the freedom necessary to devote his energies toward the development of the three State Farm companies, at his suggestion the new office of chairman of the board of directors was created. He was at once chosen to fill it.

Ramond Mecherle, who had come to the company in 1924, was elected president of the State Farm Mutual Automobile Insurance Company. G. Ermond Mecherle—who had made an outstanding record as director of personnel—was elected secretary. T. F. Campbell, who had been assistant secretary, was named vice president, and G. B. Brown was made comptroller of the companies. Adlai Rust, of course, continued as executive vice president and as treasurer, to which posts he had been elected in 1934 and 1931, and A. W. Tompkins, who had succeeded Perry Crane on the latter's death, was continued as agency vice president. George E. Beedle, who had been secretary since 1923, was named to the new office of vice chairman of the board.

Under this new alignment a new era for State Farm Mutual was ushered in.

11

INSIDE STATE FARM

Back in the 1920's, when George Mecherle bought some second-hand furniture and started an insurance company in one room in the old Durley Building in Bloomington, the least of his problems was the matter of personnel. The little handful of employees who struggled in their cramped quarters, filing the applications and issuing the policies, was less an office staff than a family. Hard-worked always, and sometimes actually overwhelmed by the flood of papers that swept across their desks, they were nevertheless an intensely loyal group. Their respect for "the Chief," as Mr. Mecherle was generally called long before he won the right to the title from the Winnebago tribe of Indians, was close to adoration. His interest in their welfare and even in their personal problems was equally sincere. In many ways he was a sort of father to the small group and all his life he continually astonished those who worked for State Farm with his knowledge of their affairs and his understanding of their needs.

This paternalism sufficed in the early days when he could keep a benevolent eye cocked on the entire office and watch the comings and goings of everyone from George Beedle down to the office boy. Such words as "personnel" or "employee relations" were never used then. He demanded and got the same loyalty to the company which he himself gave. He established an *esprit de corps* that was remarkable and that left its imprint on the organization long after it had grown beyond his wildest imaginings.

Life in the office was, in a way, much as it had been on the farm at Merna. There George Mecherle and his hired men had worked in close harmony, calling each other by their first names, but he was always the pacemaker. Since he would never ask anyone to tackle a chore he would not undertake to do himself, those who worked for him on the farm or in the office took a certain pride in keeping up with him. Physically inexhaustible, he often did not find the day long enough for all he felt he had to do. But he realized others were not always his equal and, while he always expected results and accomplishment, he did not ask it at the expense of health and happiness. His pride in State Farm Mutual as an institution of service was almost religious; and he expressed it with such convinced fervor that it was contagious. By the time the company was ten years old it had traditions as deeply ingrained as those of establishments whose roots went back half a century or more. Most of them were based on loyalty—loyalty to State Farm and loyalty to "the Chief." In the eyes of most people the man and the institution were inseparable.

The company grew so rapidly—both in volume of business and in the size of the staff needed to take care of it—that there were times when even as able an executive as George Mecherle was unable to keep up. Long before the company had grown so large that it needed its own building to house its staff, it had become apparent that the problem of personnel was a matter which could not be handled with any degree of casualness. If the selection and training of workers was not yet a science it was rapidly approaching it, and the many problems involved were becoming so increasingly complex that this aspect of the business would soon consume much time and applied attention.

Early in the company's history George Mecherle, who never forgot that an employee was an individual, was forced—as one of the largest employers in the Bloomington area—to look at him also as a statistic. Within the first five years he had arrived at the conclusion that the size of his staff was to be determined by the number of policies in force. This was not an arbitrary decision but one based upon mathematics and experience. He found the ratio was one employee for each 1,000 policies in force. It was on this basis that, for many years, the size of the State Farm working force was determined; but later the ratio changed, and for many reasons. As the number of policies grew the number of persons needed to process them increased.

As State Farm Mutual grew steadily from the staff of three girls who worked under Miss Jones in those first two hectic years before George Beedle assumed the secretaryship, to the 5,686 men and women employed in the home office and in the eleven branch offices at the end of 1954, employer-employee relationship remained at a high level. What be- gan on a sort of hit-or-miss basis in 1930, when the company signed a contract with a Bloomington physician to keep an eye on the physical well-being of the less than 200 employees, eventually developed into a well blueprinted system of personnel management. The paternalism of George Mecherle evolved into a scientifically controlled welfare pro- gram that approached its human problems on five fronts.

The first was concerned with the physical welfare of its employees. The second dealt over the years with the financial welfare. The third, which was in some ways the most important, had to do with the morale of the workers. The fourth was directed toward the training and education of those who chose to make State Farm a career. And the fifth took in some special—and very important—problems not directly connected with the others. All, of course, were interrelated; some just came about in the normal development of the company; and some were deliberately planned and far in advance of the general trend of the insurance industry.

The responsibility for the well-being of the employees from the start fell to the secretary of the company, but as far back as 1931—when the company was still less than ten years old—the variety of these duties was such that it required more attention than that hard-worked executive could give it. There was, however, a young man working for State Farm who had a decided aptitude for this type of work. The fact that his father was the head of the company was an asset to him as he laid his plans, for there was a close understanding between George and G. Ermond Mecherle which made the development of the personnel department eas- ier than it might otherwise have been. The younger Mecherle had a flair for this type of work and during the next twenty years, both before and after he became secretary of the State Farm Mutual, he devoted a great deal of time and attention to the problems of company personnel.

Because of the geographical situation of the company in the small city of Bloomington, set down as it is in the midst of the prairie in central Illinois, these problems were vastly different than they would have been had the company been located in Chicago or some other large urban community. Since Bloomington was always a county seat and a trading center for farmers, and devoid of any extensive commercial institutions or industrial plants, it did not have a variegated population from which to recruit workers. Practically all of the office force was drawn, from the beginning, from middle class families in Bloomington, and from the farms and small towns of the surrounding area. The majority were girls who came to work for the company after they had completed high school. Most of them intended to get married as soon as possible and raise their own families; few of them were "career girls." This situation not only had an effect upon the company, but upon the economy of Bloomington as well.

The first step taken toward caring for the physical welfare of the staff was a simple one—the establishment of the company's medical division in 1930. Then and for several years this consisted of a contractual arrangement with a Bloomington physician who made his examinations at his own office rather than in the State Farm building. Three years later a room was set aside in the office building for the medical department, and a nurse was engaged. She, however, was not on full-time call, but worked in one of the operating departments except when her services were needed during office hours.

During the next year Ermond Mecherle made a study of the medical problems of the staff and, in 1934, enlarged the division and placed the nurse on full-time duty. A great many of the State Farm employees, he found, lived in Bloomington rooming houses where proper medical care often was not available when needed. In order to cope with this a car was supplied for the use of the nurse who would visit any employee who telephoned in that he or she was ill, or (as sometimes happened) just failed to report. If the employee was seriously ill, the staff physician was notified and hospitalization arranged if necessary. If (as sometimes also happened) the "illness" was in reality more imaginary than real, the frowns of the nurse, and the presence of the nurse's plainly identified State Farm car in front of the house, generally sufficed to drive the malingerer back to his desk. Thus a dual purpose was served: those who needed attention got it at the right moment, and unnecessary absenteeism was materially reduced.

A natural extension of this service was the inauguration in 1937 of annual physical examinations of all employees—a well-received service which continued until the confusion and rapid turnover of employees during World War II caused its dissolution. After the war, when things had quieted down and a continuing routine had been re-established, the system was again instituted. It now included X-rays, serology, and blood-typing. In the meantime the medical division had been enlarged and two full-time nurses were on duty. The physician employed by the company had specific hours which he spent at his State Farm office, and nursing service was available for the night crew which was then regularly employed.

A milk depot was established; later Coca-Cola and candy vending machines were placed strategically around the offices. One of the State Farm legends is that the Chief was absent from Bloomington when the first soft-drink machine was installed. Walking upon his return through the corridor where it had been placed he came to a full halt, watched several clerks come up, put in their nickels, and depart with the glistening brown bottles. Astounded, he stomped off to his office. He called the maintenance department and told them, in no uncertain terms, to take that thing out—he was running an insurance company, not a soft drink parlor. Word got to Ermond, who quietly slipped into his office and explained the psychological benefits of having "the pause that refreshes" available for the girls and boys, and quickly sold the Chief on the idea. A short time later, when he knew that he was being watched, Mr. Mecherle walked down the corridor, popped in his nickel, and marched back to his office with his Coke. By this gesture he placed the stamp of approval on the new-fangled idea.

With the medical department fully established as an integral part of the State Farm setup, it was not long until it expanded its services and humanized them even further. With the co-operation of the McLean County Medical Society it began to survey the employees' own medical problems of all kinds, working closely with the individual's family doctor at all times, thus taking the onus of "institutionalism" off the service by personalizing it. In the following years several additional medical services were supplied.

In 1943, for instance, a cold-immunization program was started, and later virus A and B influenza vaccine was used with highly satisfactory results. Still later those who requested it were supplied with a special antihistamine preparation for the aborting of early colds. As anyone who has suffered the Bloomington climate will realize, such health measures were not amiss. The visiting nurse system was extended until three full-time nurses were employed. The department was now a full-time operation with a receptionist, as well as a medical director and assistant always on call. A continuing supervision was made throughout the building with respect to all health hazards.

In 1935 a sick-leave program was established. This underwent various changes until it reached its present generous provisions. As it now operates, all employees—even the most recent newcomer—are entitled to sick leave whenever it is necessary. An employee who has been with the company less than a year may be absent for illness two weeks without sacrificing salary or wage. The scale is graduated upward until an employee who has been with State Farm for fourteen years is allowed thirty weeks with full salary, fifteen weeks at half salary, and sixteen weeks' medical leave. Employees who have been with State Farm longer than fifteen years receive special consideration "because of long and faithful service." In 1946 a contributory group hospitalization and surgical benefits plan was made available for all employees.

In addition to sick leave, the company today has a well-developed vacation schedule. From the start the regulation "two weeks with pay" was accorded to everyone each summer. National holidays were regularly observed. Today, six holidays are recognized. And the vacation schedule has been put upon a graduated scale, with length of service being the measure of the period, so that most of the older employees receive a total of four weeks each year—of course with pay.

Of equal importance to the general welfare of the State Farm employees has been the company's interest in keeping up the morale of the ever-growing staff. In the early years this was not so important as it became when the company had reached its present tremendous size—a size that in some respects is too large for the community that encompasses it. When George Mecherle founded the company in 1922 he chose Bloomington for two very good reasons. One was that he insisted upon having his business where his home was, so that he might devote a major share of his time to Mrs. Mecherle, whose ill health was his gravest concern. The other was that there seemed to be no reason to go elsewhere. It was a solid town of solid citizens centrally located in the state where he fully expected his business would always be located. Twenty years later the company was doing business on a national scale with nearly 1,500 employees—most of them working in the home office.

The first real appreciation of the fact that the State Farm staff could

no longer be considered a "family," as it had been during the less com-
plicated years of its "growing pains," came about 1935. By then it had
become increasingly apparent that keeping in close, personal touch with
all the employees in the organization was no longer possible. Some
means of re-establishing the old spirit was necessary and the initial answer seemed to lie in the establishment of a publication which would
help cement the interests and loyalties of the entire staff. And so, that
year, the *Alfi News* was founded. It got its strange title from a combination of the initials of the Automobile, Life and Fire Insurance companies that together were State Farm. George Mecherle best expressed the
purpose of this brisk little publication in the first monthly issue when
he wrote:

> The predominant purpose is to arouse in everyone a feeling of the family
> spirit and to instill in you the fact that you are a very important part of
> this family. You are, therefore, partly responsible for its success or failure.
> The publication shall endeavor to strengthen your confidence in the
> company and its policies and help you acquire a wider and more thorough
> understanding of the insurance business and its various functions.
> We encourage home study and self-development, thrift and a con-
> scientious pride in your particular job. Through our personal items we
> hope to widen your acquaintance with your fellow workers. The news from
> the Life and Fire companies will enable you to keep in touch with their
> activities.
> We must work together as one, toward making our company a better
> place to work. This magazine belongs to you. . . . The credit for its suc-
> cess is deserved not only by the efforts of an individual or a few but by
> everyone in general. . . .

The *Alfi News* was not designed to supplant or even rival the other
company publication—the *Reflector*—which had been established
eight years earlier. The *Reflector* was aimed entirely at the salesmen and
agents, and was devoted to information about policies, commissions,
sales programs, and the like, whereas *Alfi News* was a "neighborhood
newspaper" for the staff of the home office. It was an immediate hit with
the employees and served the purpose of keeping the family spirit alive
in the huge office. Today, it is a weekly tabloid with all the news and
gossip of the many social activities of State Farm people. A few copies
are sent each week to the branch offices, but they too have their own
multilith publications, issued every other week.

Today there are many more activities to report in *Alfi News* than there
were when it was founded in 1935. Then, the employees were pretty

much on their own, except for such affairs as office parties, having to find their own leisure-time occupations—not always an easy thing to do in a small city like Bloomington, where communal recreational facilities were sadly lacking. Besides the Y.M.C.A. and Y.W.C.A. and three moving picture houses, there were few outside attractions. In 1946 the company recognized this situation and took steps to correct it by taking on the responsibility of creating leisure-hour activities for its workers. In this it was not entirely unselfish, realizing that some such step was necessary if it were to attract young people to its staff, having long outgrown the "labor market" of the region.

An activities director was hired in that year and a companywide activities program was instituted. This was no hit-or-miss idea, but a seriously studied proposal that led to the incorporation early in 1947 of an association known as State Farm Employees Activities Association. Incorporated under Illinois law, this organization selects its governing body by popular vote, naming its president, vice president, secretary and treasurer from among State Farm employees. It is governed by a board of directors chosen from each floor of the home office and from each of the outlying buildings which the growth of the company has made necessary in recent years to house all its offices. Membership dues are two dollars a year and every employee of the company is eligible for membership. To this, State Farm adds $2 for each $1 paid by an employee, and this —plus the revenue from the Coca-Cola and candy machines—makes up the budget on which the organization operates. The director, who has no other duties, is paid, however, by the company.

Sports, as might be expected, play the most important part in the program. Bowling has always been especially popular, among both men and women, but in the summer softball attracts both sexes. Interdepartmental rivalry is keen. Basketball is played twice each week in the season at local school gymnasiums. Golf tournaments are held each summer, with instruction in golf, swimming, and tennis being offered. Trophies and medals are awarded league winners in all sports.

To the general public, State Farm Activities is perhaps best known for its Glee Club, or Chorus. More than seventy employees are members of this extremely popular organization whose reputation—thanks to its appearance as guests on a number of network programs originating in Chicago—has spread far and wide. It has also performed at many local community events and has traveled extensively in Illinois to give concerts.

Many services—such as an "agency" for theatre or sports events tickets

in Chicago, a train reservation service, and one for chartering buses for
week-end football events—are maintained and widely used. Each activity
is encouraged by management and the greater part of their execution is
by the participating employees. It is operated on the assumption that
leadership from within is necessary for success. But the activities director
and his staff assist in co-ordinating the planning and perform many of
the detailed duties that would be impossible for the employees to accomplish during their regular working hours.

In 1947 the company realized that there was a lack of adequate facilities for use of the Activities Association and that something should
be done to correct the situation. This seemed to call for a professional
approach which would go after a solution to the problem in a more thorough manner than the administrative officers might be able to undertake.

Accordingly, the trained staff of the F. Elwood Allen organization was
called in from New York to make a detailed study of the recreational
requirements and desires of the employees and to look over the Bloomington area to find where the needed facilities might be installed. The
organization's report clearly revealed the serious need for establishing a
recreational area where the scope of the Activities Association might be
broadened as part of a program designed to better employee-employer
relationship on a long-range plan of operation.

The following spring a naturally beautiful 33-acre tract south of the
city became available and was purchased by State Farm. The Allen organization again was called in to lay out a plan for the full use of the
area. Meanwhile, a companywide contest resulted in the name Wa-Nik-
Ska-Ka Park being given the spot—that being the Indian name bestowed on G. J. Mecherle when he was made an honorary "chief" of the
Winnebago tribe. In 1951 the name was changed to the G. J. Mecherle
Memorial Park when it was rededicated to the memory of the company's
founder.

Here on these thirty-three acres, not much more than a mile south of
the State Farm building, the State Farmers of every generation find
health and happiness from early spring until late autumn. It has just
about everything for just about everyone connected with the company
—from a day nursery for the youngsters to quiet corners for spooners. It
is the center of all social activities for the employees, their families, and
their guests. Because of the latter it serves not only the State Farm group

but a great part of the Bloomington-Normal community as well. Open from ten in the morning until ten at night, with floodlights making some sports possible after sunset, The Memorial Park more than serves its purpose.

At the park, which is beautifully landscaped and arranged, there are courts and equipment for badminton, horseshoes, shuffleboard, softball, volleyball, croquet, basketball, tetherball, and tennis. In the blue lake, fishing is permitted and sections are set aside for swimming. There is a special, attended section for younger children, and lifeguards patrol the deeper areas. Picnic spots, for family groups or whole sections from the office, are plentiful, and there are tables on the porch of the clubhouse where meals, light snacks, and soft drinks are served, and picnic lunches can also be ordered there. There is a well-equipped beach house, with dressing rooms, showers, and other facilities. This is used during winter months for office parties, children's movies and meetings. A full-time custodian maintains the park—with a crew of twenty assistants during the season.

All in all, most observers of the welfare program of State Farm have found that it measures up to the highest standards of enlightened industrialism. Although supervised and, to a great extent, supported financially by the company, the program is not marred by intrusive paternalism. It makes State Farm a better place to work for it helps to keep labor-management relationships on an even keel. The steadiness of employment, the lack of "unrest" among the employees, is traceable in good measure to this system. In a larger city, with more diversified amusements and cultural interests, it might not be as necessary to all concerned as it is in the flat prairie city of Bloomington where, without this self-interested setup, boredom could well result.

State Farm Mutual has always attempted to maintain good reciprocal relationships with its employees. By virtue of his own intense pride in the company, George Mecherle never ceased to instill this pride in those who worked for him. This included not only the top executives, all of whom pledged their loyalty to his ideals at the time he retired as president and assumed the new post of chairman of the board of directors, but everyone down the line. In return for this loyalty the company has endeavored—as the record amply shows—to approach the employees in a spirit of friendliness. A few years ago a student of labor-management relationships made a doctoral study of State Farm's personnel system. In the course of his interviews he discussed the question of the size of the State Farm force. To a suggestion that in many industries the necessity to shrink the staff was an ever present problem, Adlai Rust replied:

"In order to shrink, if that were necessary, we would wait for employees to resign, and we then would not replace them. *We have a responsibility to our present force. We wouldn't do anything that would break that loyalty. The big factor in productivity is morale.*"

This spirit of friendliness plus loyalty has been shown in a number of little ways, as well as in the broad general policy towards the workers. Several years ago the company started the practice of placing a red rose and greeting card on the desk of each employee, male or female, on his or her birthday. This simple gesture was particularly appreciated by the girls—many of whom were living away from home for the first time. Any suggestion that this gesture of sentiment on the part of a "heartless corporation" be abandoned raises a storm of protest. The same is true of the ceremonious presentation of pins denoting length of service with State Farm—a practice that was started in 1938. Perhaps, today, the latter is a little more popular because, along with the pins, go cash bonus awards for five-year periods, ranging from five to thirty years' service. This additional incentive to make State Farm a continuing career was inaugurated during the second World War, when temporary opportunities often seemed greater elsewhere.

So-called "Coke parties" are held on each floor whenever an employee passes a ten-year service milestone, and all employees who have been with the company for fifteen or more years are honored annually at a special dinner party. Other "fringe benefits"—as they might be called—include an effort to keep up with modern office equipment designed for the health and comfort of desk-bound workers. This began with the purchase of posture chairs in 1935 and has, over the years, included several psychological improvements. These ranged from a short-lived effort to make easier the delivery of mail by equipping the messengers with roller skates to the installation of Muzak.

Wherever you stand in Bloomington the tan brick building of the State Farm Insurance Companies overshadows the landscape. And well it might, for State Farm in more ways than one dominates the entire community. It is, of course, the largest employer in the vicinity and the standards of employment which it has set are felt beyond its own immediate sphere. For many years its wage scale has been kept at a level which has allowed it to command the cream of office workers in the area. Always above the level for the city, it has, in turn, affected the prosperity of Bloomington by making it necessary for other employers to attempt to equal it. For this it has at times been criticized by those who have not realized its beneficial effect upon the buying power of the community. They have charged it with "monopolizing the labor market" and making it difficult for others to compete in that field. Even so, State Farm has not always found it easy to fill its own rolls with the quality of workers which the peculiarities of its business demands.

At one time, a few years ago, it was estimated that 5% of the women and girls in the Bloomington area were employed by State Farm Mutual. When the offices close at the end of the day and the girls rush for homeward-bound buses—often by way of local shops and restaurants—Bloomington streets have, for a few minutes, the illusory appearance of a teeming city. Many of this great crowd, of course, do not live within Bloomington or Normal limits, but commute by bus or pooled automobiles to nearby towns. But for the most part their lives and activities, and their dollars, are spent in Bloomington.

The number of employees in the home office varies from time to time, but not greatly. In the early days of State Farm the automobile insurance business was of a seasonal nature. It will be recalled that the City & Village Company was organized partly to take up the slack when winter snows and spring muds drastically cut down rural sales. Even then a great many city-dwelling autoists put their cars in storage during the winter months, when roads outside the city were impassable. Then there was a seasonal fluctuation in the size of the staff, it being necessary to call in part time workers when the volume of business rose. But this situation no longer prevails. With automobiles being used twelve months of the year, the result has been a stability of employment at State Farm which has been one of the reasons for the really remarkable staff loyalty to the companies.

Even bad times have had less effect upon State Farm employment than they have had upon many other comparable businesses. The record shows that State Farm suffered less than others did during the depression. In fact, the years of its greatest expansion were those of the New Deal. During the banking crisis of 1933—probably the economic nadir of our times—State Farm's business, and consequently its home office staff, suffered hardly at all. And throughout the entire depression period sales went up steadily and the company moved into state after state. Consequently, in this phenomenal situation, there was far less downward fluctuation in the staff or in the payroll. The trend was always upward.

From the installation of the first Hollerith machine, State Farm has continually mechanized its production process for the sake of increased efficiency and speed. The latest designs in business machines have been acquired and some have even been specially designed for State Farm's own use. From 1938 through 1946 a wide variety of office machinery was installed—beginning with new key punch desks and multigraph duplicators in 1938 and ranging through dumbwaiters to speed the interdepartmental transference of correspondence, check-writing and signing machines, photostat machines, modern calculators, alphabetical tabulators, and photographic machines for writing letters.

Interestingly enough, during the installation of all this labor-saving machinery, the volume of new and continuing business grew so steadily that in the decade between 1936 and 1946 the number of employees rose almost as steadily. On January 1, 1936, there were 627 workers in the home office. Ten years later there were 2,056 in all the companies' offices, including the newly established branches. A peak was reached in January, 1948, when 3,499 persons were employed. After that the size of the staff leveled off to a low of 2,730 in 1950. The reason for the decline was the vast program of reorganization—to be described in a later chapter—which took place between 1946 and 1948.

State Farm's success at keeping employee morale at a high pitch has resulted not only from careful attention to its physical and social problems and the security of steady employment. Two other major elements enter the picture: one is the financial element, aside from the reasonable wage level always maintained; and the other is the general welfare and educational element.

In 1936 Ermond Mecherle discovered that employees had great difficulty in borrowing money except at usurious rates of interest. Learning of the Filene plan for employee credit unions, he investigated the matter and one was established at State Farm. In the first fourteen years of operation the credit union suffered no losses, although it had loaned one and one-half million dollars—at an average saving of $316 to each member. Because of this favorable record it now charges the lowest rate allowed by the Federal Credit Union—½ of 1% per month.

At the annual meeting of the policyholders in 1935 George Mecherle remarked, "It looks to me as if those in charge of this organization must make some compulsory provision whereby the employees of this company are going to have something laid away for a rainy day in the future. A pension plan, if properly worked out, will not work a hardship on anyone."

Ermond Mecherle, then over-all director of personnel for the State Farm companies, had already started preliminary inquiries into the best methods of carrying out his father's suggestion. As a result, State Farm in 1938 put into effect, for most of its regular employees, the standard contributory pension plan as underwritten by the Metropolitan Life Insurance Company. This served its purpose for several years; but, in 1953, it became apparent that the system had become outmoded in several respects.

In that year a committee composed of Robert C. Perry, then actuary and now first vice president of the Life company, Edward B. Rust, and Paul L. Mitzner, vice president-personnel, conducted a survey for the purpose of bringing the State Farm pension plan up to date, bringing within its scope a broader group of employees than had subscribed to the previous plan, and making it a noncontributory plan administered through a State Farm trust fund supported by the three companies.

The trust fund offers vastly improved participation to every employee between twenty-five and sixty-five, the set retirement age, who has been employed for one year. It incorporates all those who had been under the protection of the Metropolitan contributory plan. It is integrated with the Federal Old Age Benefit, or Social Security Act. Thus, with the employer-employee contribution to Social Security, and the amounts made available through the trust fund, each employee in every salary bracket can look forward to a decent pension on which to live after reaching the age of sixty-five. At the same time, the autumn of 1953, a general group life insurance plan was inaugurated.

At the start of the war, when the cost of living began its rapid incline, a cost-of-living bonus was worked out by Ermond Mecherle, whose attention had been called to this system, not yet in general practice, by his father. Based upon the national cost-of-living index compiled by the National Industrial Conference Board, this bonus—which is in addition to wages set at base levels—is paid to all employees who are not exempt from the Federal wage and hour rulings, or all who fill out a time card for hours worked. Other salaried employees also receive a bonus, based on the purchasing power of the dollar—as determined by the National Industrial Conference Board's dollar index. The two indices are used as a basis for determining quarterly the percentage of fluctuation from the base month that has occurred within the quarter, and this percentage is applied to the base pay as a bonus every pay day. The "base pay" or salary is not affected by the rise or fall of the cost of living, or the dollar.

Along with these benefits State Farm Mutual has, for many years, endeavored to make the road to advancement as easy as possible for those with aptitude and ambition. In September, 1937, under Ermond Mecherle's leadership, a training school for prospective employees was launched and a system of selection tests was set up in the commercial departments of the regional high schools.

During 1937 ten young people, just out of high school, attended the nine-week training course and were then absorbed into the general office staff. In his report to the policyholders a year later, G. Ermond Mecherle stated that the various department heads "agreed that the knowledge of our business gained by these students in nine weeks was equivalent to the knowledge gained in three years by an employee who had not been a student in the school." During the course of instruction the students learned general office procedure, the details of the various jobs, and the meaning of insurance terms which "increases his efficiency to such a degree that the companies are able to save over a period of one year approximately $60,000 in salaries alone."

Various other training courses were tried out from time to time, but training as a staff function was not really established until 1949. This new and highly effective program has been under the direction of the personnel department—for the last several years headed by Paul Mitzner. It is a full-scale program, starting at the managerial level and carrying on down the line.

Management training started in March, 1949, with executive management participating in a capsule course preliminary to the more technical training of first-line supervisors. In the first year of operation some 147 members of first-line management participated in the three-section course which was patterned after—and based on—the well-known Training Within Industry system, but tailored to fit the special needs of State Farm. Twenty-four employees participated in the first "group conference" training that also started that year.

Altogether, 510 employees were in various training programs in 1949 —attending group conferences, round table discussions, workshop courses, and lectures, with trained instructors from the Business Management Service of the University of Illinois in attendance. Advanced groups in letter writing and public speaking continued through 1950—with 78 employees participating. Advanced management training con-tinued in various sections, with 196 first-line supervisors participating. In the autumn of 1953 courses in basic accounting and secretarial training were started, drawing 69 employees to these two courses—taught by in-structors supplied by the University of Illinois Extension and Business Management services. All told, 343 employees were trained. By 1954 al-most 1,200 were enrolled in some kind of educational program.

The following year—1951—the first programs were in executive and management training, with 177 employees participating. Instructors for these courses were supplied by Training Services, Inc., of Madison, Wis-consin. Forty-five employees took part in the second section of secretar-ial training; and group conference leadership training had ten partici-pants. In all instances the courses were conducted on company time. The training is evaluated and the results prepared for management in-spection.

Thus, State Farm has advanced in thirty years when the little group—only one of whom really was a trained office worker—started the "honest little insurance company" in a tiny office in Bloomington.

12

A MILLION OR MORE

Promptly at ten o'clock on the morning of Monday, June 13, 1938, the annual policyholders' meeting of the State Farm Mutual Automobile Company was called to order in the board room at the home office building in Bloomington. For the first time in sixteen years this function was not performed by George Mecherle—but by his son Ramond, who had been elevated to the presidency just one year before. As chairman of the board of directors, George Mecherle sat quietly while the various department heads—A. W. Tompkins, the agency vice president; T. F. Campbell, the vice president reporting for the underwriting department and the State Farm Fire Insurance Company; Fletcher B. Coleman, superintendent of claims; G. E. Mecherle, secretary and director of personnel; G. B. Brown, comptroller; R. C. Mead, actuary, and Morris G. Fuller, vice president of the State Farm Life Insurance Company—read their reports. When they had finished Ramond Mecherle arose and called upon his father to sum up the meeting.

"It has been a pleasure for me to sit in this meeting," said the Chief, fully conscious of the dignity of his new role, "and see the business conducted with such a measure of decorum. It is fine to listen to such glowing reports which denote the regular and steady advancement from year to year. . . ."

He paused, and it was obvious to those listening that he was in a somewhat strange mood this morning. He seemed to lack the fire and zest he usually manifested upon such occasions. As he continued, his listeners could not have helped but feel a change had come over him in the past year. "As we have become more important," he went on, "we are becoming more conservatively minded. This—I am satisfied—is natural, and comes from maturity.

"We may be compared," he said seriously, "in our mode of thinking somewhat to the English companies that have been in existence for years and take an exceptional pride in being able to place in their showwindows 'Established in 1840, 1850, etc.' This is indeed commendable and something which we should endeavor to emulate, as it should be our greatest desire to build for permanency on a sound business policy rather than to attempt too great a volume from this time on."

Amusing though it may have been for him to compare a company celebrating its sixteenth anniversary in the forenoon heat of a June day on the Illinois prairie to an old-established British company in the City of London, there was nothing facetious about George Mecherle's yearning for permanency. From the beginning his philosophy had been built on such a premise. Permanency through honesty had been his goal when, less than two decades ago, he had set about showing the Illinois farmers that an honest insurance company for their benefit could succeed in a field marked by failures. That—rather than a desire for bigness —was the fundamental impulse behind the exciting and tremendous achievements of the past few years. Conservative by nature, although operating on a plan that was radically different from any other in the field for many years, his great desire was for State Farm to be a sound and solid institution. He now felt that this much of his dream was realized. As he said, in ending his brief remarks, "We have very satisfactory, well-established organizations, and reasonable care and attention to fundamental business principles will enable these organizations to go on indefinitely."

Perhaps he was partly induced to make these sober reflections by the absence from the meeting—the first in sixteen years of devoted service to the company—of elderly William B. McFarland. This fine gentleman from Hoopeston—himself the soul of honor and conservatism—had been a steady and reliable guide for George Mecherle through these hectic years. A director from the beginning, he had helped the company to grow, without material reward for himself, and was generally loved and honored by everyone connected with State Farm Mutual. He was to die before the year was out, but his sane and sober sense, his good judgment and willing co-operation, were long to be remembered by those who had worked with him. As George Mecherle wrote in the *Reflector* after his death on August 3, he was "quiet and unassuming, dignified and stately at all times. His very attitude inspired confidence and a feeling of genuineness which did much to establish our organization throughout the mutual fraternities in the United States." Thinking of him, it is no wonder George Mecherle spoke that day of sound policy and of permanency.

George Mecherle had every right to be in a confident mood. The reports he had heard were indeed "glowing." The Messrs. Tompkins and Campbell had spoken of "remarkable" production, and of "excellent" underwriting. In the first five months of 1938 assets had increased $354,-000 and the surplus was up $277,000. At the same time the loss ratio was "favorable" and it had been possible, in several regions, to reduce rates. The steady increase of business had necessitated the purchase of the lot just north of the Home Office Building—the site of the old Odd Fellows Building where State Farm had been once housed in its infancy. Within a few months an eight-story addition, giving the company 80,-000 additional square feet of floor space, was to rise there to make the State Farm building even more imposing than it then was.

An analysis of *Best's Reports* for this year showed that the ratings of forty casualty companies had been reduced. Of these, twelve were mutuals, three were reciprocals, and twenty-five were stock companies. But State Farm's rating was still A-plus—the highest possible. This was at a time when business conditions were generally considered "uncertain." In the sixth year of the New Deal a "recession" had set in, the nation was still agitated over the Supreme Court issue, and President Roosevelt—in a Fireside Chat—had blamed the economic situation on "overproduction which had outrun the ability to buy." Furthermore, there was "fear of war abroad, fear of inflation, fear of nationwide strikes" and although, as F.D.R. said, "none of these fears had been borne out," nevertheless, in April, he was forced to ask Congress for a billion and a quarter more dollars for WPA and other agencies than he had estimated in January would be needed to meet the situation.

There must have been something about periods of depression and recession that inspired George Mecherle. The country had been in the midst of a postwar decline when he had conceived and launched the State Farm company. Now it was undergoing another economic dislocation. This acted as a challenge. Anyone who knew George Mecherle can hardly have taken seriously his warning not to attempt too great a volume from this time on. They knew him as too great a showman and salesman to think he would be willing to settle for the status quo. Nor was he. Within a month the pattern for his boldest venture since the great decision to start an insurance company was taking form in his active mind.

Shortly after the annual meeting Mr. Mecherle set out across the continent for a state directors' conference that was scheduled to be held at Berkeley—the site of the West Coast office—in mid-July. Accompanying him to this two-day affair, as he did on so many similar occasions, was A. W. Tompkins, the agency vice president. Somewhere between Bloomington and Berkeley, Mr. Mecherle—who never traveled without his black, loose-leaf notebook in which every detail of the companies' affairs were tabulated in the most minute detail and down to the last available report—reached a momentous decision. The final figure in that book, he decided, should be one million. This should be the aim of State Farm—one million automobile insurance policies in force. One million—or more.

George Mecherle did not pick this figure of one million out of his hat, but arrived at it almost scientifically—at least mathematically. The basis of his figuring was the number of automobiles registered in each state in which State Farm Mutual operated. From this he determined the percentage which State Farm, in competition with other companies, could reasonably expect to obtain. On this basis, one million was, in reality, a conservative estimate. Mr. Mecherle worked out the percentage of the total that each state ought to produce and set the quota to be reached each year by each division during the five years allocated for the campaign. For instance, he figured that California should account for 5.8% of the cars in the state. From the time of the Berkeley meeting to the end of the campaign that meant that California should come up with a total of about 100,000 new policies. Looked at this way, perhaps, the figure did not seem so conservative after all, and the magnitude of the task ahead of State Farm became apparent.

By the time he had reached Berkeley the idea had jelled in his mind. ("If I can sell one policy, I can sell a million," he had boasted sixteen years before.) At the meeting he broached the subject to the assembled state directors, but did not offer any concrete plan for its achievement. He was merely sowing the seed then. That summer, in Bloomington, he and Mr. Tompkins discussed at great length ways and means by which this seemingly fantastic goal could be reached. At that time there were no more than 450,000 policies on the company's books.

Early in August a carefully prepared letter went out over Mr. Tompkins's name to all the state directors—there were, by then, State Farm agents in thirty-six states—requesting that each one of them make specific recommendations whereby production of business might be speeded up to attain the one million automobile policyholders. Within a month a number of intelligent and enthusiastic replies had been received. On September 19, during the forty-ninth annual meeting of the National Association of Life Underwriters, held at Houston, Texas, another state directors' meeting was called. Two days of the busy week were spent in conference discussing specific methods and procedures. The project began to shape up. By then—or soon thereafter—it was decided to start the campaign sometime the following year. The million policyholders were to be obtained in five years. In other words—"A Million or More by '44."

Thereafter the executives' floor of the home office was a busy place. Almost everybody had some hand in whipping the project into shape. To George Mecherle it was not to be a campaign, but a crusade. One day a reporter for one of the older insurance trade journals interviewed him, and he said:

"Our fixed objective always has been to serve the greatest number of people in the best possible manner; to spread a blanket of protection over the greatest number of homes and human ambitions; and to provide sound protective service with an adequate margin of safety, seeking new fields wherein creative selling could be employed rather than seeking fields of intense competition."

The first general move toward extending the blanket of protection was made in the December 1, 1938, issue of the *Reflector*—where the first announcement of the campaign was made to the far-flung agents. This was to be big-time stuff, but in reality it was to be little more than a scientific, streamlined extension of the old township and county campaigns that George Mecherle, Mac McDonald, Bill Barthel, and Charley Wonderlin had made over the muddy back roads of Illinois seventeen years before. Then, the arrival of the teams of salesmen had been heralded by announcements in the advertising columns of the *Prairie Farmer*. Now, the nationally read pages of the *Saturday Evening Post, Country Gentleman*, and *Time* were to bring the story of State Farm Mutual to every city, town and hamlet in the United States—even in those few remaining states where State Farm did not operate. The *Reflector* told of other projects that had been planned to help the agents in their drive.

The million-policy program was to be responsible for a number of changes in State Farm policy, as it marked the emergence of the company from a relatively small company to the world's largest. Perhaps none was more indicative of the great changes that were coming than its attitude toward advertising. In the company's books the first entry actually earmarked for this purpose was in 1923, when the huge sum of $16.25 was spent. The company, of course, had been launched with appropriate paid announcements in the *Prairie Farmer*, and these undoubtedly had much to do with spreading the word about State Farm in the rural areas where it originally was designed to operate exclusively. By the mid-1930's its expenditures for all advertising purposes averaged around $15,000 annually. But by 1939, the year the million-policy campaign was begun, this was increased to the sum—astounding for those days and not appropriated until after serious and lengthy discussion by the board of directors—of $63,579.

In 1940, the company spent $151,674 to spread its message through the columns of the *Saturday Evening Post, Country Gentleman, Collier's*—and, of course, the *Prairie Farmer*. This amount included that spent for a slide film, especially made to introduce the 1944 objective to the agents, and for mailing pieces and the inevitable "advertising novelties." The following year, when the budget was increased to $202,000, the magazine *Banking* was added to the list of publications, as the company sought to increase its automobile finance plan through local banks.

During the war years the advertising appropriations were trimmed. In 1942, the advertising specialists began exploiting the name and personality of George Mecherle. A booklet, entitled *Shadow of a Man*, was issued for distribution during the company's twentieth anniversary which, of course, coincided with the Chief's sixty-fifth birthday. This was a "natural," for G.J.M.'s name was closely identified with the company he founded, as much twenty years later as it had been when he personally was crusading in the towns and villages of rural Illinois.

For the company's twenty-fifth anniversary, in 1947, Albert Reed Williamson wrote a short history of State Farm and a biography, under the happily appropriate title *An American Story*, which was widely distributed. In 1949, State Farm began using local newspapers in thirty-one states to announce rate reductions as they took place, co-ordinating the releases to appear with advertisements sponsored by local agents. By 1951 the company was spending $450,000 to advertise in *Collier's*, the *Saturday Evening Post*, in most of the leading insurance trade papers, in newspapers in thirty-nine states and Canada, in telephone directories—to list local agents and offices—and over the radio. In that year it began to sponsor, over the Mutual Broadcasting System, the comments of Cecil Brown.

In the old days George Mecherle had found that the most effective sales methods were those that were most direct. One of his favorite reminiscences dated to the rough-and-tumble period when he spent a great deal of his time out in the country training salesmen. One week he was out with a new crew in strange territory. For the first two days or so things went along well, but then the boys began to slow down and seemed to lose their pep. As he looked over his sluggish crew he remembered that sometimes, back in his farming days, his horses would act just as these men were acting now. He knew what to do for horses—maybe it would work with the men! He herded them into a drug store in a nearby village. "Pluto water, all around!" he ordered. Men, he found, were not so different from horses after all. It worked.

Not that the salesmen who had brought State Farm to its present state of stability and prosperity had been sluggish, but with this new venture at hand a variation of the old Pluto-water treatment was in order. He chose the annual agents' convention at Chicago, on February 20 and 21, 1939, for its administration. "The opening session," a company historian has recalled, "was highlighted by pageantry and showmanship that honored outstanding agents for the work they had done in the previous year. Then the convention, packing the grand ballroom of the Stevens Hotel, settled down to hard work and inspiration."

Addressing these men—assembled there from almost every part of America—George Mecherle launched into the campaign for a million or more policies by 1944 with characteristic enthusiasm. "At the outset," he said, "it was never intended that State Farm Mutual Automobile Insurance Company should be, or should become, merely another insurance organization. It was intended that it be a brotherhood of such high order that membership in it would be equal to a credit rating."

He then went back in his memory to that fateful meeting with the Farm Mutual representatives at Streator—just seventeen years ago that winter. From his address, which he gave at that time, he quoted the following: "This organization will be as distinct and separate from any other organization writing this class of insurance as sunshine is from shadow. It will not be the policy of our company to build its membership by other than straightforward business methods conducted honorably and fairly, so that no one connected with it will ever be forced to make apology." And then he added:

> It is a pleasure to say that these principles have been successfully carried throughout this organization since its inception, with the idea of building a brotherhood of protective service—rather than an institution dealing with the misfortunes of our fellow man that might be indifferent to the higher principles of charitable consideration of those who placed their trust in us.
>
> The past history of this organization tells us that—due to the unique plan of this organization and the method of its operation—it was impossible to interest the old established agencies that had been in the insurance business for many years. Due to this condition it became necessary to establish the company from those who were conversant with the practices of the old, well-established farm mutual companies, but who were unacquainted with the practices as followed by the orthodox general agencies. In this we were fortunate, as we attracted to our organization those who were grounded in the principles of service and governed by their high ideas of right, which have always been the basic fundamentals for any mutual insurance enterprise. . . .
>
> There is an old axiom which comes down to us through the ages from the teachings of Confucius, which tells us: "To make a family prosperous is like digging clay with a needle; each member must do his or her share; idleness brings ruin to the homestead like water against a sandbank."
>
> If we are to grow and prosper it is necessary that every individual and every entity with which we are associated lend its every effort toward the consummation of the idea we have in mind. It would be unfair to ask this agency force to further extend its efforts and amplify this premium volume if the company did not lend ready and willing assistance to the promotion of this idea. I am happy to state that the company, its board of directors, the state and general agencies have seen the possibilities of real

business development in this project and are in full and complete accord with the program as outlined and with the methods that will be employed.

In suggesting this five-year program with the objective of a million active policies by 1944, there may be some criticism that a program of this kind is possibly too ambitious. However, if the records of the past and the conditions of the present are any measure by which to forecast the future, there is every reason to believe that a program of this kind can be carried through to a successful conclusion.

If the program were too ambitious, the ambition at least was tempered by serious and thoughtful preparation. A great deal of advance study— the result of the co-ordinated teamwork of all the executives, directors, and department heads—went into the grand design. Some of them altered the fundamental structure; others were merely an intensified extension of normal promotional procedures; yet all added up to a campaign which probably has few equals in the history of mutual automobile insurance salesmanship. The presiding genius of the whole affair was, of course, George Mecherle, who had not had as much fun—and hard work—since the muddy spring of 1922.

One reason why George Mecherle so enjoyed himself these days was that he was meeting a new challenge which appealed to his competitive spirit. The new drive for business was launched at a time when what really amounted to rate war was in progress. Rival companies were coming out with new, special rating plans. Many of them were of such a nature that some states sought to regulate by legislation the rates charged for automobile insurance. George Mecherle let it be widely known that he was always willing to co-operate with insurance departments everywhere, and even with other companies, but that he and the State Farm company would "continue to resist attempts to force this company to give up the essential characteristics of its plan of operation or to increase its rates beyond the actual cost of this company, as reflected by its experience."

Many aids for the far-flung agency force were thought up in the executive offices of the home office building in those hectic days. The time had passed when an agent could jump into a hog pen, as the Chief had once done years before, to help a harried farmer with his sweaty chores and come out with a membership application and check duly signed. Now—besides the national advertising—the company furnished the district managers with 16-mm films, complete with sound track, especially made for State Farm Mutual. In addition to these, a whole series of strip films—together with projectors—was supplied. Also, a wide variety of promotional literature was made up in huge quantities, and all sorts of those gadgets so dear to the heart of the insurance salesman—such as mechanical pencils and key rings and State Farm shields for automobiles —were ordered by the case lot.

All this, of course, amounted to little more than an acceleration of normal procedure. Far more important was the planned expansion of the agency force through the hiring of many new agents in the metropolitan districts and, to a lesser extent, in nonmetropolitan areas. A revolving fund was set aside to assist the state directors in establishing new agencies. Service offices were set up in several key cities to assist in establishing the agents and in servicing old and new policyholders. An improved system of bonuses for agents was also put into effect. But also of importance was the establishment of the conservation department.

The creation of this division was not wholly a result of the million-policy campaign, and it undoubtedly would have come into being under normal circumstances. As its name signifies, its fundamental purpose was, as Ramond Mecherle put it, "to stop the leaks at the bottom and keep the policyholders from going elsewhere for protection"—in other words, to conserve the business already won. J. H. Parsons, who had been assistant to Fletcher B. Coleman—superintendent of claims—was called in to head the new department. Harold Mecherle was made his assistant, and Pauline Schmidt, a veteran State Farmer, was placed in charge of the corps of clerks.

Mr. Parsons' over-all instructions were threefold: (1) to secure reinstatement of as many old policies as possible; (2) to reduce the number of current lapses; and (3) to regain lost or impaired markets, particularly insurance on financed automobiles.

Gilbert F. Alcott was named supervisor of this third division. Within the first six months of operation, the conservation department began going after 368,336 former policyholders, sending full information from the files on these people to the proper agents. It set up a system whereby agents were sent out on the trail of "current lapses," of which —in the first six months of the year 1939—there were 17,374. The immediate results of this campaign were gratifying, for in that six-month period the *increase* in reinstatements was approximately 41% over the corresponding period of the previous year.

From the start, the policy of the conservation department was designed to back up the theory of George Mecherle, who felt that a State

Farm membership should carry with it something more than mere protection against the hazards of automobiling. It began a careful campaign to impress the agency staff with the importance of selecting a policyholder who could not only meet the vigorous underwriting standards of the company, but who was also in a position to maintain his insurance in full force and effect by the payment of premium notices.

"This is conservation at the source," Mr. Parsons explained in his first annual report, "and it is of the utmost importance in any well-planned conservation program."

In order to compensate for the work involved by the agents in getting policies reinstated (since this was not new business, it did not involve new commissions), the conservation department effected a tie-up with the advertising department of State Farm. A credit for $1 was allowed for each reinstatement, but this was not redeemable in cash. Instead, it could be turned in for the advertising material that was found so increasingly effective in helping to sell new policies. In the first five months of operation of this new system a total of $16,162 in such credits was chalked up—of which more than one-quarter was redeemed in advertising. Later, as reinstatements increased, the amount of the credits turned back to the home office for advertising material almost equaled the total.

At the same time the conservation department undertook a national survey to determine the underlying reasons for "lapsations" and cancellations. This was the first such undertaking on the part of the company. A report was asked from every agent explaining why each policy was allowed to lapse or be canceled on the part of the policyholder. This information was carefully classified and tabulated over the next several years, and from the data thus brought in much valuable information was obtained—enabling the company to improve relations with its policyholders.

Although up to this time the company had done no intensive research into the situation, it was aware that it was losing much valuable business to the controlled insurance carriers of the large national automobile finance companies. One of the first tasks of the conservation department was to look carefully into this matter with the hope of devising a plan which would enable the company to recapture much of this valuable business. As a result of its study a plan which well fitted the dual preferred risk policies of the company was put into operation. The plan— later widely copied—was original with State Farm Mutual.

The plan involved the co-operation of local banks and of finance organizations which were, for the first time, interesting themselves in the
financing of automobile purchasing. The State Farm plan was not designed to discourage financing of the purchase of automobiles through
these large agencies, if the policyholder so wished, but was arranged to
make financing through local institutions easier for all concerned. It
offered a policy which would run concurrently with the loan from the
bank or finance organization and which carried an endorsement fully
protecting the interests of the loan agency.

This program was a success and played its part in the eventual success
of the million-policy program. Within a year, thanks to the talks given
to agents in an extensive cross-country tour by G. F. Alcott, and thanks
to advertising in banking journals and extensive publicity in the *Reflector* and elsewhere, more than 1,300 banks were co-operating with
State Farm, whose agents sent many policyholders to the local banks for
financing the purchase of new cars. All of this publicity stressed State
Farm's "broad and comprehensive coverage," as compared to the re-
strictive fire, theft and windstorm then still being offered by many finance companies, and played up the "80% collision policy" against the
usual "$50 deductible" of finance companies. It also emphasized the
lower costs to policyholders that resulted from dealing with the local
banker.

Up to this time a majority of State Farm policyholders had carried
only liability and property damage protection—taking out their property
coverages (such as fire, theft, windstorm, comprehensive, and collision)
with the insurance affiliates of finance companies. Under the new State
Farm program they were now able to take out all their automobile insurance at one time and with one company while arranging to cover the
financing of their car with their local bank.

State Farm entered this field at a time when competition was steadily
increasing, but in spite of this its program had sufficient appeal so that
at the end of 1942 there were 2,000 or more banks co-operating with
the company. At about the time State Farm started stressing this aspect
of the business, various rulings of State Insurance Commissions and Acts
of State Legislatures reduced the commissions earned by finance companies on their insurance business.

At this time few of the finance companies wrote liability or property
damage insurance or solicited renewals of property coverages once payment of the loan had been made. One of the larger finance companies,

however, did offer a comprehensive coverage, and it was believed at this
time that the others were contemplating entering this broadened field.
Imposition of controls and the strict restriction of installment buying
during the war was soon to put a different complexion on this phase of
the business. In the early years of the million-policy campaign, however,
the tie-up between the State Farm and the local banks was the source of
much business and considerable good will.

George Mecherle was greatly interested in this source of State Farm
membership.

"Considerable thought and study," he explained to the agency force,
"has been given to this problem. . . . Our first idea was to organize and
promote a finance company of our own, but this was abandoned when
it became apparent that in order to conduct such a business on a national scale we would have to run contrary to State Farm principles and
ideals in many respects. Therefore, we definitely abandoned the idea of
organizing and operating a finance company of our own but, believing
that we could render a very valuable service to our present and prospective policyholders, we decided upon an alternate which would not em-
body any of the objectionable features of a financing operation on a
national scale, but which nevertheless would accomplish the same beneficial results.

"This plan is very simple and is based on the theory that the financing
of an automobile is rightfully a local or community problem and, consequently, should be handled by local banks in the same manner and
on the same terms as any other loan with equal security.

"Local and community banks throughout the country subscribe to
this declaration of principle. They have unusually large deposits seeking
a sound and profitable outlet. Therefore, conditions are ripe for the
launching of this phase of our conservation program.

"Our plan is very simple when boiled down to its essence. It will con-
sist primarily in establishing a contact and working agreement between
local banks and our agents, so that the bank will finance the purchase of
automobiles for deserving policyholders and will accept our policy, with
proper safeguards on the loan. Such a plan, when carried to its utmost
possibilities, will open the door to a vast new field of business, in view of
the fact that two out of three sales of new and used cars are on a de-
ferred payment basis. Furthermore, we will be able to retain many policies which we are now losing when the policyholder trades in his old car
on a new one and finances the deal."

Another State Farm innovation that played its part in the great crusade which was to build the little automobile insurance company for Illinois farmers into the biggest automobile insurance company in the world was the travel bureau. This was not a brainchild of the "million-or-more campaign" but had been, since 1935, a most potent good-will builder. A success from the start, it now was called upon to play an even larger role, which it continued to do until the exigencies of World War II and its aftermath caused its dissolution in 1947. Its major feature was the publication of the State Farm Road Atlas, specially prepared and edited and beautifully printed for State Farm in a new edition each year by the Rand McNally Company of Chicago—the nation's largest and best-known publisher of United States maps. In addition to this, it maintained an active travel bureau which worked out routes in any part of the nation for potential travelers.

Now in its fourth year, the first of the "million-or-more" campaign, it distributed 65,000 copies of the Atlas. Of these, 34,000 had been issued directly to policyholders upon request, while the other 31,000 had been purchased by members of the agency force for use in advertising, prospecting, and sales campaign. About 80% of the redeemed agents' advertising credits for reinstatements went for the purchase of the Atlas for distribution to policyholders and prospects. In 1940 the conservation department was able to report:

"We have received some very glowing testimonials from members of the agency staff with respect to the value of this advertising material in sales promotion work. The allowance of this $1 redeemable in advertising material is not only motivating the agency staff in securing reinstatements, but the distribution of this merchandise is having a definite effect on the production of new business. . . . We have had numerous instances called to our attention where the presentation of a mechanical pencil, a State Farm Road Atlas, a key case, or license holder, has resulted in sales—to say nothing of the good will that such a gift engenders."

The travel bureau was averaging 200 automobile routing requests weekly. Nearly half of these came from agents and by them were passed on to State Farm policyholders in every corner of the country. Often travelers would ask to be routed if possible through Bloomington, so that they might pass by the home office of the State Farm companies, and many of the older policyholders—stopping off in the city—would visit the State Farm Building and be shown through the busy offices. In one year more than 1,100 groups and clubs, particularly 4-H clubs, fraternities and university groups, turned to the travel bureau for information and copies of the ever popular Atlas. Although the bureau itself was discontinued in 1947, the Atlas is still published and distributed in increasing numbers annually.

The year before the great campaign began, two major policy changes had taken place. These tended to modernize the State Farm system. In 1938 the old scheme of contingent liability and assessments had been dropped, and the board of directors had been authorized to "set the amounts and conditions" for all the different kinds of insurance transacted by the corporation. The by-laws were amended to read that "no member shall be subject to assessment or contingent liability at any time." At the same time a new National Standard Policy was adopted, which included all the various forms of insurance coverage written by the State Farm Mutual. This eliminated numerous endorsements, made for economy, and greatly simplified the process of handling the policies by the agents and the home office staff.

On the eve of the million-policy campaign the company wisely decided to extend the "Advance Premium Plan" to all states where it was licensed to operate. This new plan retained all of the essential characteristics, or what R. C. Mead, the company's actuary, called the "strength and flexibility" of the original State Farm plan, but it permitted a reduction in the original premiums required for insurance—particularly on older cars. Since this reduction released excess premiums it was confidently—and accurately, as it turned out—predicted that a great number of policyholders would use this "extra money" for the purchase of further State Farm insurance, thus receiving broader protection at the same price. At the same time rates for commercial automobiles in most classes were materially reduced.

A "medical payments" coverage was also made available—an extension of the older State Farm first-aid clause in the bodily injury liability policy—whereby the company paid up to $500 for medical, surgical, or hospital expenses, or reasonable funeral expenses, for each person injured as a result of the operation of the insured automobile "regardless of the liability or negligence of the owner or operator." This was frankly designed to reduce the number of uncompensated automobile injuries and to provide almost immediate payment for medical expenses when most needed. State Farm felt that this system, which it originated in 1939, provided a more equitable basis for compensating those injured in automobile accidents than any previously offered.

During this period several other events worthy of mention took place. State Farm's long wrangle with the state of Texas came to an end when the insurance department of the Lone Star state agreed to allow the company to operate there on its regular semiannual plan rather than on the conference annual plan. With State Farm now operating amicably down to the Mexican border, it at last crossed the northern border of the United States when, in 1938, it received its license to do business in the Dominion of Canada.

Along with these good signs were portents of changes that were to be significant. For one thing, the cost of payment, settlement and adjustment of claims was to rise rapidly. In 1937, for example, a total of 114,-500 claims returned more than $5,500,000 to State Farm policyholders. This was an increase of 23% over 1936, and an average of 348 claims for every 1,000 policies. Much of this increase came about because of the new designs for automobiles which the manufacturers were putting out. The new streamlined body styles cost more to repair. Labor costs and the price of automobile engine parts were also steadily going up in those days that preceded the defense effort and the war. And, for further headaches, the annual reports now began to mention, with increasing regularity, the need for more detailed accounting information to meet the requirements of various state and federal taxing bodies and the more regulatory-conscious state insurance departments.

State Farm was, by now, definitely in the category of Big Business as it set out to accomplish in the next five years more than it had accomplished in the phenomenal seventeen which had passed. Hitherto its business had been concentrated in rural markets and it had proved without qualification George Mecherle's original contention that there was a vast, unplowed field for automobile insurance among the farmers. He had shown the way almost alone and he had done it successfully. By this time many of the Farm Bureaus which had had contracts with State Farm felt it would be more to their advantage to confine their sales to Bureau members and so they broke away, to form their own companies or other alliances.* This left gaps in the agency organization which now had to be repaired. As this took place, State Farm began

* In 1954 State Farm had contracts only with the West Virginia and Montana Farm Bureaus.

concentrating more on the metropolitan areas. But it never departed from its rural origins. In 1954 between 18 and 20% of its policyholders were farmers and 50% in all occupations lived in predominantly rural areas.

With all this went new approaches to old problems. Besides national advertising on an increasingly large scale, there was the necessity for such new departures as departments of sales analysis and research. This meant new faces, new blood: able, expert men who could thoroughly look into the potential markets in each state, find the basis for the assignment of quotas, and even set up the reassignment of territories. All this was done under the direction of George Mecherle, over whose desk passed the reports of the nationwide search for the million or more by 1944. Familiar as he was by personal contact with State Farm agents in almost every nook and cranny of the country, these figures were quickly translated at his fingertips into suggestions and recommendations to the staff and into encouraging and inspiring messages to the men in the field.

When 1939 had rolled around all this activity had resulted in a gain of 69,074 policies over the previous year. The million goal, however, still seemed far distant. But the next year saw 102,978 policies added to those on State Farm books.* This was more like it. Not only was this the greatest annual gain in the company's history, but it brought the number of policies in force, and the company's premium income, to a new all-time high. The entire industry took notice. State Farm had reached the top of the ladder. In dollars of automobile premiums written it was now bigger than any other mutual company in the United States and it was bigger than any stock company. It was exceeded only by two companies which restricted their writing to physical damage insurance on financed cars. The incredible had happened and insurance history had been made.

* At the same time (the end of 1940) the State Farm Life Insurance Company's production was $13,410,000 and the State Farm Fire Insurance Company's production was $703,000. Both were impressive increases, justifying the prophecy made the year before by A. W. Tompkins that "we are becoming more and more convinced that the attainment of a million automobile policies will carry with it a corresponding achievement of one hundred million dollars of life insurance . . . and one million dollars of premium income (in fire insurance)."

13

THE WAR YEARS

The year 1941, which was to be one of the most fateful years in United States and world history, dawned auspiciously for the State Farm Mutual Automobile Insurance Company. The great sales campaign for a million or more policies by 1944 was running practically on the schedule set for it by George Mecherle. The figures tell the story.

At the start of the year there were nearly 650,000 (actually 648,690) policies in force, and by the first of April this figure had risen to 694,995—an increase that amounted to 39.5% of the quota which had been set for the year. In one week in May alone the busy agents sent in 14,606 applications for automobile insurance, and for ten weeks in a row previously the total applications had exceeded 12,000. Never had the office force at the home office been so busy as they struggled, not always successfully, to keep up with the flood.

The task of underwriting this vast volume of new business was formidable. Seven separate underwriting divisions had to be set up to take care of it. The Illinois and Indiana, the Pacific Coast and the Eastern

States divisions each handled close to 125,000 policies. The Southern, the Iowa, Nebraska and Montana, the Michigan, Kansas and Colorado, and the Minnesota and North and South Dakota divisions each processed in excess of 65,000 policies. As A. W. Tompkins remarked, the business handled by any one of these divisions was as great as that of any good-sized insurance company. It began to look, once again, as if the thirteen-story building *and* the eight-story annex together were not going to be big enough to house State Farm much longer. The year 1941 was to see an increase of 38% in State Farm's automobile insurance over the previous year, while the State Farm fire company was to push its business ahead by 39% and the life company was to jump 29% over 1940. The premium and membership income for the automobile mutual alone was $25,007,000—which was more automobile insurance than any one casualty company had ever written in a single year.

During this period the fire company, for the first time, ended with assets of over $1,000,000, while the life company reported over $86,000,-000 worth of insurance in force. To handle all this work the home office staff had been increased from 996 men and women to 1,344, while the West Coast and other offices had been forced to enlarge their staffs proportionately. The press of business was so great that a night crew of 180 young workers—mostly students at Illinois State Normal and Illinois Wesleyan University—was engaged.

It is interesting to recall that 1941 was considered the "banner year" by the automobile insurance industry generally. State Farm was not alone in running up record-breaking production figures, although it was $6,727,000 ahead of its closest rival among the ten top leaders of the mutual field. Exclusive of State Farm's business that year, the other nine outstanding mutuals* in 1941 did a total business of $68,500,000. Add to that the $25,000,000 achieved by State Farm, for a total of $93,500,-000 done by the top ten mutuals out of the $162,400,000 worth of automobile business done by *all* mutual companies, and you get a clear idea of just how far the little insurance company of Bloomington had come in less than twenty years.

All this, of course, was not done without increased costs to the management. A few years previously G. J. Mecherle, Inc., had been reor-

* Lumbermens Mutual Casualty, Ill.; Liberty Mutual, Mass.; Hardware Mutual, Wis.; Farm Bureau Mutual Auto Insurance, Ohio; State Auto Mutual, Ohio; American Mutual Liability, Mass.; Utica Mutual, N. Y.; Auto-Owners Mutual, Mich.; and Merchants Mutual, N. Y., in that order. *National Underwriter*, April 20, 1942.

ganized under the laws of Delaware as Mutual Agency, Inc., and the management of the California office was conducted by a similar organization, also headed by G. J. Mecherle, known as Coast Agency, Inc. These still operated under a contract that was basically the same as that first written between State Farm and G. J. Mecherle, Inc., in 1922. The agencies—rather than the company itself—paid the agents their commissions. This year the memberships written by the Mutual Agency amounted to $2,173,639, for which the agency had paid, in first and incentive commissions, $2,262,408—thus suffering a loss of $88,768; while the loss incurred by the Coast Agency, which had written $476,-621 worth of memberships and paid $506,062 in commissions, was $27,440—or a grand total of $116,209 which the two agencies had paid out for first and incentive bonuses* in excess of the membership fees brought in.

This, of course, does not mean that the agencies were actually losing money. Under the contract the money paid to the agencies from the membership fees was "working money" to be put back into the field; to be used for the paying of commissions and bonuses. The fees received for renewals enabled the agencies to absorb the differences between the amount taken in membership fees and that paid out in commissions and bonuses.

Eventually the Mutual and Coast agencies were discontinued. There were several reasons for this. As we have seen in an earlier chapter some Insurance Departments were critical of such agency arrangements. Insurance history reveals instances, particularly in the era when State Farm was getting started, when some agencies took unfair advantage of their companies, collecting such high fees or commissions that the company suffered and, in some cases, became insolvent. On the other hand, many very successful mutual companies had been built on the agency arrangement and it was with these in mind that Herman Ekern and Erwin Meyers—who sensed the unimpeachable integrity of George Mecherle from the beginning—insisted upon such a contract back in 1922. At that time there was no other source of funds for organizing and maintaining the new mutual company except the management itself—in this case, George Mecherle and his quondam partner, Minnie A. Jones. Such funds could not be returned until after all obligations to

* If an agent produced a projected quota he received not only the membership fee but also a bonus, which in some cases was cumulative, *i.e.*, he got a further bonus on all business written during the period.

the policyholders had been fully provided for. As far as the advancers of the working capital were concerned, this was not the best security; some measure had to be devised to compensate the management for its risks and to provide it with the incentive to build up the company. Experience of others had shown that in the early days of a mutual company even the most competent management could expect to receive little or no compensation. Many a new company has had to operate from five to ten years before being able to accumulate much in the way of a surplus. As far as George Mecherle was concerned the records show that several years passed before he received sufficient compensation out of the agencies adequately to pay him for the time, energy and risk expended in carrying the State Farm companies through their early stages. In the long run, however, these contracts became highly remunerative.

From time to time, when the company received criticisms from one or another of the state insurance commissions as to these contracts, its answer was invariably that out of them had come three successful and sound insurance companies which, largely because of such contracts, had been able to sell automobile insurance at something like 25% less on the average than the standard board companies. Ironically, it was State Farm's ability to do this that was actually responsible for most of the criticism that was directed toward the Bloomington company. In many instances the criticisms were traceable directly to such competitors. Nevertheless, George Mecherle was sensitive to these criticisms, as he was toward anything that seemed to cast aspersions on the integrity of the companies whose name, over the years, had become almost synonymous with his own. The agencies were dissolved.

In spite of everything, the year 1941 passed in a whirl of activity. The economy of the entire country, at the time, was undergoing a radical change. The greatest preparation for defense in the nation's history was proceeding at a tremendous rate, although it had not yet reached the unprecedented acceleration it was to attain when almost all civilian production ceased and industry as a whole was enlisted for the duration of the second German war against mankind.

In 1941, the production of new automobiles was near its peak. Two years before (just a decade after the crash of 1929) the automobile industry of the United States had produced the startling number of 2,855,796 new passenger cars—out of a world total of 3,660,875—and 710,496 of the 1,118,296 new buses and trucks manufactured everywhere. Now, a State Farm analyst—reporting in the *Reflector*—estimated that there were approximately 30,000,000 new and old automobiles of every description on the roads of America, and that less than one-half of them were protected by adequate insurance. At the end of this same decade wages and salaries were being earned at a rate of $9,000,000,000 more a year than in 1929, and the farm cash income was at the highest point it had been since the 1920's. With the national defense expenditure jumping more than one and a half billion dollars in the first six months of 1941, it was hardly any wonder that State Farm agents were finding little difficulty in breaking sales records almost every week.

And then suddenly—at 7:55 in the morning of December 7—an American naval commander screamed into a microphone: "Air raid on Pearl Harbor! This is no drill!" The day which was to live in infamy had stunned the civilized world.

America's entrance into World War II brought new problems to every American—individual or corporate—as the nation sought quickly to adjust itself to its place in a war-torn world. State Farm, of course, was no exception. As George Mecherle said, in a radio broadcast for the Red Cross ten days after Pearl Harbor: "The soft, talkative days are over and we may be facing the hardest days this country has ever seen." The companies were up against a drastic necessity for readjustment. But none of the problems with which they were confronted was insurmountable. Since—like every other insurance company—the State Farm companies produced nothing tangible, they could not, like a factory, be "converted" overnight to the defense effort. Classified as a nonessential industry, they had to find their own level in the new, all-out struggle for survival.

From some quarters came the suggestion that they "pull in their horns," as far as selling automobile insurance was concerned, and concentrate their attention on "other lines." To this, George Mecherle turned a deaf ear. State Farm might lose as much as half its business, he stated firmly, but it "would come out of the war as clean as a hound's tooth," and without resorting to diversification. Nor would it abandon its now seemingly impossible goal of a million policies by 1944. The manufacture of automobiles for civilian use might cease, as it soon did, and the most drastic restrictions might be clamped down on the use of precious gasoline and rubber tires, but there would still be a public and patriotic need for at least 25,000,000 automobiles to be kept running, somehow, in order that the great army of production workers might move back and forth to the shipyards and the defense plants. There would, he reasoned, be a definite part for State Farm to play in the months to come.

Seven months and a day after Pearl Harbor, State Farm Mutual celebrated what President Ramond P. Mecherle called "a momentous occasion." On that day the automobile insurance company ended its twentieth year of operation.

As far as George Mecherle was personally concerned it also was a momentous occasion, for he was just sixty-five years old. He was torn by a decision he believed had to be made. Sixty-five was—and he felt should be in most cases—the time for a man to retire from business. But he did not want to retire, particularly at this time. The decision, however, he felt was not his to make, and so he asked his son Ramond to place the question before the membership at the annual meeting on Monday, June 8, 1942. Those two veterans of the board of directors— C. A. Asplund and J. Colby Beekman, both of whom had been helping George Mecherle make his decisions since the inception of the mutual company—now helped him to make this one. Since Mr. Asplund himself was ten years the Chief's senior, the matter of age seemed of little moment to him. The result was a rising vote of confidence in George Mecherle and a virtual invitation for him to remain as chairman of the board as long as he desired.

The reports of the various department heads reflected the immediate impact of the war economy. Already scores of home and branch office employees had gone into the armed services or left for jobs more closely connected with the defense effort. A similar situation existed in the agency force and many of the company's trained claim investigators were called upon by the Government for duty with the FBI or other agencies where their unique skills were needed. A picture of the way things on the home front partly were in the first few months of America's participation in World War II is reflected in the prosaic facts and figures of F. B. Coleman's report for the claims department:

> The results for the first four months of 1942 reflect a very noticeable reduction in claim frequency under the liability coverage, particularly a reduction in catastrophe losses. Under the property coverages the claim frequency is below that in 1941, and is more in line with what could be considered a normal year. Average costs are still mounting, and whereas this trend was not noticeable under the liability coverage in 1941, it has become very pronounced in the first four months of 1942. It is reasonable to anticipate that the average cost of all claims will be higher in 1942 than in any recent year.

The earnings of the claimants, the doctors' bill and hospital expenses, are all very important factors in the computation of the value of a personal injury claim. All of these are higher than they have been for some time. The cost of available automobile parts has increased, and the labor charges for repair work have been forced to high levels because the repair shops have been required to compete with the war industries for mechanics. The cost of property claims will not be reduced because of the scarcity of replacement parts, creating a necessity for repairing the old. The repairing of damaged parts will be costly because of high labor charges, and it is anticipated that it will cost about as much, and perhaps even more, to repair a part in the future than it would have cost to replace it in the past in those cases where there is extensive damage to the part involved.

There is not much indication so far that people are interested in conserving the available automobile parts. When parts are available and there is a question of repair or replacement, the new part is usually installed.

But, as Mr. A. W. Tompkins put it: "Despite restrictions, priorities, rationing, price ceilings, blackouts, production of war materials, mustering of men in the armed forces, and the emotional stress of the public in general, the State Farm agency force is doing an outstanding job."

That was in mid-year. At the end of 1942, when the country had been at war for nearly a year, the proof of this "outstanding job" was to be found in the record.* Up to this time the State Farm Mutual had known only one year when the total number of policies in force had declined from the previous year. That was in the depression year of 1932. Then the number dropped 34,093. Now, at the end of 1942, with no new cars being made, with gasoline being rationed, with no new tires available, and with travel cut to a minimum, State Farm had only 607 fewer policies on its books than it had at the end of 1941! And 1941 had been the biggest year that American mutual companies collectively had ever experienced, dollarwise, in the sales of automobile insurance. Perhaps even more remarkable was the fact that State Farm's premium income showed an increase of $611,321.

The next two years were to be different.

In 1943, the distance to the goal of a million policies by 1944 narrowed. Although during that year the automobile premiums of all types of mutual companies fell 11% below the 1942 figure, State Farm increased by 2.9%. This remarkable achievement took place in a year

---

* During the first months of 1942 the agency force lost 95 agents to the armed forces and more than 1,500 others left for jobs in defense plants. During the same period only 770 replacements were made. In the next few months many other agents, managers, and several State Directors were called to service.

which saw the business of seven of the ten top mutual companies decline. The business of the second largest company—the Lumbermen's
Mutual Casualty—for example, dropped 29.4%.

All this placed State Farm in a most enviable position. The company
still stood in first place among all mutual companies, with its automobile
premiums double those of its nearest mutual competitor. At the same
time it strengthened its hold on first place among *all* companies engaged in writing automobile insurance—stock, mutual, reciprocals, and
Lloyds. Its $26,393,000 in automobile premiums stood up against the
$14,617,000 of Hartford Accident, which was second among insurers
of all classes, according to the tabulation of that reliable trade journal,
the *National Underwriter*.

In its factual summary of the Big Ten for 1943 the *Underwriter* reported:

"Of course, State Farm is a composite company and the fact that it
writes all automobile lines must be taken into consideration, but its
comprehensive and collision premiums combined amount to $11,442,-
279, which is nearly double the premiums of any company specializing
in those coverages, and its automobile bodily injury and property damage premiums of $14,950,561 are second in amount only to the com-
bined bodily injury and property damage of Travelers and Travelers Indemnity."

Furthermore, State Farm Mutual and the State Farm Fire Insurance
Company combined emerged that year as the leader among company
groups—both stock and no stock—in the number of automobile premiums written, thus moving up from second among mutual groups and
third among all groups. "A notable achievement," the *National Underwriter* remarked, "is the fact that in 1943 the automobile premiums of
State Farm Mutual, for the third successive year, exceeded $25 mil-
lion."

A million or more *by* 1944 had been the goal. When George
Mecherle and his associates added up the number of policies in force
at the end of 1943 they found that they were 13,623 policies short of
what they had aimed at. This was short of the total they had been seeking by less than two-tenths of 1%.

The campaign went forward. In spite of all the adverse conditions,
when the books were examined at the end of March, they showed that
the fantastic goal had been passed. There were 1,001,519 policies in

force. Never before had any company in the field of automobile insurance accomplished such a feat. The figures told the remarkable story.

On January 1, 1939, when the great campaign began, the company—after sixteen and a half years of operation—had 476,638 policies in force. Now, five and a half years later, 524,001 policies had been added —an increase of 110%!

There were several factors that had contributed to the startling success of the plan. The foremost, as A. W. Tompkins pointed out in his report, was the definite advance planning on the part of the company executives, state directors, managers and agents. As chief of the agency force, Mr. Tompkins felt that the ready acceptance and willingness of the agents to meet the challenge—thrown at them when the drive was inaugurated in 1939—was something to be proud of.

Added to this was the reorganization of the agency force—which in many areas meant the creation of a new agency organization. Another factor was the increased compensation to the local agents which came with new bonuses resulting from increased business.

He felt, too, that the campaign had done more than increase the company's business by 110% in five and a quarter years, for it had taught the agents new and improved skills that would continue to benefit State Farm over the coming years. Looking back over the campaign, he noted the improved economic conditions—the effective buying power of the American people had gone up 101% in this same period—and and with it the growing appreciation on the part of the public as to the value of automobile insurance; and he observed that these, too, were in great measure responsible. But he felt deeply that the goal might never have been reached had it not been for what he called "the enviable record established by the company since the date of organization in writing policies designed to pay losses, promptly and satisfactorily." In the long run, he felt, this perhaps was the greatest factor—this and the "confidence of the agency force in the company management," especially in the farmer from Merna whose genius had conceived this greatest of automobile insurance companies less than a quarter of a century before.

Amazing though this achievement was, State Farm was not to stop there. Like most successful American business organizations, the company was to take the wartime conditions in its stride and keep its eye to the future. Even before the million-policy program had been completed its executives were busy making plans for a new program. Designed to offer policyholders better and broader protection and to provide the company's agents with a new incentive after the million-policy campaign had ended, it was to be introduced early in 1944.

For several months R. C. Mead, the State Farm actuary, worked out the details of the State Farm Mutual Service Policy program, which was to play a large part in the company's maintenance of its position as the world's largest automobile insurance company. He described the main purpose of the program as a means to provide the company with "a distinctive, simplified, streamlined and modernized automobile insurance policy for the greater service and protection of its policyholders."

From the company's standpoint he felt that it would "provide a constructive basis for merchandising automobile insurance that will meet the requirements of State Directors, managers, and agents by encouraging the sale of policies providing broader protection and service, thereby increasing membership and service fee income during the present period of low rates."

The new Service Policy—as evolved after much careful study—gave policyholders the choice of four so-called "package policies," embodying all the coverages offered under the old policies, but broadening the scope of protection. In addition, two new forms of protection were offered: (1) comprehensive personal and residence liability, including liability for servants, and (2) comprehensive farm and farm employers' liability insurance.

In his first report on this program Mr. Mead, whose untimely death in 1945 was to be a great loss to the company, said:

"Of particular interest is the fact that the new program marks the entrance of the company into the entire field of miscellaneous casualty insurance—a field that both from the standpoint of total premium written by other companies, as well as from total possibilities, is even larger than the automobile insurance field. While the program only contemplates the writing of comprehensive residence and comprehensive farm liability—lines which are a natural supplement to the automobile business and to our agency force—they will permit both the agency force and the company to acquire the experience and understanding that will some day allow further extension of the casualty insurance facilities of the company."

With the goal of a million policies passed and a new program for unlimited expansion launched—by mid-1944 the new policy program had been approved by all but seven of the states in which the company operated—State Farm confidently awaited whatever the successful prosecution of the war and the coming of the peace might offer. As Mr. Mead put it, they had provided as best they could for a "forward-looking basis for operation after the war is over and the manufacture and sale of new cars is resumed."

14

CHAOS AND CRISIS

The ending of the war in the summer of 1945 brought State Farm face to face with a bewildering number of perplexing problems. Some, of course, stemmed directly from the war itself, but others—and these were, perhaps, the more distressing—came about as a result of the sudden shifts in the American manner of living that came so quickly after the surrender of Japan. Problems came pouring down on State Farm like an avalanche and they called for drastic measures to meet the emergency. But when it had been met, State Farm stood stronger than it ever had stood before and was still the dominant company in the field of automobile insurance. Those first years of peace made an exciting and dramatic period in the history of the "honest little insurance company" which had been born in the period of agricultural depression that came after the first World War.

State Farm, of course, was not alone in facing the perplexities of the peace, but because it was even then the largest company of its kind in the world it undoubtedly had more and worse problems to contend with than many of its competitors. These worries began plaguing the industry the day driving restrictions were lifted and an automobile-conscious country, bursting the bonds of its long restraint, took to the highways in gay abandon, regardless of the age or condition of the cars at their command. Under such conditions claims against automobile insurance companies jumped overnight, as millions of cars, mostly rolling on worn-out tires, crowded every road and avenue. Repairs long postponed because of the shortage of parts, the lack of repair facilities, and the war-caused dearth of mechanics, were made at long last, as millions of Americans impatiently awaited the resumption of the assembly line and the appearance of new cars.

The great inrush of claims was common to all automobile insurance companies but it was greatly magnified in State Farm Mutual by the rapidly expanding number of policies in force. The very fact that business was so good intensified the seriousness of the mounting number of claims. That these were almost astronomical can be seen by a glance at the following figures.

Number of claims received

in 1944 293,045		
″ 1945 413,409	increase	41.1%
″ 1946 648,609	″	56.9%

At the same time the number of policies in force was increasing rapidly, jumping from 1,078,738 at the end of 1944 to 1,332,707 at the end of 1946.

The huge jump in the number of claims gave the mutual company the most severe headache it had ever had. There was absolutely no way for State Farm, or any company, to dam up this flood. It was beyond the industry's control. But a two-year cumulative increase of 121% in the number of claims received was a situation that called for immediate and concentrated attention. Ways and means had to be found to handle these claims after they reached the home office. But how?

This was not an easy question for the executives of State Farm to answer, for the easy answers were just not available. Obviously the first answer was to hire more help, to step up the size of the staff to handle the great inundation. And just as obviously the second two answers were to increase the office space and install new and adequate equipment. A look at the over-all situation as regards the insurance industry, and especially State Farm, at this crucial moment, will show just how and why—in the face of this sudden and uncontrollable influx of claims —the easy and obvious answers would not do.

The insurance industry, as we have seen, was not considered an essential industry, as far as the war effort was concerned. It had no priorities of any kind. It could hire only those not claimed by other industries with personnel priorities. It could command only such supplies, equipment, or space, as were not needed elsewhere. Not only could it not receive, but even much of what it had was taken away. Scores of key employees, of course, had been called into service by the country and even vital equipment had been drafted. Twenty percent of the typewriters in the various State Farm offices, for example, had been commandeered by the government. Other equipment was badly worn and needed replacement. In normal times the company would have expanded normally, increasing its office space in Bloomington and elsewhere where necessary, enlarging its staff as the ordinary demands of sales and claims necessitated.

What was needed, immediately after the war, was a breathing spell. But this State Farm was not to get. Instead, it was almost smothered by the sudden and unprecedented demands of its policyholders whose cars were literally falling to pieces now that there was gasoline to burn once again without restraint.

At this crucial period undoubtedly the most difficult situation with which State Farm had to contend was that of its personnel. Never in the history of the company had there been such a need for workers as there was now. But it was almost impossible to find workers of the high caliber which the tasks demanded and which, over the years, the company had insisted upon maintaining. Inasmuch as plans for the establishment of branch offices had been canceled during the war, when building restrictions made such expansion an impossibility, most of the recruiting of personnel in the early postwar days had to be done in the Bloomington area. As we have seen in an earlier chapter State Farm had long commanded the cream of the Bloomington labor supply, but now it had to take what it could get, and often those it had to hire were insufficiently educated, trained, or even adaptable to the kind of work they were required to do. The result was a necessary lowering of personnel standards by the company with an unfortunate but inevitable decline in the average ability and efficiency of the working force.

The dearth of top-notch workers was on all levels, but it was particularly noticeable among the supervisory personnel. A large number of trained supervisors were among the 951 employees who had been called into one or another branch of the service during the war. It was not until some time in 1947, or fourteen months after the end of the war, that all these men were back at their old desks. While they were away their work had been handled by temporary supervisors, who had borne the heavy burden of their added duties well in almost every instance, but who now cried for relief as the claims came pouring in. They were unable to keep work standards up to snuff or the morale of the workers at the pitch of efficiency which was needed to cope with the increased amount of business. This, of course, was a situation that was general throughout industry in those chaotic days and was not confined to State Farm.

Employee attitudes were not as good as they had been or as they were to become again when the crisis had passed. Workers were accustomed to the easy availability of jobs. Many of them were not then looking for stability or security, and they jumped from job to job at the slightest excuse. The turnover of workers at State Farm was at the highest level ever reached in the company's history. Situated as the home office was in the relatively small and close community of Bloomington and Normal, it was not long before everyone in the area knew that State Farm was seeking hundreds of new employees. Under these circumstances only the older and more faithful workers, who looked upon State Farm as their career, felt any compulsion to exert themselves. The others felt that a company which was hiring as rapidly as State Farm was then forced to do was not likely to release any except the most incompetent. This attitude did not make life any easier for the good, hard core of proven, conscientious, and reliable people, who had to contend with the easy attitude of the come-and-go workers of that period.

An indication of the problem of employee turnover can be seen in the fact that in 1944, when the average number of employees was 1,340, the number of persons hired was 745 and the number who left State Farm was 675. Two years later, when the average number of employees reached an all-time record of 3,126, the number hired was 1,779 and the number who left for other pastures was 1,355. In the crisis years of 1945 and 1946 State Farm hired more new employees than the average number of persons at work during the year, which meant that in those two years there was a highly abnormal rate of turnover in excess of 100%

per year. By 1948, however, various new plans of operation put into effect by management had brought the personnel problem back to normal.

In the midst of all this coming and going the company was also faced with a troublesome lack of space. The home office building was crowded to the eaves. It was sometimes next to impossible to move in any degree of comfort or even safety from one section to another. Not only was the home office jammed, but every available foot of space in Bloomington had been taken by State Farm to use as additional offices. The dining room of the Consistory Building, several blocks to the north, was a State Farm office. The ballroom of the Bloomington Club was jammed with files and filers. A former funeral parlor in the Beck Building was put to similar use, as was the floor of an ancient warehouse and the first floor of a small commercial hotel.

Equally severe was the problem of equipment. It was impossible to get enough desks, no matter where the company's purchasing agents looked. They had already mined every source, snatching them from second-hand dealers and firms going out of business. In some of the outlying offices makeshift desks were thrown together by local carpenters to serve as best they could. Every available out-moded old wooden filing cabinet in Bloomington had been bought—even the findable two-drawer files, which were highly inefficient for the use to which they had to be put. George Mecherle, looking upon this scene, must have longed for the days when he and Minnie Jones ran the company from two desks and a table in one room.

Naturally George Mecherle and his fellow executives were greatly disturbed. From the beginning State Farm had prided itself upon the speed and efficiency of its service to its policyholders. It had been George Mecherle's fundamental belief from the very beginning—indeed, it was this belief that had started him on the road to the insurance business—that an insurance company must be dedicated to service to its policyholders and that this dedication meant the difference between a successful and unsuccessful company. Even if there had not been other pressing reasons, the mere realization that if the situation were not quickly remedied the reputation of the company would suffer, would have been sufficient to force management to take drastic action. It knew that the policyholder could not be expected to understand why the machinery was faltering or to accept the excuse even if it were explained to him.

But there was one other vitally important reason why a sound revision of the methods of operation had to be undertaken at the first possible moment, revisions that would reach to the foundations of the State Farm structure and make it the sound and impregnable institution that it was rapidly to become.

George Mecherle, Adlai Rust, and the other leaders of State Farm not only had to consider the feelings of the policyholder but they had to see that the financial structure upon which the welfare of the policy-holder depended was kept in top-notch repair. It was a supreme necessity, then as always, that State Farm should be in such a sound financial position that it could immediately satisfy every contractual obligation without regard to the severity or frequency of the demands made against the company.

In the crisis years of 1945 and 1946 the increased frequency of claims and the increased cost of almost every type of claim produced a staggering underwriting loss for every casualty company in the industry. Some mutual companies at this time were threatened with liquidation and forced to curtail their writings, while a number of stock companies had to secure new working capital through the sale of stock. The total underwriting loss for the industry in those two years has been estimated at $300,000,000.

In its brief twenty-three years State Farm had grown so large that its share of this underwriting loss would have been about $15,000,000 for the two years if correct remedial actions had not been taken at the right moment by management. As it was, State Farm escaped with something less than a $9,000,000 loss in those twenty-four months. In the process the company lost about 40% of its surplus. For a few months in 1946 State Farm was losing money at the rate of $1,000,000 a month. The company's surplus by that time had dipped to about $10,000,000. The simple arithmetic of this was frightening. But through the concerted effort of almost everybody connected with State Farm, from George Mecherle down to the lowliest agent, the turning-point came in 1947, when the company's underwriting experience was once again raised to a satisfactory level. In the years that followed high profits were made and the surplus re-established at a level beyond impair, standing in excess of $70,000,000 in 1951. And this was done in spite of several rate reductions that were put into effect, aggregating about $21,000,000 annually.

One step toward decreasing the cost of claims was the decision not to accept any more applications for insurance on automobiles older than the 1938 models—then eight years old. Applications from persons under twenty-one years of age, unless members of households having their cars insured by State Farm, were also rejected. Nor were applications accepted from people over seventy years of age. Stricter rules regarding mortgaged and financed cars were placed into effect, and regulations regarding information on the present conditions of automobiles were tightened.

To further the general reduction of claims State Farm joined in national efforts to educate the public about the huge cost to themselves that carelessness on the highways brought about. Beginning in 1946, the company's national advertising and sales promotion was largely directed toward this end. It stressed the fact that even State Farm protection—"still one of the greatest bargains obtainable"—would cost more if the national accident rate continued to rise. The company co-operated with such organizations as the National Safety Council and the International Association of Chiefs of Police in their accelerated safety drives. Its advertising department worked with State Farm agents everywhere in conducting local safe-driving campaigns, as one by one the bright new cars—fresh from the assembly lines—began to appear on the streets and highways.

As these new cars began multiplying, an old problem more or less dormant during the war again became active. "We would be blind to reality," Mr. Parsons had warned in 1945, "if we did not take into consideration the threat to our business which stems from the announced purpose of the national finance companies to push their insurance services to the utmost when financing automobile purchases, even to the point of requiring their customers to cancel existing insurance in favor of taking out a policy with their insurance affiliates."

And so the promotion of the State Farm Bank Plan—the company's co-operative arrangement with local banks and lending agencies—once again assumed a leading role, with approximately 3,000 financial institutions, well distributed throughout State Farm territory, being made available to any State Farm policyholder who might contemplate the financed purchase of a new car.

Serious study, too, was given to the matter of rates. In spite of steadily increasing costs State Farm had effected no major rate changes during the war years. The postwar economy, however, dictated the need for revisions. In 1946 two general rate increases were put into effect in the hope of setting the rate level at a point where it would maintain a reasonable relationship between the surplus and the annual premium writing. And a general study was undertaken to determine the need for additional adjustments which resulted in the correction of some territorial inequities which had come into being over the years.

Here one of the fundamentals of George Mecherle's basic plan proved its merit. Because of the six-month term for premium payments, rate changes could be translated rapidly into dollars. With higher rates necessary, policyholders would pay them only as their existing insurance expired. In companies using annual policies, a full year would elapse before all policies could be converted to a new rate basis. Under the State Farm plan, this process could be completed in half the time, and funds needed to balance the mounting cost of settling claims quickly began to flow into State Farm's offices. The rate structure, in other words, could be responsive to changing conditions. And it was a two-way advantage, because as early as 1948—far ahead of almost all other automobile insurance companies—State Farm was able to launch its rate reduction program. Successive downward rate changes in each year from 1948 to 1951 added up to savings of $21,000,000 per year, figured on the company's then existing premium volume.

But the fundamental answers to the problems which management had to face in these years were not to be found alone in these measures, important though they were at the time. A long-range, revitalizing plan of action had to be devised, one which would not only cure the immediate disturbances but one so carefully thought out that it would forestall their repetition in years to come.

The situation within the organization was chaotic. One of the company's executives who went through those difficult days described it vividly when he said: "At that time you could find as many ways of doing a job as there were people doing it."

There were memoranda galore—but few people knew where to find information on any particular subject. There were files, but if they were not your own they were useless. Many of the employees, who were supposed to have complete information regarding their phase of the business, did not have it, often through no fault of their own. There was no manual of procedure. Functions which overlapped among the various departments were co-ordinated erratically and sometimes not at all. Anyone who felt he needed it could create a new form, and there were many forms serving the same purpose. There was no control point from which information could emanate and be distributed to the interested department heads. In spite of this those who had to issue rules and regulations, announce changes, and dictate policies, did the best they could. Many a Saturday afternoon was spent by harried executives not on the golf course but in informal planning sessions, held in a vain effort to lighten their burden of confusing work.

In the minds of some of the top management people these questions were formulating: Where were the flow-of-work charts? Why were there only a few individuals who carried all this information around in their heads? Why didn't someone extract this material from the minds and the files of the few, and put it in one place where it could be found and used by all?

George Mecherle was aware of this and knew the time had come when his associates would have to put their minds to work not just on how to run their own departments but how to run the business as a co-ordinated whole. He and his top aides gave days and nights of serious consideration to the seemingly overwhelming problem. What they were doing, in effect, was plotting a revolution. The times were crucial and the remedy must be drastic. The old order—which they had created—having become disorder, must give way to new.

August 12, 1946, was a day of great significance in the history of State Farm. On that day, as chairman of the board, George Mecherle issued orders creating a committee to study all the present problems of State Farm operations and find lasting answers. Twenty-one persons were named to this committee, which was under the chairmanship of J. H. Parsons. It went to work with a will. Each day it reported to George Mecherle on its progress. The next six months were hectic, as every aspect of State Farm procedure was meticulously reviewed at meetings, which were held almost daily, from mid-August until the following February.

At about the same time another committee of younger executives—a sort of task force assigned to blueprint the new technique of operation —was set up with Edward B. Rust as a chairman. Other members were Royal J. Bartrum, E. R. Warmoth, A. L. Baumann, and Elizabeth Lanham. "Bud" Rust, the son of Adlai Rust, executive vice president and for many years right-hand man of George Mecherle, was an ideal choice for this exacting task. Although at that time he had been with State Farm only five years, the younger Rust had already become well versed in the inner operations of the company. After being graduated from the Bloomington schools he had attended Stanford University, where he had been graduated *cum laude* in 1940. There he was made a member of Phi Beta Kappa, the national scholastic society. He had specialized in economics. Starting in 1941 at State Farm he had attended the claims school before starting his actual career under the late Robert Mead in the actuarial department. There, and in later assignments with G. E. Mecherle, secretary and director of personnel, he had acquired a sound background in accounting, labor relations, money and banking, public finance, and statistics. He had helped put into operation the State Farm cost-of-living bonus plan, which was later to be widely copied by other companies. As he moved through such departments as the purchasing, payroll, building and maintenance, and traffic divisions, and as he had performed the duties of the secretary's office, he had acquired a sound, general knowledge of office management and the top-to-bottom operation of State Farm.

One of the first things these committees did was to look into the future and estimate the company's potential growth as a necessary guide for their plans and programs. As of 1946, there were 1,026 full-time and 257 part-time employees working in the home office, engaged solely in handling the business of the automobile insurance mutual. These employees were responsible for the 968,134 policies then in force. Assuming, with good reason, that there would be approximately 3,000,000 automobile insurance policies in force by 1954, and that a constant ratio would be maintained between the Bloomington home office and the California branch at Berkeley, the company would be handling an average of 2,400,000 policies—or four-fifths of the total business. To do this would mean the need for 2,500 full-time and approximately 650 part-time employees—in Bloomington alone! And experience had taught that the local labor market could not fill this demand. If the life insurance objective were met, and if the fire company should reach its predicted $10,000,000 annual premium level, close to 1,000 more employees would have to be found to process this business. All told, the committee estimated that—even after taking into consideration the use of new and better machinery and the better training of employees—the company would have to increase its Bloomington staff by at least 1,500, which, under the known circumstances, would hardly be possible. Furthermore, to house these additional workers, it would have to double its present office space.

The committee estimated that even though higher wage scales might have to be met in some branch offices, the inability to find workers in

Bloomington would minimize the importance of this factor. Furthermore, "offices located in areas where there is a concentration of business are better able to give service to the public and the agent." And that intangible thing called "service," which cannot be measured in dollars and cents, had to be considered. For "service," from the very beginning, had been an integral part of the State Farm system.

As a result of its work this committee came up with a detailed plan for the establishment in strategic places throughout the country of several branch offices. Basically the plan called for a branch office for every 100,000 policies in force if there was in the proposed territory a business potential of 250,000 policies. Each branch was to have a certain amount of autonomy, although close ties to the home office were to be maintained and all matters of general policy would still be determined in Bloomington. Although, as it worked out over the next few years, the offices were not established exactly as suggested in the original report, the fundamental setup proposed by this committee was carefully followed out.

The first branch office was established soon after the committee reported. This was the St. Paul-Minneapolis office, which opened for business early in January, 1947. The next month saw the departments that handled the North and South Dakota and Montana business at work in the new quarters. Within the next sixty days an entire office force of new employees was recruited and their training was started. A total of 314 persons—70% of whom were hired in the Twin City area—were working before the middle of the year.

In October, 1947, a similar branch office was set up at Lincoln, Nebraska. Three years later, in April, 1950, the Michigan office was established at Marshall. This was followed by the setting up of the Dallas, Texas, office in October, 1951. In the summer of 1952 the Charlottesville, Virginia, office was opened. All this activity was a part of a long-range plan for expansion which, as this is written, is still going forward. The year 1953 saw the opening of the Nashville, Tennessee, branch. A new site for this branch was chosen in 1954 at Murfreesboro, Tennessee, a few miles from Nashville, with occupancy planned for 1955. Meanwhile, other branches were established during 1954 at Jacksonville, Florida, and at Birmingham, Alabama. A Southern California branch at Santa Ana, California, was under construction at the end of that year, and sites for new Pennsylvania and Missouri branches were under consideration.

Soon after the August 12, 1946, directive from George Mecherle the internal revolution got under way, with the result that the premium department was established in September. This was the first step toward ultimate co-ordination and modernization of all procedures. Prior to its establishment there had been four major fronts on which State Farm functioned. These were the agency department, the accounting department, the underwriting department, and the claims. Each was separate unto itself. Each had many functions it had acquired over the years but which, in reality, belonged elsewhere.

Typical of the confusion of system was the underwriting department, whose major responsibility was determining the acceptability and classification of risks. But in addition to this all-important task it also had charge of the issuing of policies, the billing of renewal premiums, collection, and the maintenance of many important files. With the setting up of the new premium department the underwriting department was freed for the first time to carry on the work it was designed for, without the added responsibilities.

The key to State Farm operation is a little piece of cardboard known as the "x-card." This is the card on which is written all the basic information about policy and policyholder necessary for keeping a complete record from the date the agent sold the application to the final payment and termination of the contract between State Farm and the policyholder. Until September, 1946, these cards were kept in various places, and often moved from one department to another, with resulting confusion. Because of this lax system it sometimes happened that a new applicant would receive, perhaps even in the same mail, notice of termination of his policy from the underwriting department and a premium notice from the collection department. But with the setting up of the premium department the x-cards were for the first time "frozen" or anchored in one central place. Removal of them for any purpose was forbidden. Check clerks from other departments might come to the premium department to consult them, but never to take them away. Not even George Mecherle was allowed to take one to his desk. If he, or anyone else, needed information it was supplied; but the original x-card stayed where it belonged.

But the establishment of the premium department and the "freezing" of the x-card did not end the woes of State Farm. In this period of chaos and confusion there were no clear-cut descriptions of the duties of the then existing underwriting, premium, claims, and accounting departments. Sometime after its establishment George Mecherle called a meeting of the planning committee and told them what he had in his mind. He may have been thinking back to those early days when he and E. A. Meyers and Minnie Jones were struggling with what then seemed insuperable problems but which, in the light of the State Farm of 1947, seemed so simple and easy.

"Let us assume," he said, "that we are not trying to correct our past mistakes. Let's put it this way—that we are about to start all over, *build a new company*. As you fellows go about your work remember there is nothing sacred here, nothing that can't be done away with. Be as rough as you want. The only thing I insist upon is that you do not depart from the basic principles on which State Farm has been built—the membership plan, the continuous policy, the six-months' premium, and the happiness of our agency force. Those are fundamental. Beyond them there are no restrictions. So, go to it."

With these sweeping instructions, and knowing from experience that George Mecherle meant what he said, the committees went to work. On July 15, E. B. Rust presented the first suggestions for a system of over-all reorganization as worked out by himself and R. J. Bartrum and C. A. Marquardt. This was designed to provide a more even flow of work within the various divisions and departments—but the subcommittee which devised it warned that it was only a "patch plan" and was not recommended as permanent procedure. It did, however, further alleviate the irritations arising from the maintenance by two or more departments of files on one policyholder, which, as we have seen, often resulted in one department billing a policyholder while the other was returning his money. It was adopted as a temporary measure.

But of even greater importance in getting the company out of chaos, than the acquiring of physical facilities and the adoptions of temporary plans, was the scheme of operation that became known as Plan Two. This was housekeeping at its best. This was the work of many persons, from George Mecherle downward, all of whom, as Mr. Parsons put it, "calmly and dispassionately employed their own knowledge of the business" to analyze the situation "and determine and apply the necessary corrections" in those most trying days. The plan itself was put into blueprint shape by a subcommittee of six, headed by E. R. Warmoth. The others were J. K. McLean, A. H. Dierkes, C. A. Marquardt, R. J. Bartrum, and L. L. Cox. It was presented to the company on July 21, 1947, six days after the "patch plan" was put to use.

At the time Plan Two was evolved State Farm operated on the basis of four large functional departments: agency, underwriting, claims, and investments. Two of these—underwriting and claims—had grown to such size that they had become cumbersome and unmanageable when subjected to undue pressure. The new plan was to break this old system down and set up a more flexible one in its place.

After much study it was agreed that the way to do this most efficiently was to subdivide the organization into small geographical units. Each subdivision would do its own underwriting, write its policies, handle its premium collections, adjust its claims, and render general service to members in its areas. It would also do initial key-punch accounting. Each unit was to be in the charge of a qualified manager, trained by State Farm in State Farm methods.

There were a number of advantages to this system over that then in use. The two most fundamental to the continued smooth running of State Farm business were these:

It brought high-level supervision closer to the employees.

It brought together the related underwriting and claims functions of an area and gave these departments much easier and quicker access to local information necessary to their efficient operation.

On August 8, 1947—two years after the ending of the war had brought about the conditions of crisis within State Farm—Plan Two was adopted by the management and put into immediate operation in the Indiana division, the oldest in the company. So well did it work, so quickly did the long confusion end, that within six weeks it was determined to carry the plan into all the other units of State Farm. From the very beginning results were gratifying in every respect. The log jam was broken, work was brought quickly up to date. The strained and harried looks on the supervisors' faces disappeared and smiles showed for the first time in months. Employee morale improved up and down the line. Work standards were once again raised to State Farm level.

The plan was not merely of temporary value, but of lasting effect. Four years later the pudding was shown as proof to the State Farm members in a factual report made at the annual meeting on June 11, 1951.

"The operating divisions of State Farm Mutual Automobile Insurance Company serviced an average of more than 1,000 policies per employee during this year," the report stated. "The previous record was 840 policies per employee which was the average for the 12 months ending June 1, 1950. The 1,000 policies per employee average of the past 12 months is an increase of 19% over the old record of 840. This new record of 1,000 policies per employee is an increase of 97% over the 500 policies per employee which existed when Plan Two was adopted and the operating divisions established. . . .

"Plan Two was adopted for the purpose of increasing the efficiency of our office operations. When the plan was adopted the divisions employed 2,471 persons to service 1,284,704 policies. As of May, 1951, the divisions employed 1,823 people to service 1,866,428 policies. In other words under the new Plan the employees in the operating divisions decreased 26%, while the policies in force increased 45%."

The emergency situation, the great crisis that was thrust upon State Farm at the close of the war by circumstances beyond its control, was ended. The problems were solved by prompt action from within. The operating system that was devised in those hectic days not only proved itself from the start but has shown that it possessed the flexibility necessary to the continuing growth of State Farm.

Further indication of the long-range success of this internal revolution may be seen in the following statistics: Comparing August, 1947, the date of the inception of Plan 2, with July, 1954, State Farm showed only a 45% increase in employees but a 145% increase in policies, or a 69% increase in policies per employee.

15

AS SURE AS SUNSHINE

From his large, comfortable office on the eighth floor of the north wing
of the home office, to which five new floors had been added in 1947,
George Mecherle watched the executives of his choice and training
grapple with the problems that momentarily had threatened the security
of the business he had founded a quarter of a century ago. He had im-
plicit faith in their ability and, as they reported to him constantly on
their findings and decisions, he knew that they would come through "as
sure as sunshine"—as he put it in his farm-grown phrase. But to him the
romance of the business was not now in the office, any more than it
had been in the old days when he was constantly out on the road—the
rough roads and the muddy roads of the farm country—selling State
Farm and exhorting others to sell it, too. He was always at heart the
salesman, although his understanding of the techniques of office management had grown with the years and he knew as much as anyone
about what made the wheels go around.

And so he sat there, dreaming and planning. One great worry disturbed him, wrinkled the brow of his high forehead under the hair that had grown white with the advancing years. Like every other business-man he was uncertain of the direction the economy of the country would take. The road to the new normalcy looked rougher, indeed, than it had seemed in the twenties when corn was dropping from $1.80 to 50 cents a bushel and he was dreaming and scheming about starting a new farmers' insurance business against the advice of all his business-men friends at the Bloomington Club. If, as a great many economists predicted as the war ended in the Pacific, a serious postwar depression was in the near offing, he knew that the automobile insurance business might well experience rough going. With this probability in mind he turned his attention to the State Farm Life Insurance Company.

When the life company had been founded in 1929 it was in large measure in answer to the demands of the agency force. A great many of the agents had felt that this additional line would not only add to their income but would aid them in selling automobile insurance. From the start the company had been successful. This was largely because of the imaginative leadership of its volatile director, Morris G. Fuller—another one of those executives whose choice was due to the selecting genius of George Mecherle.

Morris Fuller had come to State Farm from a wide experience in the life insurance field. He first heard of State Farm and its then president in Michigan where, acting for a life company, he had negotiated a trust agreement for the administration of the Michigan State Farm Bureau's funds. The documents were all signed when the Farm Bureau—badly in need of funds—asked him to suspend all activity until the members could hear the message of a Mr. Mecherle who, it was reported, had got the Indiana Farm Bureau out of a bad financial hole by the sale of automobile insurance policies among the farmers of the state. A week later, when Mr. Fuller returned to Lansing, he found his deal was off as a result of George Mecherle's convincing sales talk to the farm organiza-tion. That was in 1926.

During the next three years Morris Fuller often heard of the amazing man from Bloomington whose company by then had invaded nearly half the states of the union. But their paths did not cross until he re-ceived a call from Erwin Meyers, who asked him if he would consider a proposition for organizing a life company for State Farm.

"On my next visit to Chicago," he has written, "I called at his office and made an engagement to meet G. J. Mecherle. I was curious, of

course, about the plan for a life insurance company but more particularly about the plan he had installed for the Michigan State Farm Bureau. On having dinner with him in Chicago the conversation was
wholly along promotional and agency lines. He evidently had made
whatever investigation as to my experience he desired and had whatever
recommendation 'Hank' Meyers gave him, and so G.J.M. did not even
ask if I thought I could manage a life insurance company. Negotiations
for the job consumed two minutes, with him telling me how much he
would pay and my stating what my title should be and when I could
report for duty in Bloomington. Our visit was a discussion of whether
State Farm Auto agents could sell life insurance, and the experiences
of other life companies in dealing with part-time agents, the use of farm
organizations as State agents and the monetary benefit to them as a
general good to agriculture, and the need of State Farm for a more
permanent income for the local agent."

With Mr. Fuller as director, the company commenced doing business
as a wholly owned subsidiary of State Farm Mutual on April 19, 1929.*
Now, at the end of 1945, it had $169,946,833 insurance in force. While
State Farm's business was far more than that of many independent life
insurance companies, it still was not sufficient to satisfy George Mecherle. In 1945 he began studying the situation, much as he had studied
the entire picture of the automobile company in 1939, and came up
with the belief that State Farm Life should be a billion-dollar company.
With this ambitious goal Mr. Fuller agreed.

As a matter of fact, the idea of a drive to put State Farm Life on the
insurance map was conceived almost before the "million or more in
'44" automobile campaign had ended. In July, 1944, M. S. Judy, state
director of West Virginia, who had discussed the possibility of such a
campaign with A. W. Tompkins, some weeks previously, addressed the
state agents' convention on the subject "The Viewpoint of a State
Director Concerning State Farm Objectives and Their Attainments."
After reviewing the Million-Policy campaign and the manner in which

* The State Farm Life Insurance Company was organized as a legal reserve life insurance company April 8, 1929. At the annual agency convention in Bloomington
in January, 1929, the matter of the life insurance company was discussed with the
state directors, district agents and local agents in attendance. The entire group was
given an opportunity to vote as to whether or not steps should be taken for the organization of a life company. An overwhelming majority was in favor of this move,
with the result that the details were worked out to make the desires of the agency
force a quick reality.

it had stimulated many agents to an unprecedented activity, Mr. Judy urged that serious consideration be given to a campaign aimed at the same goal in life insurance.

Mr. Judy's idea was not new, for most of those concerned with the progress of State Farm had given thought over the years to ways and means of building the life company up to a position comparable to the automobile company. Initiation of the so-called "Paymaster" policy in the 1930's had resulted in the writing of a considerable amount of business in a comparatively short time, but this and other efforts had been of a piecemeal nature and had not been a part of a comprehensive plan such as was now being contemplated.

The rest of the summer of 1945 G.J.M. devoted to thinking about the proposal and in September addressed a long letter to all the state directors asking their frank opinion as to the feasibility of attempting such an undertaking. He pointed out that, in the recent history of insurance in America, the record of achievement by State Farm was one that would be hard to surpass. The five-page, single-spaced letter then reviewed the Million-Policy program, pointed out with appropriate statistics the status of life insurance with State Farm Mutual policyholders, and made clear that in his opinion the prospect for success in the next few years was tremendous if the agents would work for it with the same enthusiasm as they had shown for the auto company between 1938 and 1944.

Mr. Mecherle's challenge was the subject of two days of serious discussion at a special conference of state directors in December, 1945. Every angle of the proposal was discussed in detail and the conference finally voted to adopt the project. At once the machinery was set in motion. Training programs were arranged. Promotion schemes were originated. And within a few months the drive for "A Billion or More in '54" was under way. This, of course, was to be a purpose more difficult of accomplishment than that of the previous campaign, for it was to be supplemental to keeping the automobile company at the very top of all automobile casualty companies in the world. The first few months indicated that this was no more chimerical a goal than the 1944 campaign, for the life company ended the year with a new high of $217,922,155 —or a gain of nearly $48,000,000 ($47,975,322) insurance in force.

The good start of 1946 was not carried over into the next few succeeding years. The year 1948 saw the drive slow down and the next year saw it lag seriously behind. One of the reasons why George Mecherle had expected better results in the selling of life insurance was the proved ability of the part-time agents to sell automobile policies. But now it was obvious that these men—particularly the "old-timers" of the agency force—had not been trained for the more highly specialized field of life insurance. When, after considerable study of the situation, it became apparent that "something must be added," the first step was the inauguration of the department of agency training and education under the supervision of Henry Keller, Jr.—then assistant state director in California.

In September of 1949 the state directors held a conference in Cincinnati. From the viewpoint of many, including A. W. Tompkins, the head of the agency force, this was one of the most important meetings in State Farm history, because there it was decided that it was "imperative for the local agent's job to be definitized, personalized and individualized if we hope to attain success." At this meeting the executive officers of State Farm were convinced that they could no longer "deal with men in the agency force on a group basis but rather that management must turn its attention to the individual agent."

Following the crucial Cincinnati meeting a committee was set up charged with the responsibility of coming forth with concrete proposals for implementing the decisions reached at that time. This committee consisted of Adlai H. Rust, executive vice president, R. P. Mecherle, president of the automobile insurance company, Morris G. Fuller, vice president of the life company, and Mr. Tompkins. Long hours and many hot debates followed but, as one of the group said, "when we got our conclusions reduced to writing, we had a plan." For State Farm it was a radical plan and for George Mecherle, who was to give it his stamp of approval, it was a new departure. This change in State Farm philosophy and operation consisted of a transfer of the emphasis from a part-time agency force to a full-time agency force.

As a long-term agency objective the committee agreed as follows:

The . . . objective of State Farm Agency Department is to establish an agency force comprising men and women qualified adequately to serve the insurance needs of the public as representatives of State Farm insurance and with each individual producing a satisfactory volume of quality business in reasonable relation to the possibilities of the respective community.

Out of this generalization came the conception of the State Farm Career Man. As originally conceived, a Career Man was one who paid for a minimum of $100,000 life insurance annually, who turned in 100 automobile applications, and who (in a protected town) sold at least $1,000 of fire premiums. This obviously meant that such an agent would have to devote his entire time to State Farm, making full use of the entire organization—automobile, fire and life. Equally obvious—to men like the Messrs. Tompkins and Keller, who had made a thorough study of the agency situation—was the fact that many of the agents of State Farm were not qualified, by aptitude or experience, to become Career Men. Others whose livelihood came in part from farming or other work could not devote the time that this undertaking required. Still others did not want to write life insurance. Also obvious, however, was the belief that many of them, if given proper training and shown the advantages of making State Farm a career and not just a part-time occupation, would be able to exceed even the goals set forth.

This meant a revision of State Farm philosophy, as far as agents were concerned. It meant the end of the days of "hire and hope," as one executive put it, when the company hired a man, put a rate book in his hand, and hoped he would come through with sales. It was a great step forward in the evolution of the agency force that had really started when G.J.M. and Hank Meyers considered raising the level of agents by hiring high school superintendents. Basically it meant that from now on State Farm would start building its agency force less with the idea of pure production than with the idea of creating a permanent staff of trained and able men who would become an integral part of State Farm itself.

The ideal agent was to be a man with at least a high-school education, but preferably a college man. He was to be a man of integrity and standing in his community. Once he joined State Farm he was to be educated in the techniques of insurance as well as trained in the skills of selling it, so that he would be thoroughly aware of the nature of the product he was offering the public. He was to know the intricacies of life insurance, a field where policies are far more complex than in the automobile field. And he was to know about fire insurance.

Henry Keller had made some steps toward the educating of agents while he had been in the Iowa division before the war. After leaving the service he went to the California state office where he was able to further his ideas along this line. Mr. Tompkins, as a member and former director of the Life Insurance Agency Management Association of Hartford, Connecticut, had kept himself up-to-date on national developments in agency training, a field of study which had been receiving more and more attention throughout the insurance industry in recent years. They were readily able, when the time came, to convince George Mecherle of the need for their proposed program. Encouraged by the Chief, they went ahead and, in June, 1949, the first agency school, known as the Basic Life School, was opened in Bloomington. This was quickly followed by similar courses in North Carolina and California. It consisted of a three-day concentrated session, followed by eight weeks of personally supervised instruction in the field.

When this school was put in operation there were just forty-five men in the entire agency force who met the standards of a Career Man. The following year there were 243 men who qualified.

The policy of minimum qualifications for recruiting of new agents, of setting high standards for those who were recruited, and of the personal training and supervision of all those added to the force, paid off in more ways than one. It greatly increased the annual earnings of the average agent and bettered the morale of the entire agency force. It drew the agent closer to the State Farm organization by making him realize that he is an integral part of it. The alternative of this system, of course, would have been the hiring of thousands of agents, the grim driving of them to achieve quotas during high-pressure campaigns. The management of State Farm found that the system devised in 1949 was far superior from all points of view.

Once the State Farm organization had committed itself to the new concept of training and education as the essential basis of continuing production it had to find ways and means of putting the philosophy into practical effect. Since its 1949 beginnings this program has evolved into a highly developed system of procuring and developing agents of high caliber, of which the company can be proud. In order to accomplish this the agency department has in recent years assumed four major roles. These are: field consultation; training and education; promotion (sales, advertising, conservation and market research); and administrative services.

At the higher level is field consultation. Three regional agency vice presidents, under this setup, split between them general supervision of the far-flung agency operations of State Farm. Each of these three executives is in constant consultation with the state directors of the geographical regions to which he is assigned. On his shoulders rest several responsibilities. One of them is supervision of the selection of managers who are, in many ways, the key to the Career Man system. It is the manager who finds and trains the agents whose sales activities keep State Farm at the top of the list of automobile insurance companies. The problem of manpower development is one of the principal concerns of the regional vice president. The appointment and termination of agents goes under his scrutiny; the financing of managers and local agents, which must meet with home office approval, passes through his hands. He works with the state director in planning meetings, conferences, conventions, contests, and campaigns. He keeps his eye on the all-important training schools. To him, at his desk in the home office, the state director first turns whenever problems of policy or function arise.

The duties of the training and education department are manifold. But they are all directed toward one goal: the training of Career Men who will succeed in their full-time job of selling the three State Farm staples: automobile, life and fire insurance.

From the beginning, as we have seen, when George Mecherle selected and trained his own crew, the choice of proper agents was considered of utmost importance. In the old days no lightning-rod salesman need apply. Although the methods used today are far more scientific than they were then, the same basic principle guides—good character. For that famous sixth sense which George Mecherle applied with such startling success there have today been substituted the best tools of modern business psychology as devised in the workshops of the Life Insurance Agency Management Association. Through these it is possible, at an early stage, to winnow the wheat from the chaff and to find young men who show those natural talents which, when properly directed, can make top-notch agents and managers.

The procedure followed in creating a Career Man is a flexible one. It is based on the old but sound theory that no two men are alike, and that while all men may be created equal they do not continue through life along parallel lines. They do not travel at the same speed—nor can they all be taught from the same book. Thus the State Farm educational system is geared as much as possible to the development of the individual.

The choice of the individual is the responsibility of the manager, and since this initial test is the most important he must himself be well-trained and educated. He must not only be prepared with the knowledge, skills and habits in which he is going to train his agents but he must know how to train them. He must be an educator, versed in how men learn and how they develop skills. He must be able to teach them in the classroom and out in the field. In the first place he must impart to them the theory behind their potential career; in the second place he must show them pragmatically the ways of putting theory into practice.

Organization of the job training for the state directors and managers is the function of the training and education department, which must furnish the materials that are needed, establish field-tested procedures of selling, and equip and train both state directors and managers to use these methods effectively. The process is essentially simple but it is one arrived at only after much study on the part of men such as A. W. Tompkins and Morris Fuller, president of the life company and a nationally recognized student of insurance techniques.

Once a potential Career Man has been chosen as a trainee by a director he is given a loose-leaf, printed training-and-study course, built entirely around the activities of the State Farm multiple-line agent. At the beginning stage, which lasts approximately six months, the trainee and manager work closely together on an individual basis. Their joint efforts include study work, field projects, practice drills and, since this is designed as a practical course, actual selling experience in the field.

The service course teaches the trainee how to read and explain the contracts he has to sell, how to apply them to the needs of all types of clients, and how to conduct his business with the various branches of the automobile, life or fire companies with which he will be in contact in the future. Once the trainee has mastered this he is introduced to the esoterics of salesmanship, from "approach" to the keeping of proper records and the nurturing of clients.

All this is preparatory work. Next comes the basic school, which is conducted at the state office level. Here those trainees who have shown an aptitude for the State Farm business are brought together in small groups to study sales procedures and processes. The entire school is taught by managers who have their own agents in the school under the supervision and with the assistance of the state office staff. But, before a basic school may be set up in any state, its managers and their staffs must themselves have attended a special "pilot school," conducted on a statewide basis by agency department personnel, who coach the teachers in what they will have to teach.

The basic school and career training consists of four and a half days in the classroom and eight weeks in the field. Having successfully undergone this, a potential agent may be nominated by his manager to attend the intermediate school in career training. This calls for a study course of nine weeks followed by three and a half intensified days in the classroom and twelve weeks in the field.

But this is not all. An agent who has gone through this may be named by his manager for more advanced training in a career school. The first such school is planned for 1955. In this the class sessions will last for two weeks, conducted by highly trained personnel at the Bloomington headquarters. At these sessions advanced phases of all the multiple-line business will be thoroughly explained to the student. Specialists from each company—automobile, life and fire—will assist in conducting workshops, clinics, and special seminars during this fortnight of application. Following this, a specially planned twelve-week period of field training will be required, under the supervision of the agent's manager.

In addition to this the agency department in 1954 began developing a management training program. Here potential managers will be given a "postgraduate" course of instruction followed by field training under the supervision of state directors and the regional vice presidents. Also, each year, qualified agents are selected for enrollment at the insurance institutes of Purdue University and Southern Methodist University.

Closely aligned within the agency department with the training and education program is the promotion department, which is forever busy creating new ideas and passing upon and preparing for use those that are continually being submitted to the department from agents and managers in the field. In this department State Farm also maintains a cooperative advertising program under which the companies absorb 40% of the advertising expense incurred by local agents. This is administered by the promotion department, which prepares and distributes copy that has been approved by management, and selects advertising specialties for use by the agents. Publication and circulation of the *Reflector* is another responsibility of the promotion department. Distribution of agents' supplies, sales aids, and contest awards is also handled by the promotion department, as is all direct-mail advertising. The conservation department, also under promotion, has the responsibility of surveying loss ratios, disseminating termination reports on automobile insurance and persistency reports on life insurance. And it promotes the bank finance plan that has been in existence since the 1930's. In the field of market research it recommends programs, conducts research projects, ascertains production potentials, studies the cost and methods of insurance distribution and evaluates current results with potential possibilities.

Some indication of the successful manner in which the Career Man concept has worked is to be found in certain statistics that tell a story exciting both for State Farm and for its agents.

In 1948 State Farm had forty-six agents paying for a minimum of $100,000 of life insurance. This number dropped in 1949. But after 1950 when the company announced that it would designate as a Career Man every agent writing during the year a minimum of 100 automobile applications, $100,000 paid-for life insurance, and $1,000 of fire premiums, a change began to take place.

In 1950, the first full year of the Career Man concept, 243 agents paid for a minimum of $100,000 of life insurance, nearly five times the number in 1949. The next year, the number of $100,000 producers jumped to 338. In 1952 the number reached 563.

In 1953, 1,017 agents paid for the minimum of $100,000 of life insurance. A total of 1,007 qualified for the Leaders Club with the necessary minimum in automobile, life and fire insurance, an increase of 458, or 83%, over 1952. Of these, 998 were local agents, and they produced 28.2% of the company total in automobile insurance, 72.8% of the life insurance and 37% of the fire premiums. These men averaged 299.6 automobile applications, $118,654 paid-for life insurance on the installment basis and $3,419 of fire premiums. Out of the 1,007 Leaders, 69 were appointed agents in 1953 and 173 completed their first full calendar year.

The average earning of these 998 local agents was $8,745. A total of 173 first-year agents earned an average of $5,423 through their sales of State Farm policies, while thirteen ten-year men—all local agents—were within less than $500 of the $15,000-a-year bracket.

When one contrasts these figures alone with the $44,839 gross earnings of the State Farm Mutual Automobile Insurance Company of Bloomington, Illinois, at the end of its first year of operation on June 30, 1923 —the thirty-two-year rise of George Mecherle's "honest little insurance company" staggers the imagination.

16

RETURN TO THE FARM

One time George Mecherle was asked the question put sooner or later to all successful businessmen, "What is the secret of your success?"

"A man," he said, "has to live and sleep with his business if he wants to make a go of it. You have to take it home with you at night, so you can lie there in the darkness and figure out what you can do to improve it. In fact, you have to become sort of a 'nut' about it, so that you become so enthused that you will bore your friends talking about it. You have to be a one-man crusade."

This he believed and this he acted upon, to a great extent. In the insurance business he was widely known—and far from Bloomington—as a "crusader." The agents of State Farm, especially when they went out under his leadership to break all existing records during the campaign for a million or more policies, also had that reputation. They took their cue from him. But for all his absorption in the affairs of State Farm, he did not allow himself to become a onesided man.

Although George Mecherle never had a hobby that took up much of his time or attention—such as golf (which he did not play)—he managed to find time for some outside interests. Mostly his relaxation came at the card tables in the drab rooms of the Bloomington Club, where the leading businessmen of Bloomington gather each noon for quick lunches and long sessions of rummy or bridge. He was a good, and somewhat ruthless, player of the club's favorite game—"black deuce rummy." One night a disastrous fire broke out in the administration building of Illinois Wesleyan University. Everyone else rushed to the windows to watch the flames and smoke. Deserted by his cronies, he too watched for a few minutes and then said, with mock serious impatience, "Come on, let's get the game started. That fire's going to cost us $70,000 but it won't cost you a cent. Deal the cards."

If a friendly but stiff game of cards was his favorite means of escape and relaxation, his real "outside interest" was agriculture. He never quite got the hayseed out of his hair. But his was not entirely a sentimental attachment—the nostalgic reversal of a farm boy who, after years away from the barnyard, buys a "place in the country" where he can play at being a "farmer." His was an active interest which was strongly with him from the day he sold off his stock, turned his old home and acreage over to a tenant, and moved from the fields he had ploughed since boyhood to find new horizons elsewhere. He had never let his land go.

Instead, over the years, he added to it—as an investment, of course, but also because he loved it. The "Old Place," where he had grown up under the stern but kindly eyes of Chris and Susanna and Uncle Fred, came into his possession, and what perhaps could be called his most absorbing passion was its preservation and improvement. It was, in its way, his shrine. Into its development he poured a great deal of money, but long before its death it had paid him back many times the amount of his investment, not only in money but in satisfaction. It was, he felt, his filial duty. Land, in the eyes of his farming forebears, was not something to worship but something to use. He used his well.

When he had been a working farmer he had used his own land so well that on the day after he sold off his livestock there were thirty-seven persons begging to take it over on a rental basis. He kept these acres, and the house where his children had been born, in the best condition and later turned them over to his oldest son Ramond, who farmed it profitably until his sudden death in 1954. But it was for the Old Place that he had the most enduring attachment—the old homestead where Chris, the immigrant, had taken his Ohio-born bride so many years before. After this became his, following the death of Uncle Fred, a succession of tenant farmers worked it under his watchful eye. Some were good, others were not so good, but eventually he found a man to run it who was to develop it and its adjacent holdings into one of the most productive farms in McLean County. In the mid-1930's a young fellow took over—a fellow whose abilities under his encouragement were to assure the Mecherle place at least a footnote in the history of American agriculture.

Walter Meers—for many years George Mecherle's tenant and partner —was born on a farm in southwestern Kentucky. After two years of schooling at the Russell Creek Academy in Campbellsville he headed north for Illinois. There he worked on a number of farms, married and settled down as a tenant hopeful of buying his own place before his three baby daughters were grown up. During and after World War I it looked as if he would achieve his ambition, but the farm depression of the 1920's wiped out all his savings after making it impossible for him even to pay his rent on the farm. An ambitious, willing and clever young man, he was looking for work at a time when George Mecherle was forced to let his tenant on the Old Place go. When Mr. Mecherle set Walter Meers up in the Old Place the reputation he was later to earn— and the fortune he was to make—were still in the distant and uncertain future.

One of the Meers attributes which appealed most to George Mecherle, the former "scientific farmer without scientific education," was his readiness to experiment. This and an overweening ambition to make the farm pay in dollars and cents was the very combination for which G.J.M. had been looking. The landlord and the tenant were men who could work together in harmony. George Mecherle let Walter Meers have a free hand and under the latter's guidance the Old Place soon became one of the prize farms of the county. At the same time, with George Mecherle behind him, Walter Meers was to become one of the nation's outstanding farmer-businessmen. He prospered financially, won many honors, was made a bank director, and was even listened to (sometimes) in Washington. Before his death in an automobile accident he had become one of the wealthiest farmers in Central Illinois, holding many acres of rich farmland in his own right. The year before his death the *Wall Street Journal* told his story in a series of articles on "farming as a business" and revealed that the 3,000 hogs and 580 steers he fed in his lots—from corn raised on 1,010 acres—yielded him an income of $90,000 (before taxes) from a gross of $336,000.

In his own days as a working farmer, George Mecherle had been an avid student of ways and means of improving his stock and his land. He knew all the latest results of experiments with the blimp-like Poland China hogs and shorthorn steers, which were his choicest possessions. As a raiser of his own corn for their feed he studied soil and seeds, always with an eye to bettering the growth and increasing the yield. When he no longer was a working farmer, his curiosity was still acute, and even when he had become chairman of the board of the world's largest automobile insurance company he could talk with intelligence about what was going on at the agricultural schools of Illinois, Minnesota and Wisconsin. He was not one of those who laughed at Dr. J. R. Holbert— the Bloomington scientist attached to the Office of Cereal Crops and Diseases of the Department of Agriculture—as he poked about the corn rows at the Federal Field Station at the nearby Funk Farms. To him, the experiments on the new hybrid corn that were going on in the late 1920's and early 1930's were deserving of encouragement and support.

When "that crazy Jim Holbert" came and asked for the use of some of his land at the Old Place as a hybrid corn testing plot, George Mecherle told him to go right ahead. Meers, who was just as interested as he was, would give him all the help he needed.

In his interesting book, *The Hybrid-Corn Makers: Prophets of Plenty,* A. Richard Crabb tells the Mecherle-Meers story in fascinating detail. After describing the important early experiments in McLean County and recalling the general and costly skepticism with which they were received by many of the neighboring farmers in the dark days of the depression, the historian Crabb writes:

> Then in the mid-thirties, Holbert and the other hybrid corn breeders had a chance to prove dramatically the overwhelming superiority of their new hybrids. The drouths of 1934 and 1936 convinced skeptics as nothing else could have done in so short a time.
>
> An example of what happened from Ohio to Nebraska in those drouth years occurred in 1936 on the G. J. Mecherle farm, which was operated by Walter Meers and located nine miles east of Bloomington.
>
> Dr. Jim Holbert had one of his numerous hybrid-corn testing plots on the Mecherle farm in 1935. In October he went to study it—accompanied by A. L. Lang, University of Illinois agronomist. Mecherle told those assembled: "This is the farm on which I was born. I've always loved it as

no other piece of land on earth. You know, I've tried everything I knew or was advised by the boys over at the college, but I've never raised a hundred-bushel-an-acre crop of corn on this old farm. I don't know anything that would give me more personal satisfaction or be of more value in establishing the worth of some of these new cropping practices for farms in this part of Illinois than to raise a hundred-bushel crop here next year."

Lang, the soils scientist, and Holbert—the hybrid-corn breeder—spoke almost in the same breath.

"Why, Mr. Mecherle, there's no reason why you can't do that. All you have to do is put some extra fertilizer on your land and make a thick planting of some of the new high-yielding hybrids, and there should be no doubt about it."

Mecherle was pleased and a little surprised.

"Well, boys, you write the ticket and we'll do the work. That small field south of the house is due for corn next year. That would be a good place for you to start."

Aware that it would be disappointing to Mecherle and most embarrassing to themselves to fail, Lang and Holbert laid their plans carefully. Lang secured help from the soil physics department of the University of Illinois for some extra tile on the field, and he worked out a special recommendation for fertilizer. Holbert laid out the field in strips and planted five of the newest hybrids available from his Funk Farms Experiment Station. Just to make the results official, Meers entered the field in the University of Illinois Ten Acre Corn growing contest.

Mr. Meers prepared the seed bed with the greatest of care, and the planting was done in mid-May just as the rains stopped. Then came the test. And what happened during the next month and a half will be remembered . . . by all corn belt farmers who faced the elements in 1936.

On the last day of June, temperatures of 95° and above were reported. . . . These high temperatures continued until July 3—when the high temperature in nearby Bloomington was 102° and still no rain fell. When temperatures of 105°, 109° and 111° continued for a week, the Associated Press report from Springfield said, "Corn has reached the critical stage where serious injury will result unless drouth conditions are broken this week."

Instead, temperatures moved higher. On July 15, Bloomington's high temperature was 114°. The destructive heat was in big headlines in every newspaper. . . .

Corn was badly hurt in McLean County. Farmers were convinced that their crop had been whittled down to a half or even a fourth of normal size. But the Mecherle field looked surprisingly good, although white-fired leaves were beginning to appear at the top of the plants.

The sensational heat subsided a little on July 19 after the nation's death toll had reached ten thousand persons and livestock struck down were so numerous as to be uncounted. Still there was no rain, and corn was selling for $1.37 a bushel in Chicago—the highest price since the first world war.

July and the first half of August passed without a single shower on the . . . farm. Then, on the 16th of August, the first break came in the drouth. A half inch of rain was reported at Bloomington. Three days later a real ground-soaking shower fell, and then the new hybrids in (the) field south of the house began an amazing recovery.

In October, contest inspectors for the University's corn-growing contest checked each of the five hybrids growing in the field. The highest yielding hybrids averaged 121 bushels an acre. Three of the hybrids yielded over the 100-bushel-an-acre mark. The entire contest field averaged 101.30 bushels. The McLean County average was less than 25 bushels—a stirring testimony to what could be accomplished by careful soil management and the new hybrid corn.*

George Mecherle took a great deal of satisfaction from his connection with this experiment. With boyish enthusiasm he saved one of the best ears from this historic harvest, and had it mounted and hung in one of the most conspicuous spots in his mahogany-paneled office in the State Farm building. In the later years of his life, when he had more leisure than ever before, many an old-time prairie farmer would drop in to his office with nothing else on his mind than to chat about old times. Invariably the talk would get on to crops and cattle and their prices on the Chicago market. As chairman of the board of the world's largest automobile insurance company he was just as interested in farm topics as he had been in the long-ago days when he used to trudge to the Gould store at the Merna siding for the day's mail and the day's talk. When old friends like Billy Lausterer, who had helped introduce him at the historic Streator meeting, showed up at his office he always found time to plow old fields with them.

In other ways his close connection with farming was made manifest. Back in 1927 (when, after five years, he had shown what he could do with an insurance company) it began to be obvious that certain modern improvements had changed the way of farming in the Middle West. The old, cumbersome threshing machines of his early days had been driven almost completely to extinction by the locust-cloud of smaller machinery and the combines. And with the disappearance of the threshing machines went the need for insurance on them. This simple fact threatened a minor segment of the Middle Western agricultural economy with disaster. For many years there had been throughout the corn belt

* *The Hybrid-Corn Makers: Prophets of Plenty*, A. Richard Crabb (Rutgers University Press, New Brunswick, N.J.), pp. 133-6. Copyright, 1947, by Trustees of Rutgers College. Reprinted by permission of the publishers.

a number of threshermen's mutual insurance companies which had been built up as a sort of subsidiary to the farmers' mutuals.

When the Threshermen's Mutual of Decatur, Illinois, held its annual meeting in January, 1927, T. I. Davidson, the secretary-treasurer, said, "The threshing industry is changing so fast that it is rather hard to tell what will be done. With the combine and the small machine coming, I really see no future in the threshing machine insurance. We are not getting anywhere the way things stand now, and the only thing that I see is to take on other insurance."

So they turned to G. J. Mecherle, whom they knew as "a straightforward man" who will "do what is right." He agreed to help, but at that time he and his associates were so busy promoting State Farm that they had no time to devote to the general fire insurance business into which the threshermen believed they should turn.

He suggested that his friend and mentor, William B. McFarland, secretary of a local farm mutual insurance company at Hoopeston, Illinois, and an original director of State Farm Mutual, take the company to Hoopeston and manage it along with his local company. Its new function would be to offer reinsurance facilities to the local farm mutuals on their overlines of large risks. The name of the company was, therefore, changed to the United Farm Mutual Reinsurance Company on June 18, 1930, and the company was moved to Hoopeston, Illinois.

In 1934 the question was raised as to the acceptance by the Federal Land Bank of insurance policies of local mutual fire insurance in connection with mortgages held by the Land Bank on farm property. The question, of course, was the stability of the local mutuals operating on the assessment plan.

Mr. Mecherle became very much interested in this problem and proposed that a reinsurance plan be worked out to help the local companies over this difficulty. He called the officers of the local companies to a meeting in Peoria that year and explained his idea of an excess-of-loss reinsurance plan whereby the companies, for the payment of 5¢ per $100 of insurance in force, would receive from the reinsurance company 90% of their losses in excess of their loss ratio for the past five years.

This plan really insured the whole company and not individual risks. It insured the local company's loss ratio. It stopped the fluctuation of assessments from year to year to a great extent and it solved the stability problem.

In 1935 there were fifty-six companies under this excess-of-loss reinsurance plan. This became such an important part of the business of the United Farm Mutual Reinsurance Company that in 1939, at the request of Mr. McFarland and the officers of the member companies, the home office of the company was moved to Bloomington and Mr. Mecherle became chairman of the board of directors. Mr. Mecherle continued as chairman of the board until his death. He lived, however, to see the success of his idea and the benefits to the local mutual companies. T. F. Campbell, who supervised the operation for many years, has continued to do so after Mr. Mecherle's death and, like Mr. Mecherle, serves without compensation.

In addition to agriculture George Mecherle took more than a casual interest in politics. By instinct and upbringing, by environment and experience, he was a dyed-in-the-wool Republican. Neither he nor his father and mother—as we have seen—were at all influenced by any of the radical political movements that swept across the prairie between the time of the Mecherles' arrival in Illinois and George's departure from high school during the regime of that "eagle forgotten," Governor Altgeld. As a farmer—and later as a successful businessman—G.J.M. honestly believed his and his fellow citizens' interests were best served by the Republican Party, which had come into being in the very region where he was born and raised. Only twice had McLean County, into whose rich soil his roots went deep, strayed from the Republican fold—and then (in 1932 and 1936) by only a small margin. In that part of the country Republicanism was bred in the bone.

That he was civic-minded and always ready to work for the good of the community, regardless of any political interest, and for the welfare of his fellow citizens, no matter what their racial origin or political affiliation, is attested to by the years of financially unrewarding work he put in as road commissioner of Merna and as a director of its school. After moving to Bloomington he did not forget the township. He labored to get the broad, smooth highway that runs through his old town, several years after he had departed. As a city dweller he continued to be interested in a wide variety of civic matters although, it is true, he had little time—especially in the early years of State Farm—for active committee work. His many contributions, some tangible and others hidden, were highly regarded by his fellow citizens. In 1940 a bronze plaque bearing his profiled likeness was presented to him, to be placed in the lobby of the State Farm Building. It bears these gratifying words:

To an Outstanding Citizen
GEORGE J. MECHERLE

> in recognition of his achieve-
> ments . . . contributing to the
> progress and stability of our
> community—Presented by the
> Young Men's Club and by
> Appreciative Citizens. . . .

The words were well chosen, for a combination of stability and progress—in equal quantities—was his ideal. It was such a combination, he
was convinced, that the Republican Party traditionally offered all Americans. He was equally if paradoxically convinced that the Democratic
Party, which had been in power during nearly two-thirds of his amazingly successful business career, offered neither.

In spite of his absorption in business he found time to work for his
political ideals, although he never really became deeply involved in
political action. On local, county and state levels he was known as a
staunch and willing worker, generous with his own money, and
extremely successful in extracting contributions from others. He was a
typical "down-stater" and, although he knew and worked with many
party leaders from the Chicago area, he often did not share their view-
points, especially in national affairs. For a number of years he was an
active member of the Republican Citizens' Finance Committee and did
yeoman work raising campaign funds in the 17th Illinois District, where
his home was located.

Throughout most of his active business career, which had begun
about the time that Warren G. Harding assumed office and extended
through the astounding 1948 election of Harry S. Truman, he witnessed
many revolutionary changes in the American way of life. He did not
condemn every change that had come about through the will of the
electorate but he did disapprove of the general trend of government
administration under the New Deal and the Fair Deal. He was, in so many
ways, a rugged individualist—and his rise from an inexperienced farmer
to the chairmanship of a multi-million-dollar business had been so rapid,
and accomplished so consistently along the lines of an old-fashioned
success story, that he could countenance no political philosophy which
seemed to place any barrier in the way of private initiative. He looked
with dismay upon what he felt was the "trend toward socialism" in the
New Deal.

It was about 1943 that he began to suspect that the New Deal philosophy had become so firmly entrenched among so many people that the future of what he called "sound constitutional government, individual rights, private enterprise, and all the good things that have made this country great since 1860," was drastically threatened. And it was about this time that he began to wonder if the party he loved was ever going to awaken to its deepest responsibility. He felt that the majority of the people were essentially conservative, that they had been led astray by a lavish government, and that the Republican Party should become the party of a true conservatism.

It was not until a few years later, when he had more leisure at his command, that he was able to work out his political philosophy and set it down on paper. By then he had resigned from the Finance Committee because he felt that its dominant members were guilty of a "me-too" attitude toward certain New Deal ideas. In several letters written after the 1948 Presidential election Mr. Mecherle expressed himself as strongly apathetic to the so-called Dewey wing of the Party and as greatly impressed by the political virtues and statesmanship of Senator Robert A. Taft. Like many another Midwesterner he felt that the Eastern Republicans were leading the Party to disaster, that they were not sufficiently alarmed at what clearly seemed to him to be a dangerous trend toward socialism. It was his considered belief that the Republican Party should announce itself as the true conservative party and take unto itself the Southern Democrats—or Dixiecrats—who had come widely to think as good Republicans should and who no longer had a place in the radical party of Roosevelt and Truman. On February 26, 1951, he wrote the following letter to Senator Karl A. Mundt—a letter which is characteristic of his final thinking about national politics.

In yesterday's Chicago Tribune I read the story of how you had been traveling through the deep South and advocating the idea of a Coalition Party. Every word in this article agrees with my ideas because for eight years I have been doing everything I was able to do in order to bring about a Coalition Party between the Southern Democrats and the Northern Republicans, but it seems no one seemed to be able to find the handle. I always said it must come out of the Congress of the United States because coalition is taking place there every day of the year and if it is a good thing to use in the Congress of the United States, certainly it is a good thing to pass on down to the common people.

I said twelve years ago that the Republicans would never elect another president under the policy they were pursuing and I have been a lifelong

Republican. I was a member of the Republican Citizens' Finance Committee in Chicago for the State of Illinois for a number of years but, due to the methods pursued, I thought it best that I get off the committee, so today I find myself no longer on the committee, but a sort of lone wolf looking for some place to go.

I agree with you that the old Mason-Dixon Line should be rubbed out, that we no longer have a North and a South in these United States, but we should be one country indivisible working for the best interest of all concerned, and this can only come about by electing the proper officials to run our government. I think you agree with me in what is said in this article.

If things are not carefully watched you may find Dewey attempting to forge to the front again. I believe that the only satisfactory man to nominate for President of the United States today is Robert Taft, and if by coalition we could succeed in establishing a new name for the Party and nominating Senator Byrd for Vice-President we would have an unbeatable ticket. I am not interested in any party lines any longer but I am interested in good government, the elimination of these free spenders without sufficient forethought, and getting ourselves back to a form of government that has been so prosperous and so fine for all of us for all these many years.

This was but one of several letters he wrote on this theme in the last two years of his life. In one sent to George F. Virkus, of Elmhurst, Illinois—secretary of the Republican Round-up Committee—he wrote:

In reference to the Southern Democratic-Republican Coalition for 1952, this is a matter that I have been interested in for the last eight years. In fact, I was one of the first to make the statement that the Republican Party would never elect another President under the system they were now following, and the only salvation of our nation—in order to secure the right kind of men for public offices—would be a Coalition Party between the Southern Democrats and the Northern Republicans, rubbing out the old Mason-Dixon Line and making the nation one and indivisible.

I want to be in this movement just as deep as I can get and I am ready to co-operate with you in any way because this has been the closest thing to my heart for many, many a day. In fact, I argued in every place I have been and I think with some effect. I wrote you . . . and told you that I thought the Republicans would rather be the head of something that amounted to nothing rather than to be a part of something that might save the situation for the entire nation.

He preached this theory wherever he could but, as he told the Bloomington Rotary Club, "I am merely a voice crying in the wilderness, as at the present time I have no place to go. I do not feel that I can wholeheartedly support what has been offered by either party because in one event I see a hopeless situation and in the other I see a possibility of disaster—disaster from the standpoint of bankruptcy."

Deeply interested as he was in this idea of coalition between the conservative elements of both parties, he would undoubtedly have worked toward this goal in the election year of 1952 had not death overtaken him before he had the opportunity. Perhaps in his zeal for this ideal he would have seconded the late Colonel Robert R. McCormick's demand for the establishment of a new American Party, but it is equally probable that his ingrained Republicanism would have led him to support General Eisenhower after the candidate and Senator Robert A. Taft, whom Mr. Mecherle so greatly admired, had made their post-convention peace. His love for the Republican Party was as native to him as it was to McLean County where he was born.

17

THE LENGTHENED SHADOW

Upon more than one occasion, when called upon to explain the extraordinary growth and phenomenal achievements of the State Farm Insurance companies, more than one person familiar with their histories would fall back upon the well-worn quotation from Emerson's *Essay on Self-Reliance*: "An institution is the lengthened shadow of one man."

This was, of course, a well-deserved tribute to the capacity for leadership and the consummate executive ability of George Mecherle, the organizer and founder of the companies, whose sane influence dominated them in all respects from 1921, when he had his great idea, until his death in 1951—and, in many ways, in the years since then. It was also a tribute to the innate philosophy of a man who lived all those years by another maxim from the Sage of Concord: "No institution will be better than the instituter."

Several years before his death, upon an occasion honoring him in his official State Farm capacity, one man who had known him from the time when he was just another farmer from Merna attempted to sum up his outstanding characteristics. In his excellent, brief sketch of his close associate, Adlai Rust—the executive vice president who later was to be the guiding spirit of the companies—found these characteristics to be sincerity of purpose, patience, modesty and kindliness. Others who knew him equally well agreed that Mr. Rust had come close to the fundamental virtues of George Mecherle, and the secret of his success in the insurance industry, when he said: "Never have I known him to take a position in regard to company affairs without first applying the proposition to himself to make sure that, if he were the insured, he was being treated fairly."

George Mecherle entered the insurance business not with the single goal of making a fortune or of promoting the company destined to dominate its field. He was honestly less concerned with his own personal well-being than he was with instituting a long-needed reform among the insurance institutions then misserving the Illinois farmers. He did not enter the business to be a philanthropist, by any means; from the start he expected a fair return for his money and a fair reward for the time and effort he was prepared to devote to his "cause." But his horizons, at the start, did not extend beyond the Illinois state line; he had no vision of reaching the West Coast, the Mexican border, or the heart of the Canadian provinces. His one purpose then was merely to serve the agricultural counties of his own state with decent, honest, economical automobile insurance at a time when there was little of this type available for the farmers and their families up the back roads of the Corn Belt. His greatest measure of success was that, once his idea had exceeded even his wildest imaginings, he did not lose sight of this principle of service. He remained faithful to it, always, not only because he found that it "paid off," but because it was ingrained in the very idea that he and Erwin Meyers had forged in the Chicago law office in the late winter of 1921. "Honesty," he often said, "is not the best policy—it is the *only* policy."

Among those who worked for and with him, the second characteristic —patience—noted by Adlai Rust was appreciated. A remarkably quick thinker himself and gifted with an ability to see through a problem almost at once, he nevertheless was ever willing to listen through the whole explanation of another—no matter how long it took. His only impatience was with obvious stupidity. He was, as Mr. Rust said, "always looking for the good in his fellow man" and he was always "more than willing to overlook another's faults in his search for good qualities." Sometimes it seemed to his colleagues that he was too patient; but even he had limits to his endurance and when at last he found that the faults outweighed the good qualities he could let the axe fall with incisive finality. A case in point involves one of the very few upheavals among the top personnel of State Farm which occurred during his reign.

In the very early years he had brought to State Farm an old friend who quickly became one of the key men of the organization. Like himself, this man had had little business experience before he came to work for George Mecherle. But he was, in his end of the business, a "natural," and for several years his department functioned with remarkable efficiency. It expanded with the company. But there came a time when the growth of the business, in the opinion of its administrators, demanded fundamental changes in this department.

The old friend, who had been made an officer of the company and a member of the board of directors, disagreed. He felt the suggested changes were a reflection upon his ability and, in the opinion of George Mecherle, put his own interests ahead of those of the company as a whole. To this unhappy situation George Mecherle applied his patience —hopeful of an amicable solution. The other man, however, decided upon some kind of a showdown and, at a meeting in Chicago which G.J.M. did not attend, openly revolted against the leadership. Had George Mecherle been present he would have answered him then and there, but because he was not present he felt the action of the executive was disloyal. The axe dropped, swiftly and irrevocably.

Perhaps one of the finest tributes to the personal leadership of George Mecherle is the fact that such instances in the history of State Farm are so rare as to be almost unique. This episode and the dissolution of the original partnership with Minnie A. Jones stand by themselves in the story of the development of the company, which is all the more unusual when we consider the rapidity with which the company emerged from obscurity to the outstanding position it occupies today. In an organization which outgrew itself every few years and was always having to change its machinery to keep up with its own pace, the lack of internal explosions was amazing. Only a patient man could have exercised the calm control and restraint necessary to keep the organization in check.

Another characteristic of which Mr. Rust has spoken was his modesty. This was more real than apparent. He allowed his name and portrait to be widely exploited in the promotion and advertising of the State

Farm companies. Such a method was highly successful, especially in rural areas. It, of course, stemmed from the early days when he personally had led his teams of salesmen through the hinterlands, county on county, of Illinois. His closeness to the agency force, which he always insisted was the heart of the organization, made him a figure of great strength among the agents, and they transmitted his personality, his integrity, and his rustic simplicity far beyond his own domain. Thousands of policyholders felt that they had a personal friend in George Mecherle, and when any of them went out of his way to make personal contact with him he was always available. They found him then an understanding and unpretentious man—with as little "front" or "side" as any businessman in their home towns whom they had known and dealt with all their lives.

Modest though he was, he was never one to deprecate his own achievements. He had a healthy egotism, but it was an egotism based upon the solid achievements of the institution to which he had devoted his time and thought and energy for so many years.

"From neither a father nor an older brother," Mr. Rust wrote, "could we have had a finer or more considerate treatment in all our dealings with them." There were many others to attest to the truth of this statement. Scores of kindly and impulsive acts were to his credit, although most of them were never publicized but were kept a secret among the persons involved.

Back in 1926, when State Farm was beginning its invasion of the westward states, considerable difficulty was encountered in arranging a contract between the company and the Iowa Farm Bureau. A crucial, all-day meeting finally broke up with both George Mecherle and E. A. Meyers certain that they were licked. They went back to their hotel and were about to check out when the telephone rang. It was the home and community director of the Iowa Farm Bureau. This able lady breathlessly warned them not to leave town, as she was sure matters could be ironed out. Because of her timely intercession, they were. The contract was signed the next day.

Several years later the Iowa Farm Bureau, having profited by the contract, decided not to renew it but to enter the automobile insurance business independently. As a result the secretary—now considerably older—found herself out of a job. She wrote to George Mecherle asking if it would not be possible to find a place for her in the Des Moines office of the organization. Mr. Mecherle instead asked her to visit him at the home office in Bloomington. She and her husband got in their car and came to see him.

"Were you born on a farm?" he asked the lady. She said that both she and her husband had grown up on Midwestern farms and they had always dreamed of going back to one some day to live. This George Mecherle could understand. He thought for a minute and then said, "Well, go back to Iowa and pick one out."

A short time later they informed him that they had found one to their liking. On his next journey to that state he went to see it. It was a modest place, not worth much, pretty well run-down. The farmer from Merna said nothing much and left—to go out and find a place that *he* would call a farm. He bought it. The next day he took the couple out to see it and leased it to the lady—the one whose telephone message had saved the day for him and State Farm in Iowa many years before—for one dollar for the rest of her life.

On another occasion, however, his generosity took a different turn. One of the subcontractors involved in erecting the home office in Bloomington decided to expand and, in search of money for this purpose, approached Mr. Mecherle, who had had his eye on him as one of the up-and-coming young businessmen of the city. This is what Mr. Mecherle said:

"There will come a time when you will hate to have to send me 50% of your profits for just sitting here in my office and doing nothing. My advice is for you to take in your key men as partners. Take in those you know you can trust and who you are certain will stick to the business. For what they can put into the business you will have to pay out a smaller percentage. But that way you will also build up an organization that will be for you and with you all the way through."

The young man followed his advice and his concern grew to be one of the largest and most profitable construction companies in central Illinois.

There were many examples of the intelligent generosity of his private charities. After years of faithful service on the board of directors, one of the several gentlemen who had lent their names, time and efforts to State Farm when George Mecherle first laid his idea before the farmers at Streator found himself in serious difficulties. He was growing old when certain business reverses forced him to mortgage his home. Some time later his unexpected inability to meet this obligation left him faced with the tragedy of probable foreclosure. Word of this reached George Mecherle a few days before the annual meeting. When the old gentleman arrived for the occasion, as he had done without fail since 1922, George Mecherle took him aside. After much gentle prodding he got him to admit the circumstances. A man of great probity and pride, he did so only with the greatest reluctance. Probably he would not have told his troubles to anyone except George Mecherle. Mr. Mecherle told him to go back and see his banker, that he was sure that, if he told him all the details (which were highly to his credit, for he had taken the mortgage to meet obligations of a company he was connected with and for which he had no more than a moral responsibility), the bank would not press too hard. What he did not tell the old gentleman was that as soon as he had heard of the situation he had put his personal responsibility behind the mortgage, to the full satisfaction of the banker.

Although essentially an extrovert—he would not have been the successful salesman and magnificent showman that he was if he had not been—he never allowed his personal charities to be publicized in any way. They were performed quietly and achieved without ostentation. In most cases only he and the other principals involved knew anything about them.

18

END AND NEW BEGINNINGS

In March, 1940, when State Farm was well on the road to becoming the largest automobile insurance company in the United States, George Mecherle moved from his office on the twelfth floor of the original State Farm building to larger, more sumptuous quarters at the north end of the building. His old office had been the nerve center of the organization, located as it was at the center of all State Farm activity. Now he was somewhat removed from the hustle and bustle of the greatly expanded offices in a large, comfortably furnished room lined with Philippine mahogany, overlooking the broad expanse of the county. It was an office befitting his position as chairman of the board, but although it was expensively furnished it was plain and solid, like the man who sat in the big, overstuffed chair between the two big desks. And, as might be expected of George Mecherle, there were reminders of his prairie farm origin scattered about.

Entering this room from the elevators, one saw covering the walls large photographic murals, taken by Jim Holbert of the Funk Seed Company and showing the corn fields and feed lots and farm buildings of the "home place." In his large private office, reached through two offices occupied by his secretaries, Mrs. Sylvia Caldwell and Mrs. Mary Dearth, both veteran employees of State Farm, were further pictures of the farm and the prairie. Dominating one corner was a gilded ear of corn from the famous experimental acres planted by Holbert and Meers in the year of the drought. Off to the left of his desks was his treasure room and library. This was typical of the man. There in glass cases he kept his State Farm mementos—his collection of mechanical pencils picked up during his many travels over the United States, his Indian chief's bonnet presented him by the Winnebago Indians when they made him an honorary chief, scrolls, testimonials, pipes, and other articles which had a great sentimental value to him, treasures from his busy life. This room was lined with books in fine bindings, mostly importations from England of first editions of the classics.

George Mecherle never retired from business, never stopped working day and night on the affairs of State Farm. But in the latter years of his life he "slacked off" somewhat, leaving more and more details to the staff of executives he had hand-picked and trained. He traveled less, and made fewer speeches to conventions and meetings of the agents, but he still kept every detail of the business at his fingertips. He kept the facts and figures of State Farm up to the very last minute in his worn black loose-leaf books. He knew what was going on in every department. In spite of the growth of the State Farm he still kept his interest in the individual welfare of the staff, and knew the names and personal histories of an incredibly large number of them.

When he had retired from farming in 1918 the most compelling reason for doing so had been the illness of his wife. Over the ensuing years the arthritis from which she suffered had grown steadily more crippling until she had been forced to spend most of her time in a wheelchair. George Mecherle never ceased trying to find some surcease for her, but in this he did not succeed. A long session at the Mayo Clinic in Rochester, Minnesota, had failed to bring her relief. Frequent visits to Hot Springs, Arkansas, did her no good, nor did a lengthy visit to a hospital in St. Louis. But, physical invalid though she was, she never ceased to take a cheerful and encouraging interest in all his affairs. Nor did George Mecherle ever tire of telling of how she had been his chief encouragement back when he was first starting his own insurance company. They were a more than ordinarily devoted couple. Day after day he would leave the office, go home and, after placing her comfortably in the car, drive her out to the "home place," where she loved to sit and watch the activities on the farm. She loved to have him drive the car right up to the feed lot where she could see the fattening cattle. That George Mecherle enjoyed these visits as much as she did goes without saying, for both were children of the prairie, farm-born and farm-raised.

After living for many years in Normal the Mecherles had moved to Bloomington. George Mecherle bought a large, comfortable house far out on East Washington Street. His reason for taking this house, aside from the fact that it was a well built, quietly located, and attractive home, was that the former occupant had installed an elevator in it. This made it easier for Mrs. Mecherle, for in spite of her illness she still "ran the house," superintending the servants, planning the meals, and doing such household chores as she could from her wheelchair. In the large yard running narrowly in the back of the house were two flower gardens, where she liked to sit and read on good days, and farther down was a vegetable garden which she superintended.

In the summer of 1942 Mrs. Mecherle was taken ill, and on August 22, at the age of sixty-one, she died at her home. Her passing led the *Pantagraph* to publish the following editorial:

> In the ideal team of husband and wife, the wife more often than not, chooses to serve in the inner councils of the home. She advises, encourages, and helps the husband at times when he needs advice, encouragement and help the most.
>
> Mrs. George J. Mecherle, whose death has saddened the community, was such a wife. Mr. Mecherle has often, publicly and privately, acknowledged the dependence upon his wife's intimate understanding and intuition in the years when he was building in this city one of the outstanding business structures of the nation.
>
> Overcoming frail health, which was a handicap to her much of her life, her unfailing cheerfulness was a source of strength in the family and in the community. Her generosity towards many organizations demonstrated her concern for general community interests. Her life was well and truly lived.

The death of Mrs. Mecherle left a void in George Mecherle's life that was difficult to fill. Their children were now grown, embarked on careers of their own, and established in their own homes. The large house on East Washington Street was an empty place to return to after his long day at the office or after a wearying trip out of town. He traveled less than he had in the past, but now, as throughout his whole business life, he insisted upon getting to his office by eight o'clock in the morning, and often he was the last to leave at night. In spite of his work, his card sessions at the Bloomington Club, or his outside interests in the Masons and other organizations, there was a loneliness in his life at this time. All his friends were pleased when, in January 1944, he remarried.

Mrs. Sylvia Caldwell, who became his second wife, was one of the veterans of the State Farm "family." She had come to the company as a policy writer in September, 1925, when State Farm was little more than three years old. She was a brilliant woman, with a better-than-average education, who had demonstrated her abilities early in her career. Since 1927 she had been George Mecherle's chief secretary. In this capacity she knew the affairs of State Farm inside and out, and since State Farm was George Mecherle's one great interest in life he could hardly have chosen a more amiable or understanding companion with whom to spend the declining years of his life.

A native of Alleghany, Pennsylvania, where she was born Sylvia Mae Harbaugh in 1887, she had married Albert Caldwell shortly after finishing her education and had gone with him to Siam to teach at a Presbyterian college in Bangkok. Their first son, Alden, was born in that faraway land. After three years there they started back for the United States by way of England and, at the last moment, found passage for New York on the new liner *Titanic*. All three survived the dreadful ordeal of the sinking of the "unsinkable" ocean liner. Later a second son, Raymond, was born to them. Eventually they moved to the Middle West, but after they had settled in Bloomington Mr. Caldwell's business kept him in the East a great deal of the time. Eventually they had separated and been divorced.

Mrs. Mecherle made as gracious a mistress of the home on East Washington Street as she had made an efficient secretary in the office, which was George Mecherle's other home. She devoted herself to his welfare and, for the next seven years, quietly but firmly kept him from spending all his time and strength on his business affairs. During the strenuous years since his first retirement from the farm George Mecherle had seldom taken an extended vacation. He was one of a group of Bloomington businessmen who used to go fishing each spring at Lake Gogebic in northwestern Michigan, and who with other fishermen formed Bloomington's noted Fish Club. He used to delight in their fortnightly sessions at the Tilden Hall Hotel. But aside from this diversion he had taken little time off for rest and recreation. Now Sylvia began to convince him to

"ease off," as he put it, and in 1948 the couple took their first "real vacation." This was a cruise to South American waters, the first time that
George Mecherle, who knew every large town and city in the United
States, had ever been at sea (unless his Florida fishing expeditions in
1918 could be called that).

The next year, travel in Europe once more being possible, Mr. and
Mrs. Mecherle went abroad. On his part it was a sentimental journey.
Before leaving he had a Chicago travel agency locate exactly the little
village of Untermasholderbach whence the brothers Mögerle had started
on the journey that led them at last to Bloomington in the middle of
the nineteenth century. The arrangements made by the travel agency
went without a hitch and, accompanied by two young German guides,
the couple reached the ancestral village. They searched the records of
the little church and found to their surprise and pleasure that the old
papers gave a picture of the Mögerle family exactly as George's father
and uncle had recalled it on the farm at Merna. They found the name
well known in the region, but were unable to locate any living members
of the family. Afterward they traveled across Europe and went to England. The historic palaces and cathedrals and other points of tourist interest failed to excite George Mecherle, who was happiest when motor-
ing through the farming regions. There he would stop and talk with the
farmers, comparing their way of doing things with the McLean County
way.

The last years of his life were pleasant. He had more leisure and he
made good use of it, but he never relinquished his hold on State Farm
affairs. All his life he had been healthy. His tremendous, farm-built
physique had served him well. The only time he had been hospitalized
in his life was for an appendectomy. The only warning that he, like all
others, was subject to the ills that flesh is heir to came one summer after
his second marriage, when he suffered a slight stroke. At the camp at
Lac Court Oreilles in Wisconsin, where he and Sylvia spent several
pleasant summer weeks, he ripped a finger with a fish-hook and always
thought that this injury had caused the upset. He paid little attention to
it, however, except to try, without too much success, "to take it a little
more easy."

On Friday, March 9, 1951, he spent the day at his office. That evening he attended the annual spring reunion of the Masons at Bloomington Consistory and the next day went to lunch at the Bloomington
Club. He spent a pleasant afternoon playing "black deuce rummy" with

friends. After dinner at home with Mrs. Mecherle he read for a while and retired at his usual hour. That night he awoke in pain, called Sylvia, and died quietly with her at his side. His stout, tireless heart had failed at last. He was seventy-four years old.

The high esteem in which George Mecherle was held by the citizens of Bloomington, who had already declared him an outstanding citizen when they placed the plaque in his honor in the lobby of the State Farm building, was made manifest by the huge crowd which attended his funeral in the Consistory building. The large auditorium was crowded and an overflow audience listened to the dignified service over loud-speakers in another large room downstairs.

The year of George Mecherle's death saw State Farm Mutual in sound condition. It had 2,183,092 policies in force. The company which had started with such modest financing had a premium and membership income of $119,117,303. Of this amount $114,700,000 was in automobile insurance premiums and membership, representing 2,155,971 automobile insurance policies in force. The man who had trudged the back roads and beaten the highways of the great Corn Belt of America in order to give the farmer a better deal in automobile insurance had builded better than he had ever dreamed. He had sold his one million policies, just as he had said he would, and a million more.

In one of his many inspirational messages to the agents in the field George Mecherle had one time written:

"Remember this: Every man who accomplishes anything worthwhile in this life will leave behind him many temples still unfinished when he departs this life."

The unfinished temple he left behind was State Farm Mutual.

In that same message he had also spoken of those who "are not fearful of the morrow" and who, like himself, were "more anxious to leave behind an indelible record which all men may read, which will tell to all the world that we were aggressive. . . ."

For nearly thirty years George J. Mecherle had been the dominant figure in all the affairs of the State Farm companies. It was his vision of an honest insurance company for the farmers of Illinois that had brought State Farm into being in 1922. In those early, uneasy days that followed his visit to the St. Louis convention, his Chicago talks with Herman Ekern and Erwin A. Meyers, and the historic presentation of his radical plan to the farmer mutual secretaries at Streator, State Farm Mutual had been very nearly a one-man operation. His magnificent presence and dynamic personality had towered over all who came to work with him in those days. And even when the company had grown to the tremendous size it was in the last years of his life this same personality and presence continued to shine over the entire organization.

George Mecherle did not look upon himself as a dictator. In all honesty he thought of himself as a father, sometimes stern but always benevolent, of a family.

"We have never permitted strife to creep into the family of this organization," he said upon one occasion. "No matter what the outside may think, this is a family, although at times we might have to take some individual and give him a good larruping. We might have differences of opinion, but no man's opinion has been ridiculed—because out of the wildest ideas have been formulated workable plans that have been used to advantage."

He never forgot his own wild idea and how, out of it, came the most workable plan in the history of automobile insurance.

"I was kind of a lucky dog to think about this business," he once wrote a boyhood friend, "and maybe not so lucky at that. You know, the greatest troubles we have are what we bring on ourselves. The rulings and regulations and laws with which we have to comply cause us an unending amount of trouble. But I suppose anyone who deals with the human family, to the extent which we are engaged with it, will always find a lot of trouble."

George Mecherle's philosophy was simple and true. He thought of insurance as a benefit to the whole human family; he was more concerned with its humanity than with those "esoterics of insurance" that so long occupied his old friend and associate, E. A. Meyers. In the later, more leisurely years of his life he often turned to the books in his comfortable library that adjoined his office in the State Farm building. He was neither a deep nor wide reader. For the most part the books had been selected by the second Mrs. Mecherle. He unerringly found the volumes containing old Benjamin Franklin's wise writings and he took several of them home for more careful reading. Like Henry Ford, in the manufacturer's later days, he found passages in Emerson that were both stimulating and comforting. He was a much more literate and articulate man than Henry Ford, and his talks and speeches were always in his own homely words and never in the polished words of an amanuensis. Had he found the time before he became so absorbed in his business he undoubtedly would have devoured serious books at a rapid rate.

One day shortly before his death he was browsing in his library when he came across the Modern Library edition of Richard McKeon's *The Basic Writings of Aristotle*. That evening, after dinner, he read in it for a long, quiet time. Just before bedtime he turned to Sylvia Mecherle and exclaimed, "By golly, I didn't know anybody wrote things like this." It was one of his great intellectual discoveries. Just what passages excited him we do not know, for he did not mark them. But the next day he was still stimulated by the philosopher, and talked about him to everyone who came to his office. He wanted his boys to read Aristotle.

An unlearned philosopher he may have been, but he was instinctive in the pragmatic application of his simple theories to useful ends. One thing he knew, without having to find it in books, was that no one man was indispensable. This was coupled with a nearly infallible judgment of human nature. From the beginning he had chosen his associates wisely and had been quick to discover and dispose of those who did not reach the high mark of his exacting demands. He seldom erred in finding the right man for a job, or the right job for a man. At the time when he and Minnie Jones were on the verge of breaking up their brief association, Ekern, Meyers & Janisch sent George Beedle down from Chicago to handle the office affairs. George Mecherle quickly spotted his worth and never let him return to the law office. When he first needed someone to handle claims he went out to a Merna farm and tapped his old friend E. J. Carmody, who had never done such work before, because he recognized in him a natural talent for this kind of work. And so it went, year after year, as he built State Farm into the "unfinished temple" he left behind.

From his associates on every level he demanded three things: willingness to work hard, faith in the organization, loyalty to the "spirit" of State Farm. Few were those who did not give him all three in good measure. In return he gave to his associates what he demanded from them. He was no swivel-chair commander, but the hardest worker of them all. His faith in the high purposes of State Farm as an organization dedicated to the service of its members was all-absorbing. And his loyalty to the men and women who were loyal to him and his ideals was legendary.

A former associate once wrote this picture of him in the last years of his life: "True, he wasn't on the road as much as he had been in the early years, when by the force of his enthusiasm and personality he was constantly travelling from one end of the country to the other, organizing, selling, teaching, building the business. But he was at his desk early every morning and many times until after the offices had been closed.

"The matter of reorganizing and often rebuilding various agencies, weeding out bad business here and strengthening manpower there; the job of instilling into new men the principles by which State Farm organizations had been built, and reinspiring older men; leading the way in smoothing out difficulties in procedure and practice—in short the leadership that had built the organizations—kept him very much occupied, despite the staff of officers he had to assist him."

That his presence was deeply missed at the State Farm offices after his death is unquestionable, but it is unlikely that from the other world he looked down upon the organization with any misgivings. He had left behind him a group of men who were dedicated to his ideals, not only because they had won a personal stake in the welfare of the companies but because he had impregnated them over the years with his own belief in State Farm as a great institution. At the first annual meeting following his death—the twenty-ninth annual meeting since that first fateful one in the cramped room in the Durley Building—recognition of his continuing influence over the policies of State Farm was made manifest. By unanimous vote the directors, some of whom had been with the company from the beginning, kept vacant the chairman's seat which he had occupied for the past fourteen years and ordered that it be kept vacant until the date his term would have expired. Those present at this meeting felt they could do no less.

Men like Ramond Mecherle, Adlai Rust, G. Ermond Mecherle, Gilbert Brown, Morris G. Fuller, Fletcher B. Coleman, Arthur W. Tompkins, Theodore F. Campbell, James H. Parsons and H. E. Curry, who occupied positions of trust under George Mecherle, were more than eager to carry on the traditions "the Chief" had established. Each had been associated with State Farm for many years and had worked closely with Mr. Mecherle. To their ideas for the advancement of the company he had given a welcome ear, and he had encouraged them in the development of the company's policies, which more often than not, as we have seen, were the product of their collective thinking. The postwar crisis, brought about by the sudden and exaggerated number of claims that followed the lifting of wartime restrictions, had shown their joint ability under fire.

In years of service, except for Adlai Rust, the oldest of these veterans was Ramond Perry Mecherle, oldest of George and Mae Perry Mecherle's sons. He had come, as we have seen, to State Farm, when he was a young man of twenty. Later, at the Babson Institute near Boston, he had received a good business education which was enhanced by practical work as the company's first superintendent of commissions. From that post he went "through the mill," growing up with State Farm and becoming a vice president of the automobile mutual in 1933. Four years later, when his father advanced to the newly created post of chairman of the board of directors, he was elected president of the State Farm Mutual Automobile Company, a post he continued to hold until his sudden death in 1954 at the age of fifty. During his thirty years with State Farm he served as a member of the executive committee, vice president of the life and fire companies, and as a member of the board of directors of the three State Farm affiliates.

Like his older brother, George Ermond Mecherle spent his entire business career with State Farm. After his schooling at the Normal Community High School, the University of Illinois at Urbana, and at the University of Arizona at Tucson, he came to State Farm in 1928. He began in the underwriting division, moved on to become registrar of the Life Company. In 1930 he was made assistant to the chief underwriter of the automobile company. The next year he found his real place with the organization when he was made director of personnel. As we have seen, his development of this important part of the business was an outstanding contribution to the advancement of the State Farm trio's standing in the insurance industry. Harried for several years by ill health, he felt impelled to resign all his official positions with the State Farm companies on October 4, 1954, although he remained as a vice president of the automobile company in an advisory capacity. At the time of his resignation he was secretary and a member of the board of directors of the State Farm Mutual and a director of the fire and life companies, and vice president of the automobile company. His ill health had required him to relinquish his work as personnel director in 1952, and this post was taken over by Paul Mitzner.

The sudden death of Ramond Mecherle and the resignation of his brother from his several positions brought about a realignment of the top echelon of the three companies. Adlai H. Rust was elected president of the State Farm Mutual Automobile Insurance Company. T. F. Campbell succeeded Ermond Mecherle as secretary of the automobile company, and Morris G. Fuller took his place on the executive committee. E. B. Rust became a member of the investment committees of the three companies and a member of the executive committee of the fire and casualty affiliate. Robert C. Perry took Mr. Mecherle's place on the life company's executive committee.

Among State Farm executives few if any were closer to George Mecherle than Adlai H. Rust, whose long-held title of executive vice president indicated the position of high responsibility he had long held in State Farm affairs. When he first started his association with State Farm as a young lawyer in Bloomington he had no intention of devoting most of his life to the insurance business. He had a bright future with his growing law practice in the county seat. But when State Farm affairs began more and more to take up his time George Mecherle, who had admired him for years and respected his business as well as legal judgments, persuaded him to come to the company on a full-time basis. It was not long before he was regarded throughout the organization as George Mecherle's right-hand man. As the companies grew he undertook the important assignment of handling the investment of its funds. He has handled hundreds of millions of dollars in this capacity. Upon George Mecherle's death, as executive vice president, chairman of the board of the fire and life affiliates, and treasurer of all three companies, he became the central figure around which the large affairs of the company revolved. Like his old chief, he was a native of McLean County and was born on a farm. His interest in farming has never waned. Owner of two prairie farms, he is one of the country's well known breeders of Aberdeen-Angus cattle.

When Mr. Rust celebrated his thirtieth anniversary in June, 1952, Ramond Mecherle paid tribute to him in these words in the *Alfi News*: "Many times I have heard Dad say, in different ways, that he and Adlai Rust made a pretty good team together. Each one seemed to understand the other perfectly. Their different abilities somehow meshed together in a sort of happy harmony. Dad used to say, 'I'm not a detail man.' He could see the broad sweeping outlines of a plan, but Adlai could see the details and facts needed to make it work. Each complemented the other. As a team they were unbeatable. Working closely with each other, they guided State Farm policies from one sound decision to another—on and on, until the time came when the little automobile insurance company which they had nursed back in 1922 became the largest in the world." In this same article Mr. Mecherle quoted his father as saying of the man who was largely responsible for company investments then totaling more than $175,000,000: "Adlai is the kind of man you would like to have handle your own money."

The men who are carrying on after Mr. Mecherle's death are all well versed in insurance lore. Under their co-operative management, State Farm continues to maintain its enviable position as leader in the industry, and to expand. Several of the principal officers make up the executive council, which serves as a consulting body to President Rust on major questions of policy. There is A. W. Tompkins, executive vice president in charge of the far-flung agency force, who first helped Mr. Mecherle bring State Farm to the Western states in 1925; there is Theodore F. Campbell, president of the fire company, secretary and vice president in charge of underwriting, who came to State Farm in 1928; Morris G. Fuller, who arrived the following year to take over the life company end of the business; Fletcher B. Coleman, who came to Bloomington in 1931 and rose to be in charge of claims; Gilbert Brown, who, after a varied experience as a public accountant, became comptroller in 1935; and J. H. Parsons, vice president, and secretary of the executive council. Then, of course, there is Edward B. Rust, executive vice president in charge of operations; H. E. Curry, vice president in charge of the Actuarial Department, who had succeeded Robert Mead in 1945; Thomas C. Morrill, vice president in charge of public relations and related management problems, who had come from the New York State Insurance Department and had learned insurance under Alfred M. Best, and E. L. Hiser, who was picked by George Mecherle years ago to head McLean County agency operations and is now also a director of the company and a member of the board's executive committee.

Then, too, there is Erwin A. Meyers, whose counsel has helped guide State Farm affairs from the first, and his younger partner Russell H. Matthias, who has handled much of State Farm's corporate and legislative work since 1933 with extraordinary vigor and success. In 1951, the firm of Meyers and Matthias had succeeded Ekern, Meyers and Matthias, to which Russell Matthias was admitted as a partner in 1942.

Each of the two "line functions"—agency and operations—has its own senior management group. The agency staff with A. W. Tompkins at its head, seconded by Henry Keller, Jr., as vice president-agency, is bulwarked by three regional agency vice presidents—T. J. Kiesselbach, who brought to his agency department post a substantial background of successful experience as a State Farm agent; Merritt C. Ackland and

Myron E. Dean, each of whose State Farm careers is fortified with extensive insurance experience elsewhere.

As the head of operations, Edward B. Rust is chairman of the eleven-man operating committee. All of its members are State Farm veterans, men who combine specialized technical training with a broad understanding of the State Farm system. Richard F. Stockton, vice president-operations, is chief aide to Edward Rust. Then there are R. J. Bartrum, vice president-claims; A. L. Baumann, assistant comptroller; Carl A. Marquardt, vice president-planning and research; Frank L. Mittelbusher, vice president-statistics; Paul L. Mitzner, vice president-personnel; E. R. Warmoth, vice president-underwriting; Robert O. Noel, assistant vice president, and James H. Turner, director of administrative services. Henry Keller, Jr., also serves on the operating committee as one means of maintaining liaison between agency and operating functions.

The branches, in turn, are each headed by capable members of the management team. Norval P. Goelzer, vice president, heads the Western branch at Berkeley. Resident vice presidents are Cranford W. Ingham at St. Paul, W. A. Sherman at Santa Ana, C. E. Beadles at Marshall, C. F. Adam at Murfreesboro, E. A. Breyvogel at Charlottesville, and Sumner Roberts at Dallas. At Toronto, Mark Ashley is chief agent, while Merrill Grafton fills the post of resident manager at the Jacksonville branch, Vincent D. Fehringer at Birmingham and Keith Jump at Lincoln.

Each of the affiliated companies—life and fire—has its own strong coterie of officers. Aiding President Fuller in State Farm Life are Robert C. Perry, first vice president; J. H. Miller, senior vice president; George R. Davies, vice president and counsel; Burnell H. Miller, vice president and controller; John C. Morris, vice president and secretary; and vice presidents R. R. Hanback, Everett O'Brien and I. M. Spear.

President Campbell of State Farm Fire and Casualty has as his chief lieutenants R. C. Thoele, who is vice president and secretary, and assistant vice presidents James H. Hazard and A. W. Kohlhagen, in charge, respectively, of underwriting and claims.

On one of the happiest occasions of his life, the dedication of the north wing of the State Farm building on June 7, 1939, George Mecherle put his finger on the secret of State Farm success. He said:

"Things do not happen—they are brought about by careful planning, diligence, application, and direction.

"The tiny seed planted in the year 1922, which has been nurtured by the sunlight of agency devotion and sustained by the life-giving waters of policyholder persistency, has grown in root and branch—spreading a mantle of service and protection throughout the nation—until today the ripened fruit of its many branches is falling as a benediction into the lives, homes, and hearts of our people."

To the 3,370,217 policyholders in the three State Farm companies, to the 5,686 workers in the home office and the eleven branch offices of the company, and to the 7,500 agents of State Farm in forty-two far-flung states of the Union and in Canada, these words were as true at the end of 1954 as they were when the farmer from Merna spoke them in the shadow of the Bloomington courthouse, where his immigrant father ended his long trek across the prairie just ninety-seven years ago.

INDEX

ABOUT THE AUTHOR

KARL SCHRIFTGIESSER, a native of Boston, Massachusetts, has been on the staffs of the old *Boston Evening Transcript*, where he "broke" the famous book censorship story of the 1920's, the *Washington Post*, where his daily column was widely read in the early days of the New Deal, and the *New York Times*. For six years he was book critic for *Newsweek Magazine*. He has contributed articles on a wide variety of subjects to such magazines as the *Atlantic Monthly, Collier's*, the *New Yorker* and the *New York Times Magazine*. His book reviews have appeared in the *Times*, the *Herald Tribune* and the *Saturday Review* for the past twenty years. His first book, *Families*, appeared in 1940 and was a study of ten outstanding American families, ranging from the Adamses to the Roosevelts. This was followed by the first full study of the two branches of the Roosevelt family, *The Amazing Roosevelt Family, 1613–1942*. Then came *The Gentleman From Massachusetts*, a biography of Senator Henry Cabot Lodge, the man most responsible for the American rejection of the League of Nations in 1920. This led to *This Was Normalcy*, an account of the personalities and political activities of the twelve years of Republican rule between Wilson and Franklin D. Roosevelt. His most recent book is *The Lobbyists: The Art and Business of Influencing Lawmakers*, a historical account of the third house of Congress. He is also the author of *Oscar of the Waldorf*. At present Mr. Schriftgiesser is working on a study of Fisher Ames and other New England Federalists, founders of the conservative political tradition in America. The present work is his first venture into the realm of business history. His home is on a farm in Londonderry, Vermont, but he spends much time in New York and Washington.